WANDERING
ON THE
WAY

EARLY TAOIST TALES AND PARABLES OF CHUANG TZU

Translated with an Introduction
and Commentary by
Victor H. Mair

BANTAM BOOKS
NEW YORK TORONTO LONDON SYDNEY AUCKLAND

WANDERING ON THE WAY
A Bantam Book / September 1994

Book design by Donna Sinisgalli

Map on page lv designed by Laura Hartman Maestro

Library of Congress Cataloging-in-Publication Data

Chuang-tzu.
[Nan-hua chen ching. English]
Wandering on the way : early Taoist tales and parables of Chuang
Tzu / translated with an introduction and commentary by
Victor H. Mair.
p.   cm.
Includes bibliographical references.
ISBN 0-553-37406-0
I. Mair, Victor H., 1943–   . II. Title.
PLI900.C46E5   1994
299'.5I482—dc20   93-46775
                                                        CIP

Published simultaneously in the United States and Canada

Bantam Books are published by Bantam Books, a division of
Bantam Doubleday Dell Publishing Group, Inc. Its trademark,
consisting of the words "Bantam Books" and the portrayal of a
rooster, is Registered in U.S. Patent and Trademark Office and in
other countries. Marca Registrada. Bantam Books, 1540 Broadway,
New York, New York 10036.

PRINTED IN THE UNITED STATES OF AMERICA

FFG   0 9 8 7 6 5 4 3 2 I

For Susan Rebecca and Heidi Lynné,
two women of strength;

And for Joseph Richard,
the wandering Van-Man.

Kə   vātāi dvạnmaibyascā yaogaṭ āsū

Who yoked the pairs of swift (steeds) to wind and welkin?

Zend-Avesta, Yasna 44.4

CONTENTS

PREFACE   xi

INTRODUCTION   xvii

NOTES ON THE TRANSLATION   xlvii

MAP OF CHINA CIRCA 330 B.C.E.   lv

INNER CHAPTERS

1. Carefree Wandering   3
2. On the Equality of Things   10
3. Essentials for Nurturing Life   25
4. The Human World   29
5. Symbols of Integrity Fulfilled   42
6. The Great Ancestral Teacher   51
7. Responses for Emperors and Kings   66

OUTER CHAPTERS

8. Webbed Toes   75
9. Horses' Hooves   80
10. Ransacking Coffers   84
11. Preserving and Accepting   90

12. Heaven and Earth   102
13. The Way of Heaven   119
14. Heavenly Revolutions   130
15. Ingrained Opinions   144
16. Mending Nature   148
17. Autumn Floods   152
18. Ultimate Joy   166
19. Understanding Life   174
20. The Mountain Tree   185
21. Sir Square Field   198
22. Knowledge Wanders North   210

MISCELLANEOUS CHAPTERS

23. Kengsang Ch'u   225
24. Ghostless Hsü   237
25. Sunny   254
26. External Things   268
27. Metaphors   278
28. Abdicating Kingship   284
29. Robber Footpad   298
30. Discoursing on Swords   312
31. An Old Fisherman   317
32. Lieh Yük'ou   324
33. All Under Heaven   333

GLOSSARY

Names   349
Places   364
Terms and Allusions   370

BIBLIOGRAPHY   387
DELETED PASSAGES   393
ACKNOWLEDGMENTS   401

PREFACE

The *Chuang Tzu* is far and away my favorite Chinese book. Although this fascinating collection of essays, tales, and anecdotes presents many difficult problems of interpretation, for two decades it has been the work that I wanted more than any other to render into English. To prepare myself for the task, I gathered together scores of traditional and modern commentaries. Although I have consulted them closely and carefully during the course of my research, I seldom refer to them directly in the Notes on the Translation. The main reason for this is that I view the *Chuang Tzu* primarily as a work of literature rather than as a work of philosophy and wish to present it to the reading public unencumbered by technical arcana that would distract from the pleasure of encountering one of the most playful and witty books in the world.

There have been a few previous translations of the *Chuang Tzu* into English, French, German, Mandarin, Japanese, and other languages (the majority of them incomplete or abridged, others very much out of date) although nothing like the hundreds that have been done for the *Tao Te Ching*, that other well-known Taoist classic. A couple of these renditions are quite competent, but I believe that none of them has succeeded in capturing the quintessential spirit of the book. Both the style and the thought of the *Chuang Tzu* are extraordinary. If we try to approach them by ordinary means, we will surely fail. Therefore, in making this translation, I have not been afraid to experiment with new modes of expression to simulate the odd quality of writing in the *Chuang Tzu*. The chief aim of this book is philological accuracy. Beyond that, however, I wish to present Chuang Tzu as a preeminent literary stylist and to rescue him from the clutches of those who would make of him no more than a waffling philosopher or a maudlin minister of the Taoist faith. Consequently, this is the only complete translation of the *Chuang Tzu* that renders the poetic portions of the text as verse in English. Furthermore, I have endeavored to reflect the overall poetic quality of the book in my translation. As the noted sinologist Burton Watson has so aptly observed (*Basic Writings*, p. 17):

> Chuang Tzu, . . . though he writes in prose, uses words in the manner of a poet, particularly in the lyrical descriptions of the Way or the Taoist sage. In the broader sense of the word, his work is in fact one of the greatest poems of ancient China.

To ignore the poetics of the *Chuang Tzu* by treating it simply as a piece of philosophical prose would do it a grave injustice.

The main reason I fell in love with the *Chuang Tzu* so long ago, and why my fascination with the book has only increased over the years, is the sheer literary attraction of this strange and wonderful collection of Taoist writings. Reading the *Chuang Tzu*, even after the hundredth time, gives me pure pleasure and helps me to relax in times of stress or anxiety. As imaginative literature, there is no other Chinese work that even remotely compares to it before the introduction of Buddhist narrative and dramatic traditions from India and Central Asia. The *Chuang Tzu*, however, is not simply entertaining. It is also a highly edifying work in the sense that it is full of profound wisdom and insights on life.

Inasmuch as this is a book that has meant so much to me for decades, I wanted to share it with others. That is the simplest explanation for the genesis of the present work. Another impetus for the creation of this translation is my strong feeling that the *Chuang Tzu* deserves to be better known in the West. The popularity of the *Tao Te Ching* outside of China is nothing short of phenomenal. Almost unbelievably, a new translation of that little book appears at the steady rate of about one per month. There are now so many different English editions of the *Tao Te Ching* available that enthusiasts who have no familiarity with Chinese are emboldened to make their own translations by relying solely on previous versions. As a sinologist, I will not comment on the reliability of such secondary renderings, but at least they demonstrate that the *Tao Te Ching* has by now become a thoroughly domesticated American classic.

It is sad, by contrast, that few Americans beyond scholarly circles have ever even heard of the *Chuang Tzu*, much less experienced the thrill of dipping inside its covers. In a way, I feel a sense of injustice that the *Tao Te Ching* is so well known to my fellow citizens while the *Chuang Tzu* is so thoroughly ignored, because I firmly believe that the latter is in every respect a superior work. We may account for the enormous popularity of the *Tao Te Ching* by pointing to its brevity and its ambiguity: everybody can not only find in it what they want, they can find what they're looking for quickly. The *Tao Te Ching* in its many American renditions is a kind of Taoist fast food—you devour it in several bites and it doesn't cost much. The *Chuang Tzu*, on the other hand, is more like a banquet or a buffet—you are obliged to spend more time savoring its tremendous variety of delightful dishes, and of course you have to pay a bit more because it is bigger.

This is a book to help you slow down and unbend. Some readers may be so captivated by it that they will want to plunge from beginning to end in just two or three sittings. For most, however, a more leisurely approach is recommended. You can open the *Chuang Tzu* to virtually any of its scores of sections and experience them separately, or you can read one of its thirty-three chapters at a time. The point is that no matter where in the *Chuang Tzu* you turn, there is food for thought.

Here you will learn about the usefulness of uselessness, the joy of wandering, the insignificance of the difference between big and little, what it means to follow nature, and a thousand other stimulating topics. Within the pages of the *Chuang Tzu*, you will discover the weirdest cast of characters this side of Bedlam, most of them invented out of whole cloth by the author(s). You will laugh uproariously at the eccentricities and antics of the most zany bunch of sages ever assembled. This is not some dry, moralistic treatise, nor is it a demanding, philosophical disquisition. Rather, the sublime wisdom of the *Chuang Tzu* is imparted to us by poking holes in our conventional knowledge and assumptions about what is good and bad. It accomplishes all of this, furthermore, with a divine sense of humor throughout. The *Chuang Tzu* deals with very heavy stuff, but it does so with a feather-light touch.

Before proceeding further, I should explain what the name of the book means and how it should be pronounced. "Chuang" is the surname of the supposed author of this marvelous work and "Tzu" simply implies "master" in the sense of a leading figure in a given school of thought in ancient China. Hence, we may render "Chuang Tzu" as "Master Chuang." (I generally refer to the title of the book as the *Chuang Tzu* and the name of the reputed author as Master Chuang.) While the pronunciation of the title is not such an easy matter as its meaning, I would console my poor reader who is afraid to attempt it by saying that speakers of Sinitic languages themselves have pronounced (and still do pronounce) the two sinographs (Chinese characters) used to write it in widely varying ways depending upon where and when they lived. For example, a Cantonese of today would read them quite differently from a Pekingese, and a resident of the Chinese capital 2,600 years ago would have pronounced them in a manner that would be unrecognizable to either the Cantonese or the Pekingese. Therefore, it does not really matter that much how each of us says the title of the book in his or her own idiolect. For those who are fastidious, however, the "correct" pronunciation in Modern Standard Mandarin may be approximated as follows. The "Chu-" part of Chuang sounds like the "ju" of juice or jute, except that the "u" functions as a glide to the succeeding vowel and thus comes out as a "w"; the "-a-" must be long, as in Ma and Pa; the "-ng" is the same as in English. Perhaps the best way to approximate Tzu is to lop off the initial part of words such as "adze," "fads," and so forth, striving to enunciate only the "d" and the sibilant that comes after it, hence -dze or -ds. To end this little lesson in Mandarin phonology, then, we may transcribe Chuang Tzu phonetically as *jwawng dz* or *jwahng dzuh.*

"Chuang Tzu" is the traditional sinological transcription of the name of the putative author and of the title of the book attributed to him that is translated here. Recently a new transcription system has come into vogue in China according to which the name is transcribed as "Zhuang Zi." The Mandarin sounds these two transcription systems indicate remain the same (as given at the end of the previous paragraph).

Even though the *Chuang Tzu* was written over two millennia ago and in a language that is at times well nigh impenetrable, it still has a vital relevance today. Communist theorists in China continue to debate vigorously the significance of the text, whether it is materialist or mystical, positive or negative. There are those who also perceive distinctly modernist strains in the *Chuang Tzu.* Considering the wide familiarity of the contemporary world with his compatriot, Lao Tzu (the Old Master), who is a far less interesting and stimulating writer, it is likely that we will be hearing more of Master Chuang in the not-too-distant future.

As we shall see in the Introduction under the heading "The

Question of Authorship," the *Chuang Tzu* was clearly not all written by a single thinker. Nonetheless, there is an essentially inimitable spirit that informs the book as a whole. For the purpose of discussion, we may refer to that spirit as Chuang Tzu (Zhuang Zi) or Master Chuang (Master Zhuang).

In spite of the fact that it is richly rewarding, the *Chuang Tzu* is not an easy book. It has been a challenge to me, the translator, to devise means for bringing it alive in English while at the same time remaining faithful to the extraordinary qualities of the original Chinese text. I predict that the *Chuang Tzu* will be equally challenging to you, the reader. But, in the end, you will emerge from your encounter with this wonderful anthology a wiser and happier person. That is my promise to you, reader, so long as you promise not to get hung up on mere words. For, as the *Chuang Tzu* (end of Chapter 26) says:

> A fish-trap is for catching fish; once you've caught the fish, you can forget about the trap. A rabbit-snare is for catching rabbits; once you've caught the rabbit, you can forget about the snare. Words are for catching ideas; once you've caught the idea, you can forget about the words. Where can I find a person who knows how to forget about words so that I can have a few words with him?

INTRODUCTION

THE HISTORICAL CONTEXT

The core of the *Chuang Tzu* was probably originally composed in the latter half of the fourth century B.C.E., but the text as a whole was not completed until toward the end of the second century B.C.E. To understand the nature of its compilation, we need to become familiar with the historical background and intellectual currents of the era when the book came into being.

The Chou dynasty (circa 1111–255 B.C.E.) was founded on feudalist principles that worked fairly well for a little over four centuries. During the Spring and Autumn period (771–476 B.C.E.), however, the authority of the Chou kings began to be undermined. While the Chou dynasty had not yet broken up entirely, it was divided into spheres of influence controlled by a dozen or so small feudal duchies. Late in this period, the *shih* ("retainer; knight") arose as an important new intellectual force in China. Gradually, they evolved from a warrior class to an influential group of scholars and political theorists who actively sought to alter the policies of the various dukes. Confucius is a good example of one such knight-scholar. Many of China's most prominent early thinkers came from this class, one of the four main classes of Chinese society during the latter half of the Chou period, the other three being farmers, artisans, and merchants.

The Spring and Autumn period was followed by the Warring States period, also called the period of the Contending Kingdoms (475–221 B.C.E.). The deterioration of the Chou dynasty continued apace, with the imperial house being reduced to mere symbolic status. Real power was vested in the hands of the kings of the increasingly independent states who vied for hegemony. The number of significant states during this period was reduced to only half a dozen (see map, p. lv). Among themselves, they continually struggled for supremacy. Out of this constant conflict, two of the warring kingdoms, Ch'in in the far northwest and Ch'u in the south, finally emerged as the key powers. In 223 B.C.E., Ch'in defeated Ch'u and captured the heartland of China. A couple of years after that, Ch'in (whence the name China) established the first unified Chinese empire, the basic bureaucratic structure of which lasted until 1911, though undergoing countless rebellions and dynastic changes throughout history. To be brief, we may say that the Warring States period witnessed the demise of the old feudal regimes and their replacement by a centralized monarchy.

In spite of the political disruption and the social chaos of the Warring States period, intellectually this was by far the most exciting and lively era in the whole of Chinese history. Peripatetic philosophers wandered through the length and the breadth of the land trying to get the attention of any ruler who might be willing to put their ideas into practice. The Warring States period offers many interesting parallels with developments in Greek philosophy that were going on at the same time. We shall touch upon some of them here and in the Notes, but others deserve separate, intensive investigation for comparative purposes. Suffice it for the moment to say that the majority of China's seminal thinkers lived during this period and that it corresponds to the classical period of Greek philosophy.

CONFUCIANISM AND MOHISM

To understand the *Chuang Tzu*, it is necessary to realize that virtually all of the philosophical schools of the Warring States period were in dialogue with each other and, furthermore, that their vigorous debates are reflected in the pages of this book. Consequently, we would do well to make a survey of the most important thinkers of the age, especially those to whom the *Chuang Tzu* reacts most strongly.

The first intellectual tradition to coalesce as an identifiable school was that of the Confucianists. They were under the leadership of their namesake, the renowned early Chinese thinker, Confucius (551–479 B.C.E.). Confucius was active at the very end of the Spring and Autumn period, just before the outbreak of the Warring States period. Appearing during a time of sociopolitical upheaval, Confucius strove to restore order by propagating his doctrines.

Confucius was a man of great stature, both physically and in terms of his reputation. A profoundly conservative moralist who hearkened back to an imagined golden age at the beginning of the Chou dynasty, it was he who set the tone of reversion instead of progress that characterized the mainstream of Chinese social and political thought until this century and still has a profound influence on traditional Chinese intellectuals. His rationale for glorifying the past was based on the firm belief that the legendary sage-kings of antiquity could provide a model for good government in his own chaotic times.

Confucius' teachings are preserved in the *Analects* which consists largely of conversations between him and his disciples. In the *Analects*, Confucius asserts that a king should rule through virtuous suasion rather than through sheer power. His ideal leader was the superior man (*chüntzu*), a person who was guided by the highest principles of conduct. Confucius and his followers were very much concerned with issues of benefit and harm, right and wrong, good and bad. The Confucians were moral absolutists, stressing *yi* ("duty; righteousness; justice") and *jen* ("humaneness; benevolence"). At the same time, they were very much status-oriented in their approach to social relationships, insisting that there was an unalterably fixed pattern of domination and subservience between ruler and subject, father and son, husband and wife, elder brother and younger brother.

For Chuang Tzu (Master Chuang), the Confucianists were much too stiff and stuffy, too hidebound and hierarchical. Master Chuang took great delight in making fun of Confucius and his disciples. So formidable were Master Chuang's indictments of the Confucianists that the syncretists who were somewhat sympathetic to them tried to co-opt him by writing several sections subtly espousing their cause and sneaking them into his book. These will be pointed out below ("Structure and Composition of the Text") and in the appropriate chapter introductions.

The Mohists, who were active during the fourth and third centuries B.C.E., were the first to challenge the heritage of Confucius. Their founder, Mo Ti or Mo Tzu (Master Mo), lived during the second half of the fifth century, having been born a few years after Confucius's death. It is significant that Master Mo was almost an exact contemporary of Socrates and that there are so many analogies between the system of thought that he propounded and various schools of Greek philosophy from the same period, but especially the Stoics. Tradition holds that Master Mo was originally a follower of Confucianism until he realized that it overemphasized rituals at the expense of ethics, so he parted company and founded his own school.

Master Mo was a skillful military engineer but devoted his talents solely to defensive works. In this sense, he might best be characterized as a militant pacifist. From the titles of ten important chapters of his works, we can gain an idea of the sorts of issues that occupied him and his followers: religion ("The Will of Heaven" and "Elucidating the Spirits"), philosophy ("Rejecting Destiny" and "Universal Love"), politics ("Elevating the

Worthy," "Conformity with Superiors," and "Rejecting Aggression"), morals ("Economy in Funerals," "Economy in Expenditures," and "Rejecting Music"). Master Mo was associated with workers, craftsmen, and tradesmen, quite unlike Confucius and his followers who were aristocratic in their orientation. The Mohists were fiercely egalitarian and tested all dogmas by whether or not they benefited the people. For Mo Tzu, everything was measured in terms of social utility. He criticized the Confucians for their skepticism of heaven and spiritual beings as well as for their fatalism. Consequently, a debate of huge proportions ensued between the Confucians and the Mohists. The Mohist style of argumentation was dry and wooden. This is one of the reasons why their teachings virtually disappeared after the third century B.C.E. and have only been brought to light again in this century. Because of the ostensible similarity in their doctrines, Christians have been especially interested in the Mohists.

The Mohists were scientifically minded. Their works include estimable treatises on optics and other technical subjects. So practically oriented were they that they even adopted the use of some simplified sinographs in an attempt to ease the burden of a difficult writing system. The Mohists subscribed to an ascetic discipline and behaved like religious fundamentalists. After the death of the founder, Mohism was organized into a church headed by a succession of Elder Masters that lasted for several centuries. As a man, Master Mo was admired by all, but his teachings are considered by most Chinese to have been far too demanding. In a nutshell, we may describe Master Mo as a spartan, populist activist and theoretician of rather dour disposition who advocated universal love, inveighed against excess and luxury, and believed that the only justifiable war was a defensive one—not at all to be scoffed at but, by the same token, not at all to the lighthearted taste of Master Chuang either. He considered the Mohists to be far too preachy and pragmatic, too mechanical and maudlin. We will encounter much wry ridicule of them in these pages.

OTHER DOMINANT PHILOSOPHIES

Chinese historians speak of the Hundred Schools of Thought that flourished during the Warring States period, a round number serving to indicate the many competing schools. It was indeed the most vital period in the development of Chinese thought. All the schools came forth in response to the burning realities of the day and suggested a broad spectrum of solutions to cure the ills of the body politic. The leading thinkers were often government officials themselves or itinerant scholars who traveled from one feudal state to another promoting their programs for social and political reform, trying to find a sympathetic ruler who would put them into action. The ideas of these Hundred Schools are preserved in the conversations between their masters and disciples, in memorials and other types of documents, and in treatises of varying lengths. The chief concepts that all of the schools debated included the following:

Tao (pronounced *dow*)—the Way, or to be more etymologically precise, the Track

Te (pronounced *duh*)—integrity or virtue; etymologically rendered as "doughtiness"

Jen (pronounced *ren*)—benevolence; etymologically equivalent to "humaneness"

Yi (pronounced *yee*)—righteousness; etymologically rendered as "justice"

T'ien (pronounced *teeyan*)—heaven; etymologically equivalent to "divinity"

Each school had its own particular Way or Track. The Confucians, for example, promoted the Way of man, and the Taoists advocated the Way of the Way (cosmos or a universalized concept of nature). The *Chuang Tzu* responded to nearly all the other schools of thought during the middle and late Warring

States period. Since Master Chuang reacted to these schools, elements from a wide variety of sources are operative in his book. To understand the *Chuang Tzu*, then, it is necessary to have some sense of the competing schools of thought that were present during the Warring States period, beyond just the Confucians and the Mohists.

During the fourth century, a new figure enters the fray. This is the individualist Yang Chu. Most of what we know about Yang Chu may be found in the seventh chapter of the *Master Lieh* which bears his name. It shows him as an unorthodox personage, but not as someone who was truly licentious. His enemies called him an egoist and it was unfairly said of him (by a prominent Confucian) that he would not sacrifice a hair to benefit all under heaven. (What he actually said was "If nobody would sacrifice a hair, if nobody would try to benefit the world, then the world would become orderly." In other words, we should live and let live, not imposing ourselves on others nor letting others impose themselves on us. The Confucian distortion is both obvious and self-serving.) This was in direct contrast to Master Mo who was renowned as an extremely hard worker for the public good. The Yangists were intent upon protecting themselves from the dangers of involvement in political strife. Yang Chu held that man must nourish his Heaven-endowed nature by keeping it intact and striving for happiness. We may characterize his philosophy as a brand of moderate hedonism.

It was in this context, then—after Confucius, Mo Tzu, and Yang Chu—that Master Chuang appeared upon the scene. It is not surprising that these three thinkers loom so large in his book, because they had set the terms of the Warring States period's intellectual debates. But Master Chuang does something very unusual. Instead of joining them in a debate, he deflates them by undermining both their basic premises and the methods by which they argued them. Over and over again, Master Chuang demonstrates the futility of debate. Simultaneously with his attacks on disputation, however, a new group materialized who espoused argument as a legitimate professional pursuit in its own right.

Appearing in the late fourth century, at about the same time as Master Chuang, were the Sophists or Logicians. Perhaps it would be more accurate to refer to them by the literal translation of their designation in Chinese, the School of Names (or Terms), or the School of Names and Debate, because they did not actually develop any syllogistic reasoning nor discover any laws of thought. In diverse ways, this new school affected all the other schools that were active during the fourth century. The leaders of the Sophists were Hui Shih and Kungsun Lung. Like the Mohist school, from which they derived, they were in favor of universal love and opposed to offensive war, but they differed from their predecessors in practicing disputation for its own sake. It was the Sophists who devised a whole set of celebrated paradoxes, such as Kungsun Lung's famous "A white horse is not a horse." Many of these paradoxical statements are preserved in the *Chuang Tzu*, but they are included there almost as a sort of joke. Master Chuang was actually a close friend of Hui Shih's. He mischievously debated with him and poked fun at his logic-chopping.

It is worth noting that the author of the final chapter of the *Chuang Tzu* gives great prominence to Hui Shih, not only by placing him in the culminating position, but simply by devoting so much space to this otherwise largely neglected philosopher. There is, in fact, some evidence that this section of Chapter 33 may originally have been part of a separate chapter devoted to Hui Shih. Like Master Mo, he truly deserves to be called a philosopher in contrast to the vast majority of other early Chinese thinkers who dealt primarily with social and political problems rather than logic, ontology, epistemology, and so forth. Master Mo, interestingly enough, is similarly highlighted in this survey by being placed first and by being awarded generous coverage.

Another major personality who appeared on the scene at

about the same time as Master Chuang was Mencius (circa 372–289 B.C.E.). Whereas Master Chuang satirized Confucius, Mo Tzu, and Yang Chu, Mencius ardently defended Confucius and criticized the other two. For his advocacy of collectivism based on universal love, Mencius singled out Mo Tzu as Confucius's most dangerous rival. His focus was on human nature, a subject that had actually been brought to the fore by Yang Chu. Still, Mencius criticized Yang Chu sharply for his assertion of the primacy of the self over society. Mencius emphasized that human nature is basically good and that all men could become sages by fulfilling their inherent potential. He tempered the aristocratic side of Confucianism by being a champion of the common people and speaking out for humane government. This he did by stressing the role of the scholar-official in inculcating moral values in the ruler who, as a result, would be encouraged to treat his subjects more kindly. Of all the early Confucian thinkers, Mencius was the most concerned with individual human development, but always within the context of creating a good society. During the third century, Master Hsün, another Confucian thinker who was influenced by several other schools, declared human nature to be fundamentally bad, that it could only be kept in check by education and strict moral inculcation. Given these presuppositions, it is not surprising that he believed in authoritarian principles of government.

By the end of the fourth century, all but the Confucians had recognized that the authority of the ancient sages could no longer be depended upon as an adequate guide to the contemporary world that had changed so tremendously. Master Chuang was among those who denied the relevance of the ancient sages for the contemporary world. Furthermore, while Confucian humanism definitely put man at the center of things, Master Chuang thought of man as but one among the myriad things.

Wing-tsit Chan (*Source Book*, p. 178) has pointed out that the Confucians have by and large been critical of Master Chuang. Hsün Tzu (Master Hsün, flourished 298–238 B.C.E.) said that he was "prejudiced in favor of nature and does not know man." Chu Hsi (1130–1200), the preeminent Neo–Confucian, complained, "Lao Tzu at least wanted to do something, but Master Chuang did not want to do anything at all. He even said that he knew what to do but just did not want to do it."

This antagonism to Master Chuang on the part of the Confucians is understandable, of course, because Master Chuang himself was so critical of them. Master Chuang often plays tricks on us by sometimes having Confucius speak like a Taoist and sometimes like himself. We can never be sure which is which unless we pay very close attention to the drift of an entire tale. The multiplicity of ambiguous personae in the *Chuang Tzu* is part of the exhilarating reading experience that it presents. Sometimes even Master Chuang himself is made to appear antithetical to what we would expect of Master Chuang by sounding Confucian, pedantic, or technical.

To summarize this survey of Chinese thought during the Warring States period, we may say that the Confucians were primarily interested in family relationships as the model for organizing good government, the Mohists were preoccupied by societal obligations, the Yangists were concerned with the preservation and enhancement of the individual, the Sophists were consumed by questions of logic, and the Legalists were focused wholly on the advancement of the ruler and his state. In opposition to all of these were the Taoists who viewed human society and politics as inevitably corrupting and sought to merge with the Way by returning to nature as contemplative quietists and hermits.

Perhaps the best and most authoritative introduction to Warring States philosophy is the concluding chapter of the *Chuang Tzu* itself. A systematic account of the outstanding thinkers of the age, this chapter presents—in tightly argued, analytical fashion—many of the themes and figures that appear in narrative form elsewhere in the book. From a strictly scholarly point of view, therefore, it may well be the most valuable chapter of the *Chuang Tzu*, even though it was clearly not written by Master Chuang himself, but probably by the editor(s) of the book who brought together the disparate materials that go to make it up. "All Under Heaven" amounts to a critical review of the major (and some minor) thinkers of the pre-Ch'in period. Considering the unprecedented nature of its accomplishment, the last chapter of the *Chuang Tzu* is a most remarkable document, a veritable intellectual tour de force.

RELATIONSHIP TO THE *TAO TE CHING*

Of all the philosophers who were active during the Warring States period, Master Chuang's closest affinities are naturally with Lao Tzu (the Old Master or Masters—there were probably more than one of them). Like the Old Masters, Master Chuang held that what can be said of the Way is not really the Way, and there are many other points of similarity between them. The Old Masters were the originators of the sayings that were compiled as the *Tao Te Ching* around the end of the third century B.C.E. Master Chuang quotes from the *Tao Te Ching* repeatedly; dozens of examples could be cited. Those who are well acquainted with the *Tao Te Ching* will frequently notice echoes of that text in the pages of the *Chuang Tzu*. What is intriguing, however, is that they usually are not exact quotations. In other instances, sayings attributed to the Old Masters are not to be found in the standard edition of the *Tao Te Ching*. This indicates that the *Tao Te Ching* was still probably circulating as oral tradition at the time of Chuang Chou and had not yet coalesced as a written text, certainly not the text that we know today.

The *Tao Te Ching* is extremely terse and open to many different interpretations. The *Chuang Tzu*, on the other hand, is more definitive and comprehensive as a repository of early Taoist thought. The *Tao Te Ching* was addressed to the sage-king; it is basically a handbook for rulers. The *Chuang Tzu*, in contrast, is the earliest surviving Chinese text to present a philosophy for the individual. The authors of the *Tao Te Ching* were interested in establishing some sort of Taoist rule, while the authors of the *Chuang Tzu* opted out of society, or at least out of power relationships within society. Master Chuang obviously wanted no part of the machinery of government. He compared the state bureaucrat to a splendidly decorated ox being led to sacrifice, while he preferred to think of himself as an unconstrained piglet playing in the mud. The *Tao Te Ching* offers the Way as a guide for life and it propounds nonaction as a means to achieve one's purpose in the workaday world. Master Chuang believed that the Way had supreme value in itself and consequently did not occupy himself with its mundane applications. Rather than paying attention to the governance of human society (the fundamental concern of most early Chinese thinkers), he stressed the need for transcendence and the freedom of the individual from such worldly concerns. In spite of all the differences, however, Master Chuang was clearly attracted by the doctrines of the Old Masters and many of his writings may be thought of as expanded metaphors or meditations on the brief sayings of those early Taoist luminaries whose ideas have been enshrined in the *Tao Te Ching.*

There is no text listed in the earliest authoritative catalogue of Chinese books as having been written by the Old Masters (Lao Tzu), nor is there a *Tao Te Ching* in 5,000 sinographs (its legendary length) or in eighty-one chapters (the number in the received version) that can be dated to the pre-Ch'in period. This fits with my contention that a single Old Master never existed, that the text associated with the Old Masters is a Ch'in period (or from a time shortly before then, in the latter half of the third century B.C.E.) compilation of adages and wise sayings attributed to a type of sage, many of whom were active during the Spring and Autumn and Warring States periods (722–221 B.C.E.), and that the text in question only came to be called the *Tao Te Ching* several centuries later under the impact of the rise of religious Taoism (which itself came into being as a result of the massive influence of Buddhism upon Chinese society and thought around that time). The questions of the dating and authorship of the *Chuang Tzu* are no less complicated than those for the *Tao Te Ching*. We shall devote a special section to them below.

Although the problems surrounding the authorship of the *Tao Te Ching* and the *Chuang Tzu* may be dissimilar, their respective literary forms can give us some insight into their composition. The *Tao Te Ching* is written entirely in verse, snatches of which are also to be found in other texts dating to about the same period in which it took shape. One of the functions of gnomic verse, especially when it is rhymed, is that it is easily memorized. Indeed, in traditional societies where the technology of writing is not widespread, the regular structure of verse itself is a sort of mnemonic device. In contrast, unrhymed prose with its varying cadences is much harder to commit to memory and is a sign of the emergence of cultures premised upon the written word as the primary technology for preserving and transmitting information.

The *Tao Te Ching* is renowned for its density and brevity. The *Chuang Tzu*, on the other hand, is best characterized as being written in a "rambling" mode. This expansive style reflects the freedom of life advocated by Master Chuang. The very first parable in the book, about the inability of little fowl to comprehend the stupendousness of the giant P'eng-bird, is typical of the relaxed quality of the book as a whole.

The shape of the *Tao Te Ching* is exactly what we would expect of a body of sage wisdom that was normally conveyed orally—it was poetic and communal in the sense that its authorship was shared (that is, it cannot readily be attributed to a single, easily identifiable creator). The *Chuang Tzu* evinces a stage when writing was just starting to free itself from the exclusive control of priests and diviners (esoteric specialists in sacred lore

and ritual), and authorship by identifiable intellectuals was beginning to take on a more definite role in Chinese society.
Therefore, the *Chuang Tzu* is fundamentally a work of prose, but
it still includes sizable chunks of verse having an oral heritage,
some of it gnomic as with the *Tao Te Ching*, some of it epic
(though severely fragmented, as was all early Chinese myth that
encountered the stridently anti-mystical strains of Confucianism), and some of it oracular (notably the stunning series of
cosmic riddles that opens Chapter 14). I consider the verse
portions of the *Chuang Tzu* as being oral wisdom embedded in
the prose matrix of a single thinker and his followers and
redactors. The transitional nature of the *Chuang Tzu* is further
evident in the fact that much of its prose is highly rhythmic and
parallel, partaking of certain qualities of verse. It might have
been possible to set off more passages as verse or semiverse, but I
have resisted the temptation to do so on the grounds that the
Chuang Tzu, in the final analysis, is a work of prose. We must
remember, however, that the Warring States philosophers, of
whom Master Chuang was one, were mostly peripatetic per-
suaders who went about trying to convince the rulers of the
contending kingdoms to adopt their policies and, through them,
to bring peace to the empire. The word for persuasion in
Classical Chinese is *shui*, which is cognate with *shuo* ("to say,
speak"). Hence, even though the *Chuang Tzu* represents one of the
earliest attempts in China to write discursive prose, it is still
imbued with the oral tradition out of which it grew.

The third major Taoist text, the *Lieh Tzu*, is of questionable
authenticity. Most scholars would agree that it was put together
during the third century C.E. and that it was much colored by
Buddhist sources. Nonetheless, the *Lieh Tzu* does contain some
passages that undoubtedly are based upon pre-Ch'in lore. Master
Lieh figures prominently in the *Chuang Tzu* and was even awarded
his own chapter (32). The fourth major Taoist collection is the
Master Huainan which dates to around 130 B.C.E. It is a highly
eclectic work, selecting elements from a variety of sources.

The Question of Authorship

The *Chuang Tzu* in its present form was certainly not written by Chuang Chou, the putative author. Before explaining how we know this to be the case, let us examine what facts may be gleaned about the life of our supposed author. Born around the year 369 B.C.E., Chuang Chou was from Meng, a district of the northern state of Sung (it lay south of the Yellow River near the border between the modern provinces of Shantung and Honan). Though Sung was considered to be a northern state, Meng was very close to the border with the powerful southern state of Ch'u and consequently strongly influenced by southern culture. It is not surprising that later, in an imperial proclamation of the year 742, the *Chuang Tzu* was awarded the honorific title *True Scripture of the Southern Florescence (Nanhua chen ching)*.

Not much else is known of Chuang Chou's life except that he seems to have spent some time in Ch'u and in the Ch'i (a northern state) capital of Lintzu where he must have associated with scholars from the celebrated Chihsia "academy" that was located there. Chuang Chou probably died in about 286 B.C.E. In fact, the evidence for the existence of a historical Chuang Tzu (Master Chuang) is only slightly greater than that for a historical Lao Tzu (Old Master), the alleged author of the *Tao Te Ching*, which is virtually nil. In fact, as we have seen, the Old Master was most likely not a single historical personage at all but a congeries of ancient sages. Nonetheless, the great historian Ssuma Ch'ien managed circa 104 B.C.E. to devise a sort of "biography" for Chuang Chou in scroll 63 of his celebrated *The Grand Scribe's Records (Shih chi)*. Ever since that time, devotees have believed that Chuang Chou really did exist and that it was he who wrote the *Chuang Tzu*.

Here is what Ssuma Ch'ien actually had to say about Master Chuang:

> Master Chuang was a man of Meng and his given name was Chou. Chou once served as a minor function-

ary at Lacquer Garden and was a contemporary of King Hui of Liang and King Hsüan of Ch'i. There was nothing upon which his learning did not touch, but its essentials derived from the words of the Old Masters. Therefore, his writings, consisting of over a hundred thousand words, for the most part were allegories. He wrote "An Old Fisherman," "Robber Footpad," and "Ransacking Coffers" to criticize the followers of Confucius and to illustrate the arts of the Old Masters. Chapters such as "The Wilderness of Jagged" and "Master K'angsang" were all empty talk without any substance. Yet his style and diction were skillful and he used allusions and analogies to excoriate the Confucians and the Mohists. Even the most profound scholars of the age could not defend themselves. His words billowed without restraint to please himself. Therefore, from kings and dukes on down, great men could not put him to use.

King Wei of Ch'u heard that Chuang Chou was a worthy man. He sent a messenger with bountiful gifts to induce him to come and promised to make him a minister. Chuang Chou laughed and said to the messenger of Ch'u, "A thousand gold pieces is great profit and the position of minister is a respectful one, but haven't you seen the sacrificial ox used in the suburban sacrifices? After being fed for several years, it is garbed in patterned embroidery so that it may be led into the great temple. At this point, though it might wish to be a solitary piglet, how could that be? Go away quickly, sir, do not pollute me! I'd rather enjoy myself playing around in a fetid ditch than be held in bondage by the ruler of a kingdom. I will never take office for as long as I live, for that is what pleases my fancy."

Judging from the dates of King Hui of Liang (reigned 370–355 B.C.E.), King Hsüan of Ch'i (reigned 319–301 B.C.E.), and

King Wei of Ch'u (reigned 339–329 B.C.E.) who are mentioned in this account, Chuang Chou was roughly a contemporary of Mencius (372–289 B.C.E.). Ssuma Ch'ien states that Chuang Chou was born in Meng, located just north of Shang Hill City (Shangch'iu shih) in eastern Honan province. The location of the Lacquer Garden, where he is supposed to have held a minor position, is not certain. In fact, Lacquer Garden may not even be a place name at all but only a general designation for a plantation. Some scholars hold that it was located about fifty miles northeast of the modern city of Kaifeng (also in Honan province). It is noteworthy that none of the five chapters from the *Chuang Tzu* cited by Ssuma Ch'ien as written by Chuang Chou himself occur among the "inner," supposedly more authentic, chapters of the book.

We must remember that this skimpy biographical sketch was written more than two centuries after the time of Chuang Chou and that, during the intervening period, there were no other works that provided any useful information about his life. Furthermore, most of Ssuma Ch'ien's brief portrait of Chuang Chou is drawn from anecdotes in the *Chuang Tzu* itself. Since the *Chuang Tzu* is full of hyperbolic invention, this means that they have no necessary basis in fact. Aside from those recounted by Ssuma Ch'ien, there are a number of other memorable anecdotes about Chuang Chou in the later chapters of the *Chuang Tzu,* but these are largely apocryphal. According to these anecdotes and to the hagiographical legends that have grown up around him, it would appear that Chuang Chou was a highly unconventional person who paid no attention to physical comfort or social status. He is said to have worn raggedy clothing and to have tied his shoes on with string to prevent them from falling apart. Although he was poor, Chuang Chou by no means thought of himself as unfortunate or miserable.

There are a number of tales in the *Chuang Tzu* that indicate that Chuang Chou did not consider death as something to be feared. For example, when his philosopher-friend Hui Shih came to console him upon the death of his wife, he found Master Chuang sitting sprawled out on the floor beating on a basin and singing.

> "When she first died, how could I of all people not be melancholy? But I reflected on her beginning and realized that originally she was unborn. Not only was she unborn, originally she had no form. Not only did she have no form, originally she had no vital breath. Intermingling with nebulousness and blurriness, a transformation occurred and there was vital breath; the vital breath was transformed and there was form; the form was transformed and there was birth; now there has been another transformation and she is dead. This is like the progression of the four seasons—from spring to autumn, from winter to summer. There she sleeps blissfully in an enormous chamber. If I were to have followed her weeping and wailing, I think it would have been out of keeping with destiny, so I stopped." (18.2)

When Master Chuang himself was about to die, his disciples planned an elaborate burial, but he protested, saying that all he wanted was for heaven and earth to be his inner and outer coffins, the sun and moon to be his paired jades, the stars and constellations to be his pearls, and all natural phenomena to be his mortuary gifts. Apparently, Master Chuang viewed death as a natural process or transformation. Death to him was but the giving up of one form of existence and the assuming of another. Master Chuang believed that the wise man or woman accepts death with equanimity and thereby achieves absolute happiness.

Occasionally, the names of ancient Chinese philosophers afford a clue to their affiliations or intentions (like Master Mo ["Ink," as used by carpenters in drawing a straight line], Master Kuan ["Tube," purpose unknown], Old Master [a hoary sage], and Lieh Yük'ou ["Resist Tyranny"]). Chuang Chou's surname and name, which ostensibly mean "Solemn Round," do not help us much in this regard because he was anything but sedate, though he may well be thought of as slipperily circular.

The connection between Chuang Chou and the *Chuang Tzu*, though less tenuous than that between Lao Tzu and the *Tao Te Ching*, still presents obstacles of its own. As a historical personage, Chuang Chou remains an enigma. Inasmuch as there are almost no hard facts available about Chuang Chou the man, we are forced to rely on information that may be gleaned from the *Chuang Tzu* itself in an attempt to figure out what sort of person he was. As we have seen, however, this is not a very reliable procedure either, given the playful propensities of the author(s) of the text. Even the synoptic Chapter 33, "All Under Heaven," gives only an enigmatic, though endearing, account of Chuang Chou the individual.

Whether or not there ever was a Chuang Chou (there probably was), of one thing we can be sure: he did not write all of the *Chuang Tzu*. The sheer amount of blatantly contradictory ideological materials that occur in the various chapters alone is proof enough of that. The literary quality of the chapters is also tremendously uneven, some of them being among the finest masterpieces of Chinese writing, brilliantly conceived and expressed, while others are tritely composed and sloppily executed. The Sophist, Kungsun Lung, is mentioned three times in the *Chuang Tzu*. Since he was active after Chuang Chou, this indicates that the *Chuang Tzu* was compiled after the time of the master himself. In the survey of schools of thought that constitutes Chapter 33 and elsewhere in the text, Chuang Chou is discussed from a historical viewpoint. This is further evidence that the *Chuang Tzu* was put together by someone other than Chuang Chou. In order to find out who that might have been, we need to discuss in more detail the separate strands and layers of the book.

Structure and Composition of the Text

Since the middle of the third century C.E., scholars have regarded the *Chuang Tzu* as a composite text. The current edition (standard from the fourth century C.E.) has thirty-three chapters, but there is good evidence that a fifty-two-chapter edition of the *Chuang Tzu* existed as late as the first century B.C.E. Kuo Hsiang (d. 312 C.E.), basing his work on that of a previous commentator named Hsiang Hsiu, wrote the first extant and what many consider to be the best commentary on the *Chuang Tzu*. By doing so, he secured its position as the primary source for early Taoist thought. Kuo Hsiang was undoubtedly also the compiler of the *Chuang Tzu* in its present form.

The *Chuang Tzu* as we now have it is divided into three parts: the Inner Chapters (1–7), the Outer Chapters (8–22), and the Miscellaneous Chapters (23–33). The first seven chapters, the Inner Chapters, are considered by the majority of scholars to reflect best the thought of Master Chuang himself. Of the three sections, they are the most often translated and are widely considered to be the most authentic. This is not to assert, however, that they are the only excellent parts of the book. Many connoisseurs of the *Chuang Tzu*, for example, would claim that the most beautiful chapter is 17, which includes the magnificent dialogue between the Earl of the Yellow River and the Overlord of the Northern Sea. And Chapter 29, which contains the long, bizarre conversation between Robber Footpad and Confucius, is held by many devotees of the book to be the most humorous.

The great discrepancies among the contents of the various chapters are due to a number of factors. First are the doctrinal differences among the Taoist factions that came after Master Chuang and were identified with him. Some of these were undoubtedly affected to one degree or another by other schools and hence would have brought in material from them. Next are the non-Taoist thinkers who recognized the enormous appeal of

Master Chuang and wanted to appropriate part of his popularity to advance their own programs. The incorporation of sections by such thinkers in the *Chuang Tzu* further complicated the text. The *Chuang Tzu* is thus a very heterogeneous work that does not speak with a single voice. The number of ways of looking at the *Chuang Tzu* are as plentiful as the disparate facets of the text itself.

No one has yet discovered a trustworthy method for firmly attributing even the Inner Chapters to Chuang Chou, although a growing consensus tends to do so. Beyond the first seven Inner Chapters, some scholars see a number of other identifiable strands operative. Chapters 8–10 and parts of 11 reflect a primitive, naturalist cast associated with the followers of the Old Masters (Lao Tzu). Chapters 12–16 and perhaps 33 are said to belong to the Syncretists who probably edited the book as a whole. Their role will be further examined in the following paragraph. Chapters 16–27 are thought to represent the ideas of later members of Master Chuang's own school. Finally, there are the individualists of a somewhat Yangist disposition who seem to be responsible for Chapters 28–31. This breakdown by no means exhausts the complexity of the *Chuang Tzu*, but it does give some notion of the difficulties inherent in dealing with early Chinese texts.

The precise responsibility for the composition of the separate portions of the *Chuang Tzu* is shrouded in mystery. Nor are we on much firmer ground when it comes to determining who first collected them into a single volume. Several critical scholars now believe that the *Chuang Tzu* was compiled by Liu An (d. 122 B.C.E.), the Han dynasty Prince of Huainan, with the assistance of attendants at his court. The lavish, un-Chuang Tzu-ish praise of the sovereign in some of the Outer Chapters and Miscellaneous Chapters seems like the kind of sycophancy expected of the court literati who danced attendance upon Liu An. Liu An and his circle of scholars did espouse a brand of philosophical syncretism (aimed at reconciling differing schools of thought into a single system) that seems to be compatible with the overall composition of the *Chuang Tzu* and especially the signaturelike final chapter. Still, we lack hard data to ascribe with confidence the initial editing of the *Chuang Tzu* to anyone in particular.

Kuo Hsiang's standard edition of the *Chuang Tzu* that has been transmitted down to us contains many commentaries that appear to have worked their way into the text. In the present translation, I have removed some of the more egregious instances (they have been transferred to the section at the back entitled Deleted Passages). All thirty-three chapters of the Kuo Hsiang edition of the *Chuang Tzu* have titles, but they do not derive from the period of the initial composition of the text and thus are not to be taken overly seriously.

The original heart of the *Chuang Tzu* probably consisted of relatively short, vivid parables and fables such as the opening paragraphs of the book. Another good example is the first paragraph of 5.5. The ensuing paragraphs beginning "Thus" and "Therefore" may be later explanatory additions. This pattern is frequently repeated elsewhere in the book: a short, graphic tale or parable followed by more abstract expositions of the point that it makes, e.g., 24.10. The two types of materials frequently clash in mood and in style. Naturally, it is the concrete narratives that are more memorable than the abstract expositions.

In short, Chuang Chou did not write the *Chuang Tzu*. For the sake of convenience, however, we may collectively refer to the nominal author(s) of the core passages of the *Chuang Tzu* as Master Chuang (Chuang Tzu), which is to say that we associate the text with the school of thought that was grouped around that shadowy name.

IMPORTANCE OF THE *CHUANG TZU*

After the Old Master(s), the fathers of the Taoist church have always looked upon Master Chuang as the most important fountainhead of their tradition, but one wonders how much of Taoist religion the wag would have been able to stomach. A wide

spectrum of Chinese thinkers has similarly tried to pre-empt
Master Chuang, or parts of him, for their own. But this is
perhaps the most serious mistake in dealing with the protean
Master Chuang, namely, to treat him as a systematic philosopher. Master Chuang's game is to put dents in, if not annihilate
altogether, human thought processes. Rather than rationality, it
is intuition that he favors. Such a figure can scarcely be taken as a
model upon which to build a system of thought. The importance of the *Chuang Tzu* lies far more in its function as a literary
repository than as a philosophical disquisition.

There are scores of famous passages from the *Chuang Tzu*
that are among the most memorable in all of Chinese literature.
Here I shall cite only two:

> The emperor of the Southern Sea was Lickety, the
> emperor of the Northern Sea was Split, and the emperor
> of the Center was Wonton. Lickety and Split often met
> each other in the land of Wonton, and Wonton treated
> them very well. Wanting to repay Wonton's kindness,
> Lickety and Split said, "All people have seven holes for
> seeing, hearing, eating, and breathing. Wonton alone
> lacks them. Let's try boring some holes for him." So
> every day they bored one hole, and on the seventh day
> Wonton died. (7.7)

This demonstrates graphically the disastrous consequences of
going against nature. What makes us remember the lesson is not
so much the contents of the doctrine espoused but the inimitable
manner in which it is expressed.

> Once upon a time Chuang Chou dreamed that he
> was a butterfly, a butterfly flitting about happily enjoy-
> ing himself. He didn't know that he was Chou. Suddenly
> he awoke and was palpably Chou. He did not know
> whether he were Chou who had dreamed of being a

butterfly or a butterfly who was dreaming that he was Chou. Now, there must be a difference between Chou and the butterfly. This is called the transformation of things. (2.14)

Here Master Chuang is playing on the theme of transformation. So striking is the imagery that whole dramas have been written on this theme. If Master Chuang had been merely a pedestrian, prosaic philosopher, no one would pay any particular attention to his claim about the "transformation of things."

Conveyed by the literary grandness of Master Chuang is a grandness of soul. Through it, we are led to liberation. In the very first chapter, Master Chuang tells us that there are varying degrees of happiness. The greatest happiness is achieved through a higher understanding of the nature of things. For the full development of oneself, one needs to express one's innate ability. This is *te*, whose basic meaning for Master Chuang, as for the Old Masters, is integrity or character. *Te* is the manifestation in the individual of the universal Way/Track or Tao. The Tao is thus immanent in all creatures and things, even in excrement. (22.6)

That which belongs to beings and objects by nature is intrinsic or internal; that which is imposed upon them by man is extrinsic or external. All the myriad things in the world are different by nature and they have different innate abilities, but they are equal (each in their own way, of course) when they freely exercise their innate abilities. In other words, for Master Chuang equality exists only in the universal Way that both permeates and embraces the enormous variety of the myriad things. Yet, instead of letting a duck keep its short legs and the crane its long legs (8.1), man intervenes and tries to impose an artificial equality (that is, uniformity) by making them have legs of the same length. This runs counter to the nature of both the duck and the crane. Artificiality forcibly attempts to change things according to its own conceptions and enforces uniformity (not equality). This is the purpose of all morals, laws, institutions, and governments, namely, to promote sameness and to eradicate difference.

The motivation of those who promote uniformity may be entirely laudable. For example, if they believe that something is good for themselves, they may wish to see others enjoy it too. In the process, however, they are more than likely to demean, if not destroy, those whom they intend to help because they oppose their individual natures. We may say, then, that Master Chuang was the first great proponent of true diversity and that he had the good sense to recognize that it could not be achieved through government fiat.

Master Chuang strenuously opposed the formal mechanisms of government. In his view, the best way to govern is through no government at all. In this, he agreed with the Old Masters, but for different reasons. The Old Masters were deeply concerned with governance, but advocated a minimalist policy simply because they felt that the more government there was the less effective it would be. For Master Chuang, however, the whole notion of government was problematic because of the opposition between man and nature. Better to let things take their own course, he would say, and not govern them at all, not even minimally. Lest he be misinterpreted, it is questionable whether Master Chuang's position is tantamount to anarchy, and he was by no means in favor of violence. It was not Master Chuang's business to describe what sort of governing apparatus there should be; his purpose was to tell us what government should not do.

According to Master Chuang, every person can achieve happiness for himself or herself. Just let them be. Master Chuang's social and political philosophy is quite different from every other thinker in early China in that it was directed toward the private person rather than to groups. He encouraged individuals to seek inner happiness rather than trying to enforce happiness through government policy. To him this was a contradiction in terms. As soon as government intervenes in natural affairs, it destroys all possibility of genuine happiness.

Another lesson taught by Master Chuang through his parables is that of the humble artisans whose perfect mastery of their craft reveals a mastery of life itself. Butchers, wheelwrights, bell-stand makers, and others are shown to possess a superior wisdom that cannot be expressed in words and can only be acquired through experience and practice.

Modern critics often assert that Master Chuang was an anti-rationalist. The situation, however, is not quite so straightforward as that. While he is dubious about the efficacy of reason to solve all human problems, he does not assert its utter futility. To come to grips with Master Chuang's ambivalent attitude toward human rationality, we must explore the sources of his discontent with it. Master Chuang's animus toward rationality stems from historical circumstance. It was the Mohist plodding predilection for logic that left Master Chuang so disenchanted with this dull species of rationality. Master Mo's doctrines were so unusual in the context of Chinese thought that they had to be defended in open debate. As a result, he and his followers were the first thinkers in China regularly to engage in formal disputation. Honing their elocutionary expertise in this fashion, the Mohists came the closest of all schools in ancient China to constructing a coherent system of logic. Their initial success with this new technique of persuasion encouraged other schools to follow suit in developing the techniques of debate they had introduced. Consequently, philosophical disputation became endemic to the period. More than ever before, debaters paid attention to defining their terms, structuring their arguments, and seizing upon the fallacies of their opponents. Ultimately, as with Hui Shih and Kungsun Lung, logic became a pursuit for its own sake. Master Chuang was a younger friend and perhaps even initially a disciple of Hui Shih. His intimate familiarity with paradox and sophistry indicate that he must have dabbled with logical subtleties himself when he was young, but he obviously outgrew them.

Master Chuang's fascination with Hui Shih's brand of rationality stemmed from a desire to probe the limits of reason, not to deny its validity altogether. Master Chuang uses reason to put reason in proper perspective.

The late Mohist *Canons* (circa 300 B.C.E.) contain the most logically sophisticated texts from early China. In them, we see clearly the resort to reason as the arbiter of conflicting viewpoints. This approach, which had already become the hallmark of Greek philosophy and subsequently characterized the whole of the Western philosophical tradition, in the end was decisively rejected by later Chinese thinkers who preferred to rely more on moral persuasion and intuition. Master Chuang played a vital role in the emergence of Chinese skepticism toward rationality, turning it on its head and satirizing it trenchantly. In the *Chuang Tzu*, arguments that seem to have the appearance of reason are ironically designed to discredit it. Master Chuang was also very much interested in the intricate relationship of language and thought. His work is full of intentional non sequiturs and absurdities because he uses these devices to explore the inadequacies of language itself, an approach similar to that later taken by Zen masters with their koans. Again, we find Master Chuang ironically using a device to cast doubt upon the infallibility of that same device. This proves that he abandoned neither language nor reason; he only wished to point out that overdependence on them could limit the flexibility of thought.

Another key theme in the *Chuang Tzu* is that of relativity. A person who understands that big and little, soft and hard, good and bad are not absolutely counterposed transcends the ordinary distinctions among things and the distinction between self and other. In this way, he or she identifies with Unity and essentially becomes immortal.

Above all, Master Chuang emphasized spontaneity. He was a mystic who recommended freedom from the world and its conventions. Most philosophers of ancient China addressed their ideas to a political or intellectual elite, but Master Chuang focused on those who were striving for spiritual achievements.

The *Chuang Tzu* was involved in a vibrant interaction with Buddhism as this originally Indian religion developed in China. Chinese Buddhists received more inspiration from the *Chuang Tzu* than from any other early Chinese text. This is especially true of members of the Zen (Ch'an) school. We may, therefore, say that one of the major contributions of the *Chuang Tzu* to Chinese culture was the role that it played in the evolution of Zen, which has now become a world religion, particularly in its Japanese guise. But this is a phenomenon that occurred long after the composition of the original text. There is, however, evidence of Indian influence in the very formation of the *Chuang Tzu*, some of which has been pointed out in the Notes on the Translation (see, for example, the entries on "breathing . . . from the heels" and "bear strides and bird stretches" in the Glossary of Terms). We should also pay attention to the ancient Iranian elements in the *Chuang Tzu*. To give only one instance, the story of Chi Hsien and Master Hu (7.5) is about a contest of spiritual powers between an Iranian-style mage and an Indian-style sage. The mage, Chi Hsien, also appears in 14.1 playing the role of dispenser of cosmic wisdom who can answer riddles that would stump even an ancient Chinese sage. The puzzles that he solves have an even broader, trans-Eurasian compass since they take the form of an extended series of riddles uncannily like those posed by early Indo-European seers and priests. Also awaiting further investigation is the striking resemblance of the colloquy on the joy of fishes between Master Chuang and Master Hui (17.7) to many philosophical dialogues found in the works of Plato. Master Chuang was not an isolated Chinese thinker, but the impressive product of a long process of national and international cross-fertilization.

Master Chuang is claimed by both religionists and philosophers, but I think of him more as a fabulist, that is, as a composer of fables and apologues. It is as a literary stylist that Master

Chuang had his greatest impact on culture—probably more than any other single Chinese author, succeeding generations of writers have turned to him for allusions, themes, turns of phrase, and modes of expression. Painters likewise have found abundant stimulation in the tales of Master Chuang.

The *Chuang Tzu* is, first and foremost, a literary text and consequently should not be subjected to excessive philosophical analysis. Unfortunately, this is practically the only way that scholars have viewed the text during this century. In my estimation, this distorts its true value. What is more, the *Chuang Tzu* is not merely a literary text; it is actually an anthology or compilation of literary texts. Hence it is even less susceptible to systematic philosophical analysis. This is by no means to say that the *Chuang Tzu* is devoid of importance for the history of Chinese philosophy. To be sure, it contains much valuable information that documents intellectual trends during the Warring States period, but these must be sorted out very carefully. Because of the heterogeneous nature of the text, it is extremely difficult, if not altogether impossible, to determine a system of thought to which Chuang Chou subscribed. The *Chuang Tzu* is a monument of Chinese literature; it is in this light that we should read and interpret it.

NOTES ON THE TRANSLATION

Among the dozens of scholarly commentaries that I have examined during the course of my translation and annotation, the most useful are listed in the Bibliography. All of them suggest various emendations and revisions. I have tried to make the best of the text as it stands, permitting only the most limited changes, in spite of the fact that it is obviously corrupt (i.e., containing errors or alterations) in some places. My aim throughout has been to duplicate as closely as possible in English the experience that a trained student of Classical Chinese would have when he or she reads the *Chuang Tzu*. I should mention that an abstruse, ancient work such as the *Chuang Tzu* has always been inaccessible to all but a minute percentage of the Chinese population who possessed special preparation in grappling with its enormously refractory and artificial language. It is "artificial" in the sense that it is book language only, a dead language that may never have lived or lived only partially in the mouths of priests, seers, and bards, and that for more than two thousand years has not been capable of being understood when read aloud unless the auditor had previously memorized the passage in question. The monumentally difficult nature of Classical Chinese has become even more accentuated in this century with the demise of the imperial institutions that fostered and sustained this "unsayable" hieratic language as a mechanism of control through the powerful literati officials who had spent decades in mastering it. Since 1919, less than a decade after the revolution of 1911, which toppled the last dynasty, the Manchus, Classical Chinese has been replaced as the official written medium of China by the demotic vernacular, Modern Standard Mandarin. Today, modern citizens of China are at least as far removed from the language of the *Chuang Tzu* as modern speakers of English are from *Beowulf*, or as modern speakers of Greek are from Plato's *Republic*—if not further.

Classical Chinese is by its very nature problematic in that it has been dramatically divorced from spoken language for no less than two millennia and may always have been so because of the fact that it was written in a script that was only partially phonetic. The language of the *Chuang Tzu* is even more peculiar in that it purposely distorts and impishly tampers with the conventions of Classical Chinese itself. To render faithfully an extraordinary text like this into a living language such as English or Mandarin requires a stupendous act of transformation, not merely a mechanical translation. Against this need for a creative response to the *Chuang Tzu*'s linguistic mischief is the duty of the conscientious philologist to be as consistent and accurate as possible.

In the Introduction, I have stated that I believe the verse portions of the *Chuang Tzu* to be more nearly reflective of oral tradition than is the prose matrix in which they are embedded. But to assert that an early Chinese work such as the *Tao Te Ching* or the verse portions of the *Chuang Tzu* were of oral derivation is not to assert that the texts as they have been recorded accurately mirror the rhythms, structure, and grammar of the Eastern Chou speech upon which they were presumably based. To be sure, precise linguistic evidence indicates that, in the process of committing utterances to writing in ancient China, various conventions were employed that automatically omitted or simplified certain syntactic, morphemic, and grammatical features of the spoken languages. This was largely due to the partially phonetic nature of the Chinese script which made it virtually impossible to capture in writing with fidelity and facility all of the significant elements of speech.

Consequently, while written Chinese verse may not be a direct reflection of spoken language, it nonetheless reveals a bias in favor of gnomic and oracular modes of discourse which normally are associated with the realm of orality. The Chinese prejudice in favor of poetry at the expense of prose persisted throughout the imperial period and hearkens back to antiquity when knowledge was transmitted by seers and sages who commanded a body of wisdom verse. Chinese prose itself was continually contaminated (or, from another viewpoint, we may say "embellished") by the cadences and structures of poetry, and it is often well-nigh impossible to determine whether a given piece is written in prose or in poetry. This also accounts for the distinctive Chinese literary genres known as the rhapsody (*fu*) and parallel prose (*p'ient'iwen*), which lie somewhere between the realms of prose and poetry. Throughout Chinese history, there have been occasional efforts to "reform" and "purify" Chinese prose by making it less euphuistic, mannered, elevated, and poetic, and more straightforward, simple, practical, and prosaic. But, until the cataclysmic political revolutions of this century, which radically transformed the fundamental premises of Chinese society, there was always a continual reversion to poetry as the preferred form of writing.

As we have seen in the Introduction, the *Chuang Tzu* is an anthology composed of heterogeneous components. The many disparate voices in the text make it one of the most difficult of early Chinese works with which to grapple. The translation strives not to homogenize these various strands into a single, undifferentiated style, but to let the various voices of the whole text, no matter how discordant they may be, sing through by themselves. Where the original shows the hand of a genius, the translation attempts as best as possible to re-create in English its excellences, but where the original is awkward or clumsy, the translation makes no effort to camouflage its inferiority.

Even with the superior parts of the text, there is a natural tendency for translators to improve them to suit the tastes of Western readers. For example, Classical Chinese nearly always relies on the word *yüeh* to introduce a quotation. It basically means just "said" (or "asked" if a question is involved), but translators are given to rendering it as "responded," "exclaimed," "cried," "expostulated," and so forth. This dressing up of the text gives a false sense of the quality of the original work.

The reader should also be warned about the recurrence in the book of certain tales and parables, sometimes only barely modified. Another perhaps somewhat jarring quality of the book for a modern reader is the manner in which it jumps from one tale or parable to another within a given chapter. If one understands that these phenomena are due to the fact that the *Chuang Tzu* is essentially an anthology, rather than the product of a single mind, this will make it easier to accept. Furthermore, not only is the *Chuang Tzu* an anthology, it is an anthology that expresses the viewpoints of many different schools that debated with and borrowed from each other. Generally, however, each chapter expresses certain broad themes and the tales and parables within it are intended to illustrate them. These primary themes have been highlighted in brief introductory notes by the translator at the beginning of each chapter. Occasionally, the same story will be repeated in several chapters of the book with a slightly different twist because a different message is intended. Yet, regardless of the lack of seamless unity to the book, the scintillating language and wonderful imagery are sure to captivate the reader.

Aside from its notorious heterogeneity, another aspect of the *Chuang Tzu* that makes it so hard to deal with is the fact that it is occasionally textually corrupt. This is the result of a long and complicated process of redaction and transmission. All conscientious students of the text are frustrated by those parts of the *Chuang Tzu* that are manifestly garbled or have evident contradictions. In many instances, I have been able to solve these problems by resorting to various text-critical methods, but in some I have simply had to make difficult decisions about what I thought the authors were really trying to say. In my deliberations on the most complicated points, I have usually come up with two or three alternative interpretations, but in the end had to choose the one I thought most probable for the translation.

My policy is always to stay as close as possible to the Chinese text without becoming unintelligible or overly awkward in English. Occasionally, I have had to add a few words for grammatical or syntactical clarity in English. As a rule, however, I have endeavored to keep such additions to a minimum, not going beyond what is in the Chinese text itself. This accounts for the spareness of the English rendition, which is a deliberate attempt to convey a sense of the terseness of the Chinese original. In a few cases, I have provided brief parenthetical explanations to help the reader who has no background in Chinese history or culture. The notes in the Glossary should suffice to solve most of the remaining difficulties initiates will encounter.

For all of the reasons outlined in the preceding paragraphs, the reader will swiftly come to the realization that the *Chuang Tzu* is not as easy to read as a collection of Chinese folk tales. While the demands placed upon the reader are thus heavier, the rewards are correspondingly greater.

So as not to interfere with the reader's appreciation of this inimitable work itself, I have refrained from excessive annotation and commentary. In general, I have provided only those notes that I felt were essential for comprehending unfamiliar material. These are listed in the Glossary, which is divided into three sections: Names, Places, and Terms and Allusions.

I have found it convenient to invent one new word to match

an ubiquitous Chinese technical term, namely, "tricent" (three hundred [paces]) for *li* (one third of a mile), on the model of the word "mile," which literally means "a thousand [paces]." This was necessary to avoid confusion because the syllable *li* may also be employed to indicate so many other important concepts in Chinese, e.g., "principle," "ritual / ceremony / etiquette," "benefit / profit / gain," "one third of a millimeter," and so forth, which are also often cited by sinologists in their romanized form.

It has been my practice to translate (rather than simply to transcribe) the names of characters who appear to be fundamentally the product of the author's (or, more precisely, the authors') imagination. Often these names constitute puns or are otherwise intimately operative in the unfolding of a given tale; to ignore them would be to eviscerate a key feature of the diction. Sobriquets and other types of pseudonyms are also often translated if their meaning is sufficiently transparent, even for historical figures, since they were often chosen by individuals to express an aspect of their personality that they wished to emphasize. When, however, an individual is already relatively well known in Western sinology by the transcribed form of his name, then I provide only that.

Ideally, all transcribed proper nouns should be given in the reconstructed form that is appropriate for the time when and place where they were current. Unfortunately, our reconstructions of the sounds of ancient and archaic Sinitic languages, topolects, and dialects are still grossly inadequate, so we must resort to the makeshift of citing them in Modern Standard Mandarin. This is often deceiving, especially when the phonetic quality of a word is operative in what an author is trying to express. In the present translation, I have regularly given the archaic pronunciation of the names of two southern states to indicate that they were originally inhabited by speakers of non-Sinitic languages.

For the information of sinologists and other scholars who

may need to know, the basic text that I have relied upon in making this translation is that of CH'EN Kuying, although I do not always follow his recommendations for emendations and excisions. Therefore, those who may wish to compare this translation with the original Chinese should also consult the standard edition as presented in the first section of the Harvard-Yenching *Concordance*. The latter, incidentally, has been my most important tool in producing this rendition. When deciding upon the best English equivalent of a given word or expression in the *Chuang Tzu*, I have constantly checked its occurrences elsewhere in the text. Without the *Concordance*, this would have been a maddening, virtually impossible task.

The next most important research work that I have relied upon are the splendid scholarly tomes in Japanese by AKATSUKA Kiyoshi. There are two primary reasons for this. First, Akatsuka points out those portions of the *Chuang Tzu* that are in verse. This is not evident from the format of the original, since ancient Chinese texts consisted wholly of unpunctuated strings of sinographs. To determine whether or not a given passage is in verse, one must analyze the rhymes at the ends of clauses and sentences. Because the phonology of archaic Sinitic and Modern Standard Mandarin is so different, this is no mean task. The second great contribution of Akatsuka lies in interpreting the semantic content of the names of the fictional figures who people the pages of the *Chuang Tzu*. This, too, requires formidable learning because many of the names are disguised by the device of employing homophonous sinographs to write them. Few commentators, interpreters, and translators pay any attention to these two tremendously vital aspects of the *Chuang Tzu*. Consequently, in my estimation, they do not succeed in conveying to their readers the unique literary qualities of the work. Both in identifying portions of the text that were originally composed in verse and in construing the names of characters who appear in it, I have gone beyond Akatsuka, but his superb contributions in these areas have lightened my burden immeasurably. His generous accounts of the historical background for events and persons mentioned in the *Chuang Tzu* have also been highly appreciated.

More extensive annotations (including indication of parallels to the *Tao Te Ching* and other early Chinese texts), together with an introduction directed to specialists, have been separately published in *Sino-Platonic Papers* and are available by writing to the author.

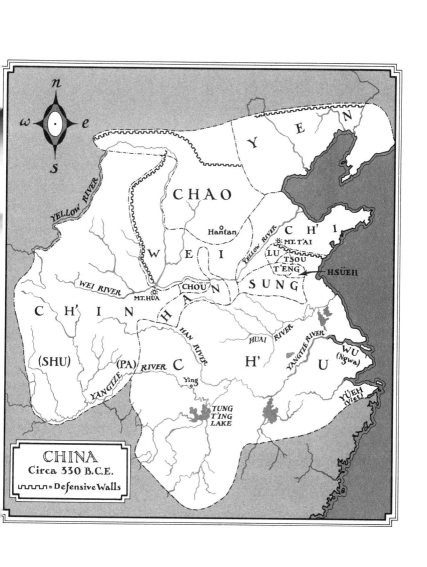

n
w · **e**
s

YELLOW RIVER

CHAO

Hantan

Y E N

YELLOW RIVER

CH'I

MT. T'AI

W E I

LU

TSOU

T'ENG

HSÜEH

WEI RIVER

MT. HUA

CHOU

S U N G

C H' I N

H A N

HAN RIVER

HUAI RIVER

YANGTZE RIVER

WU
(Ngwa)

(SHU)

(PA) RIVER C

H'

U

YANGTZE

Ying

YÜEH
(Viet)

TUNG
T'ING
LAKE

CHINA
Circa 330 B.C.E.
ᴸᵁᴸᴸᵁ = Defensive Walls

INNER
CHAPTERS

1

CAREFREE WANDERING

The Chuang Tzu *begins with an examination of the relativity of big and little. The benefits that result from creative spontaneity are illustrated by several of the most memorable tales in the book.*

1

In the darkness of the Northern Ocean, there is a fish named K'un. The K'un is so big that no one knows how many thousands of tricents [three hundred paces] its body extends. After it metamorphoses into a bird, its name becomes P'eng. The P'eng is so huge that no one knows how many thousands of tricents its back stretches. Rousing itself to flight, its wings are like clouds suspended in the sky. When the seas stir, the P'eng prepares for its journey to the Southern Ocean, the Lake of Heaven.

In the words of *The Drolleries of Ch'i*, a record of marvels, "On its journey to the Southern Ocean, the P'eng beats the water with its wings for three thousand tricents, then it rises up on a whirlwind to a height of ninety thousand tricents and travels on the jet streams of late summer."

There galloping gusts and motes of dust are blown about by

the breath of living organisms. Is azure the true color of the sky? Or is the sky so distant that its farthest limits can never be reached? When the P'eng looks down at the sky from above, it must appear just the same as when we look up. . . .

A cicada and a dovelet laughed at the P'eng, saying, "Wings aflutter, we fly up until we land in an elm or a dalbergia tree. Sometimes, when we don't make it, we just fall back to the ground and that's that. What's the use of flying up ninety thousand tricents to go south?"

If you're going on an outing to the verdant suburbs you only need to take along three meals and you'll still come back with a full stomach. If you're traveling a hundred tricents, you need to husk enough grain for an overnight stay. But if you're journeying a thousand tricents, you've got to set aside three months' worth of grain. What do these two creatures know?

Small knowledge is no match for great knowledge, nor is a short lifespan a match for a long one. How do we know this is so? The mushroom that sprouts in the morning and dies by evening doesn't know the difference between night and day. The locust doesn't know the difference between spring and autumn. These are examples of short lifespans. In the southern part of the state of Ch'u, there is a tortoise called Dark Spirit for whom spring and autumn each lasts five hundred years. In high antiquity, there was a large cedrela tree for which spring and autumn each lasted eight thousand years. These are examples of long lifespans. Nowadays Progenitor P'eng is famous for his more than seven hundred years of longevity. Isn't it pathetic that people try to emulate him?

A question put by T'ang, the first emperor of the Shang dynasty, to his wise minister Chi is similar. T'ang asked, "Do up, down, and the four directions have a limit?"

"Beyond their limitlessness there is another limitlessness," said Chi. "In the barren north there is a dark sea, the Lake of Heaven. In the sea there is a fish named K'un that is several thousand tricents in breadth, but no one knows its length. There is also a bird named P'eng whose back is like Mount T'ai and whose wings are like clouds suspended in the sky. It rises upon a twisting whirlwind to a height of ninety thousand tricents, pierces the clouds and then heads south on its journey to the distant Southern Ocean with the blue sky touching its back.

"A marsh sparrow laughs at the P'eng, saying, 'Where does he think he's going? I spring up into the air and come back down after not much more than a few yards. Flitting about amidst the bushes and brambles, this is the ultimate in flying! So where does he think he's going?'

"This shows the difference between the great and the small."

Thus there are those whose knowledge qualifies them for a minor bureaucratic appointment, those whose conduct is suitable for overseeing a village, and those whose virtue befits them for rulership and who can win the confidence of an entire country. Their self-estimation is like that of the marsh sparrow, so Master Sung Jung smiled at them complacently.

Here was a man who would neither feel flattered if the whole world praised him nor frustrated if the whole world censured him. Master Sung was able to be like this simply because he could tell the difference between what was intrinsic and what was extrinsic, because he made a distinction between honor and disgrace. Although he was not embroiled in worldly affairs, still there was something that he was unable to achieve.

Master Lieh could ride upon the wind wherever he pleased, drifting marvelously, and returning only after fifteen days. Although he was not embroiled in the pursuit of blessings and thus was able to dispense with walking, still there was something that he had to rely upon.

Supposing there were someone who could ride upon the truth of heaven and earth, who could chariot upon the transformations of the six vital breaths and thereby go wandering in infinity, what would he have to rely on?

Therefore, it is said that the ultimate man has no self, the spiritual person has no accomplishment, and the sage has no name.

2

Yao wished to abdicate his rulership of all under heaven to Hsü Yu, saying, "If one did not extinguish a candle when the sun and moon come out, wouldn't it be hard to discern its light? If one continues to irrigate the fields when the seasonal rains fall, wouldn't it have little effect upon the amount of moisture in them? Once you are established on the throne, master, all under heaven will be well ordered. Yet I am still the ruler and consider myself inadequate to the task. Allow me to hand over the empire to you."

"You are governing all under heaven," said Hsü Yu, "and the empire is already well ordered. If I were to replace you, would I be doing it for the name? A name is but an attribute of reality. Would I be doing it for the sake of attribution? The wren nests in the deep forest, occupying but a single branch. The mole drinks from the river, merely filling its little belly. Return, oh lord, and forget this business. I have no need for all under heaven! Even supposing that the cook were not attending to his kitchen, the impersonator of the dead would not leap over the pots and pans to take his place."

3

Chien Wu said to Lien Shu, "I have heard Chieh Yü speak. His words are impressive but not to the point. Once he goes off on a tangent, he never comes back. I was astounded by his words, which were limitless as the Milky Way. They were extravagant and remote from human experience."

"What did he say?" asked Lien Shu.

" 'Far away on Mount Kuyeh there dwells a spirit man whose skin is like congealed snow and who is gentle as a virgin. He does not eat any of the five grains, but inhales the wind and drinks the dew. He rides on the clouds, drives a flying dragon, and wanders beyond the four seas. His spirit is concentrated, saving things from corruption and bringing a bountiful harvest every year.' Thinking this madness, I refused to believe what he said."

"Indeed!" said Lien Shu. "The blind cannot share in the display of pattern and ornament, the deaf cannot share in the sound of bells and drums. Not only are there physical blindness and deafness, they also exist on an intellectual plane. It would appear that Chieh Yü's words were directed at you. The spirit man is of such integrity that he mingles with the myriad things and becomes one with them. Worldly strife leads to chaos. Why should he exhaust himself with the affairs of all under heaven? Nothing can harm the spirit man. He would not be drowned in a flood that surges to heaven, nor would he be burned in a fierce drought that melts minerals and scorches the hills. One could mold a Yao or a Shun from his dust and residue. Why should he be willing to bother himself with such things?"

4

A man of Sung who traded in ceremonial caps traveled to the state of Viet. But the people of Viet cut off their hair and tattooed their bodies, so the caps were of no use. Yao brought order to all the people under heaven and brought peace to all within the four seas. He went to distant Mount Kuyeh to visit the Four Masters. Upon returning to his capital on the north bank of the Fen River, he fell into a daze and forgot all about his empire.

5

Master Hui said to Master Chuang, "The King of Wei presented me with the seeds of a large gourd. I planted them and they grew to bear a fruit that could hold five bushels. I filled the gourd with liquid but its walls were not strong enough for me to pick it up. I split the gourd into ladles but their curvature was so slight they wouldn't hold anything. Although the gourd was admittedly of huge capacity, I smashed it to bits because it was useless."

"Sir," said Master Chuang, "it's you who were obtuse about utilizing its bigness. There was a man of Sung who was good at making an ointment for chapped hands. For generations, the family occupation had been to wash silk floss. A stranger who heard about the ointment offered him a hundred pieces of gold for the formula. The man of Sung gathered his clan together and said to them, 'We have been washing silk floss for generations and have earned no more than a few pieces of gold. Now we'll make a hundred pieces of gold in one morning if we sell the technique. Please let me give it to the stranger.' After the stranger obtained the formula, he persuaded the King of Ngwa of its usefulness. Viet embarked on hostilities against Ngwa, so the King of Ngwa appointed the stranger to the command of his fleet. That winter, he fought a naval battle with the forces of Viet and totally defeated them [because his sailors' hands didn't get chapped]. The king set aside a portion of land and enfeoffed him there.

"The ability to prevent chapped hands was the same, but one person gained a fief with it while the other couldn't even free himself from washing floss. This is because the uses to which the ointment was put were different. Now you, sir, had a five-bushel gourd. Why didn't you think of tying it on your waist as a big buoy so that you could go floating on the lakes and rivers instead of worrying that it couldn't hold anything because of its shallow curvature? This shows, sir, that you still have brambles for brains!"

Master Hui said to Master Chuang, "I have a big tree people call Stinky Quassia. Its great trunk is so gnarled and knotted that it cannot be measured with an inked line. Its small branches are so twisted and turned that neither compass nor L-square can be applied to them. It stands next to the road, but carpenters pay no attention to it. Now, sir, your words are just like my tree— big, useless, and heeded by no one."

"Sir," said Master Chuang, "are you the only one who hasn't observed a wild cat or a weasel? Crouching down, it lies in wait for its prey. It leaps about east and west, avoiding neither high nor low, until it gets caught in a snare or dies in a net. Then there is the yak, big as the clouds suspended in the sky. It's big, all right, but it can't catch mice. Now you, sir, have a big tree and are bothered by its uselessness. Why don't you plant it in Never-never Land with its wide, open spaces? There you can roam in nonaction by its side and sleep carefreely beneath it. Your Stinky Quassia's life will not be cut short by axes, nor will anything else harm it. Being useless, how could it ever come to grief?"

2

On the Equality of Things

The Great Clod, a metaphor for the Earth and the Way, is introduced. An extended discussion of self and other, right and wrong, affirmation and denial, ensues. Transcendent knowledge goes beyond all such dichotomies.

1

Sir Motley of Southurb sat leaning against his low table. He looked up to heaven and exhaled slowly. Disembodied, he seemed bereft of soul. Sir Wanderer of Countenance Complete, who stood in attendance before him, asked, "How can we explain this? Can the body really be made to become like withered wood? Can the mind really be made to become like dead ashes? The one who is leaning against the table now is not the one who was formerly leaning against the table."

"Indeed," said Sir Motley, "your question is a good one, Yen. Just now, I lost myself. Can you understand this? You may have heard the pipes of man, but not the pipes of earth. You may have heard the pipes of earth, but not the pipes of heaven."

"I venture," said Sir Wanderer, "to ask their secret."

"The Great Clod," said Sir Motley, "emits a vital breath called the wind. If it doesn't blow, nothing happens. Once it starts to blow, however, myriad hollows begin to howl. Have you not heard its moaning? The clefts and crevasses of the towering mountains, the hollows and cavities of huge trees a hundred spans around: they are like nostrils, like mouths, like ears, like sockets, like cups, like mortars, or like the depressions that form puddles and pools. The wind blowing over them makes the sound of rushing water, whizzing arrows, shouting, breathing, calling, crying, laughing, gnashing. The wind in front sings *aiee* and the wind that follows sings *wouu*. A light breeze evokes a small response; a powerful gale brings forth a mighty chorus. When the blast dies down, then all the hollows are silent. Have you not seen the leaves that quiver with tingling reverberations?"

"The pipes of earth," said Sir Wanderer, "are none other than all of the hollows you have described. The pipes of man are bamboo tubes arrayed in series. I venture to ask what the pipes of heaven are."

"As for the pipes of heaven," said Sir Motley, "the myriad sounds produced by the blowing of the wind are different, yet all it does is elicit the natural propensities of the hollows themselves. What need is there for something else to stimulate them?"

2

Great knowledge is expansive;
Small knowledge is cramped.

Great speech blazes brilliantly;
Small speech is mere garrulousness.

When people sleep, their souls are confused; when they awake, their bodies feel all out of joint.

> Their contacts turn into conflicts,
> Each day involves them in mental strife.

They become indecisive, dissembling, secretive.

> Small fears disturb them;
> Great fears incapacitate them.

Some there are who express themselves as swiftly as the release of a crossbow mechanism, which is to say that they arbitrate right and wrong. Others hold fast as though to a sworn covenant, which is to say they are waiting for victory. Some there are whose decline is like autumn or winter, which describes their dissolution day by day. Others are so immersed in activity that they cannot be revitalized. Some become so weary that they are as though sealed up in an envelope, which describes their senility. Their minds are so near to death that they cannot be rejuvenated.

Pleasure and anger; sorrow and joy; worry and regret; vacillation and trepidation; diffidence and abandon; openness and affectedness. These are all like musical sounds from empty tubes, like fungi produced from mere vapors. Day and night they alternate within us, but no one knows whence they arise. Enough! Enough! The instant one grasps *this*, one understands whence they arise!

3

"If there were no 'other,' there would be no 'I.' If there were no 'I,' there would be nothing to apprehend the 'other.'" This is near the mark, but I do not know what causes it to be so. It seems as though there is a True Ruler, but there is no particular evidence for Her. We may have faith in Her ability to function, but cannot see Her form. She has attributes but is without form.

The hundred bones, the nine orifices, and the six viscera are all complete within my body. With which am *I* most closely identified? Do you favor all of them equally? Or are there those to which you are partial? Assuming that you treat them equally, do you take them all to be your servants? If so, are your servants incapable of controlling each other? Or do they take turns being lord and subject among themselves? If not, do they have a True Lord over them all? Whether or not we succeed in specifying His attributes has neither positive nor negative effect upon the truth of the Lord.

Once we have received our complete physical form, we remain conscious of it while we await extinction. In our strife and friction with other things, we gallop forward on our course unable to stop. Is this not sad? We toil our whole life without seeing any results. We deplete ourselves with wearisome labor, but don't know what it all adds up to. Isn't this lamentable? There are those who say that at least we are not dead, but what's the good of it? Our physical form decays and with it the mind likewise. May we not say that this is the most lamentable of all? Is human life really so deluded as this? Am I the only one who is so deluded? Are there some individuals who are not deluded?

4

If we follow our prejudices and take them as our guide, who will not have such a guide? Why should only those who are intelligent make such mental choices for themselves? The foolish do the same thing. If one claims that right and wrong exist before they are established in the mind, that is like saying one sets out for Viet today but arrived there yesterday. To do so is to make something out of nothing. Even Holy Yü couldn't make something out of nothing. How could I alone do so?

5

Speech is not merely the blowing of air. Speech is intended to say something, but what is spoken may not necessarily be valid. If it is not valid, has anything actually been spoken? Or has speech never actually occurred? We may consider speech to be distinct from the chirps of hatchlings, but is there really any difference between them?

How has the Way become so obscured that there are true and false? How has speech become so obscured that there are right and wrong? Could it be that the Way has gone off and is no longer present? Could it be that speech is present but has lost its ability to validate? The Way is obscured by partial achievements; speech is obscured by eloquent verbiage. Thus there are controversies between Confucians and Mohists over what's right and what's wrong. They invariably affirm what their opponents deny and deny what their opponents affirm. If one wishes to affirm what others deny and deny what others affirm, nothing is better than lucidity.

Everything is "that" in relation to other things and "this" in relation to itself. We may not be able to see things from the standpoint of "that," but we can understand them from the standpoint of "this." Therefore, it may be said that "that" derives from "this" and that "this" is dependent upon "that." Such is the notion of the cogenesis of "this" and "that." Nonetheless, from the moment of birth death begins simultaneously, and from the moment of death birth begins simultaneously. Every affirmation is a denial of something else, and every denial is an affirmation of something else. "This" and "that" are mutually dependent; right and wrong are also mutually dependent. For this reason, the sage does not subscribe to [the view of absolute opposites] but sees things in the light of nature, accepting "this" for what it is.

"This" is also "that"; "that" is also "this." "This" implies a concept of right and wrong; "that" also implies a concept of right and wrong. But is there really a "this" and a "that"? Or is there really no "this" and no "that"? Where "this" and "that" cease to be opposites, there lies the pivot of the Way. Only when the pivot is located in the center of the circle of things can we respond to their infinite transformations. The transformations of "right" are infinite and so are the transformations of "wrong." Therefore, it is said that nothing is better for responding to them than lucidity.

6

To use a finger as a metaphor for the nonfingerness of a finger is not as good as using nonfingerness as a metaphor for the nonfingerness of a finger. To use a horse as a metaphor for the nonhorseness of a horse is not as good as using nonhorseness as a metaphor for the nonhorseness of a horse. Heaven and earth are the same as a finger; the myriad things are the same as a horse.

Affirmation lies in our affirming; denial lies in our denying. A way comes into being through our walking upon it; a thing is so because people say that it is. Why are things so? They are so because we declare them to be so. Why are things not so? They are not so because we declare them to be not so. All things are possessed of that which we may say is so; all things are possessed of that which we may affirm. There is no thing that is not so; there is no thing that is not affirmable.

Thus, whether it be a tiny blade of grass or a mighty pillar, a hideous leper or beauteous Hsi Shih, no matter how peculiar or fantastic, through the Way they all become one. To split something up is to create something else; to create something is to destroy something else. But for things in general, there is neither creation nor destruction, for they all revert to join in Unity.

Only the perceptive understand that all things join in Unity. For this reason they do not use things themselves but lodge in commonality. . . . It is all a result of their understanding the mutual dependence of "this" and "that." To have achieved this understanding but not be conscious of why it is so is called "The Way."

To weary the spiritual intelligence by trying to unify things without knowing that they are already identical is called "three in the morning." Why is this called "three in the morning"? Once upon a time, there was a monkey keeper who was feeding little chestnuts to his charges. "I'll give you three in the morning and four in the evening," he told them. All the monkeys were angry. "All right, then," said the keeper, "I'll give you four in the morning and three in the evening." All the monkeys were happy with this arrangement. Without adversely affecting either the name or the reality of the amount that he fed them, the keeper acted in accordance with the feelings of the monkeys. He too recognized the mutual dependence of "this" and "that." Consequently, the sage harmonizes the right and wrong of things and rests at the center of the celestial potter's wheel. This is called "dual procession."

7

The knowledge of the ancients attained the ultimate. What was the ultimacy that it attained? They realized that there was a stage before there were things. This is the ultimacy they had attained, the utmost to which nothing can be added. Next, there were those who recognized that there were things, but that there was a stage before which things were distinguished. Next, there were those who recognized that there were distinctions among things, but that there was a stage before there was right and wrong. Now, the manifestation of right and wrong is what diminishes the Way. What causes the diminution is what leads to the creation of preferences. But, after all, are there really diminution and creation? Or are there, after all, really no diminution and creation? That there are diminution and creation may be seen from clansman Chao's playing the lute. That there are no diminution and creation may be seen from clansman Chao's not playing the lute. Chao Wen played the lute, Maestro K'uang beat the rhythm with a stick, and Master Hui commented philosophically beneath a parasol tree. The knowledge of these three masters was virtually complete, so they practiced it till the end of their lives. However, they believed that they were different from others in what they were fond of and wished to enlighten others about their fondness. Yet, try as they may to enlighten them, others were not to be enlightened. Thus one of them ended his life in muddleheaded discussions of "hard" and "white." And Chao Wen's son carried on his father's career his whole life without any accomplishment. If this can be called accomplishment even I, who am without accomplishment, can be called accomplished. But if this cannot be called accomplishment, neither I nor anything else is accomplished. Therefore, the sage endeavors to get rid of bewildering flamboyance. For this reason, he does not use things himself, but lodges in commonality. This is called "using lucidity."

8

Now I have something to say here. I do not know whether or not what I have to say is of the same category as "this." But, whether it is of the *same* category or not, like them it is *a* category, thus in the end it is no different from "that." Nevertheless, let me try to explain myself.

There is beginning. There is a time before beginning. There is a time before the time before beginning. There is being. There is nonbeing. There is a stage before nonbeing. There is a stage before the stage before nonbeing. Suddenly there is being and nonbeing. Still, as for being and nonbeing, I do not know which is really being and which is nonbeing. Now I have just said something, but I do not know whether what I have said is really saying something or not.

There is nothing under heaven larger than the tip of a downy hair at the end of autumn, but Mount T'ai is small. There is no greater longevity than that of a child who dies in infancy, but Progenitor P'eng died young. Heaven and earth were born together with me and the myriad things are one with me. Since all things are one, how can there be anything to talk about? But since I have already *said* that all things are one, how can there be nothing to talk about? One and speech makes two, two and one makes three. Continuing on in this fashion, even the cleverest mathematician couldn't keep up, how much less an ordinary person! Therefore, if in proceeding from nonbeing to being we arrive at three, how much farther we shall reach when proceeding from being to being. We need not proceed at all if we understand the mutual dependence of "this" and "that."

9

The Way has never been divided up, speech has never been constant. It's all because of "this" that there are demarcations. Let me explain what I mean by demarcations. There are left and right, discussions and deliberations, analyses and disputes, arguments and altercations. These are the eight types of demarcative assertions. The sages set aside without discussion what lies beyond the world. The sages discuss what lies within the world, but do not deliberate upon it. As for annals and other records of the statesmanship of the former kings, the sages deliberate over them but will not dispute about them. Therefore, wherever there is analysis, something is left unanalyzed. Wherever there is dispute, something is left undisputed. You may ask, "How can this be?" The sages embrace all things, but ordinary people dispute over them to show off to each other. Therefore it is said, wherever there is dispute, something is left unseen.

The great Way is ineffable, great disputation is speechless, great humaneness is inhumane, great honesty is immodest, and great bravery is not aggressive. The way that displays itself is not the Way. Speech that is disputatious fails to achieve its aims. Humaneness that is constant cannot go around. Honesty that is aloof will not be trusted. Bravery that is aggressive will not succeed. One who does not abandon these five precepts will be more or less headed in the right direction.

Therefore, she who knows to stop at what she does not know has attained the ultimate. Who knows the disputation that is without words and the Way that cannot be walked upon? If one can have knowledge of them, this is called the Treasury of Heaven. You may pour into it, but it never fills; you may dip from it, but it never empties; and you never know where it comes from. This is called the Inner Light.

10

Long ago, Yao inquired of Shun, "Wishing to make a punitive attack against Tsung, K'uai, and Hsü'ao, I sit on my throne feeling all preoccupied. Why is this so?"

"The rulers of these three states," said Shun, "are still living primitively amidst brambles and bushes. Why are you preoccupied? Of old, ten suns appeared simultaneously, illuminating the myriad things. How much more should a ruler like yourself, whose virtue excels that of the sun, be able to tolerate other rulers!"

11

Gnaw Gap inquired of Princely Scion, "Do you know wherein all things agree?"

"How could I know that?"

"Do you know what you don't know?"

"How could I know that?"

"Well, then, is it possible to know anything at all?"

"How could I know that? Nonetheless, I'll try to say something about it. How can we know that what I call knowledge is not really ignorance? How can we know that what I call ignorance is not really knowledge? But let me try to ask you a few questions. If people sleep in damp places, they develop lumbago or even partial paralysis. But would the same thing happen if a loach did so? If people dwell in trees, they will tremble with vertigo. But would the same thing happen if a gibbon did so? Of these three, which knows the proper place to dwell? People eat meat, deer eat grass, giant centipedes savor snakes, hawks and crows relish mice. Of these four, which knows the proper food to eat? Gibbons go for gibbons, buck mates with doe, loaches cavort with fish. Mao Ch'iang and Hsi Shih were considered by men to be beautiful, but if fish took one look at them they would dive into the depths, if birds saw them they would fly high into the sky, if deer saw them they would run away pell-mell. Of these four, which knows the correct standard of beauty for all under heaven? As I see it, the principle of humaneness and righteousness, the paths of right and wrong, are inextricably confused. How would I be able to distinguish among them?"

"If you," asked Gnaw Gap, "do not know the difference between benefit and harm, does the ultimate man likewise not know the difference between them?"

"The ultimate man is spiritous," said Princely Scion. "If the great marshes were set on fire, he would not feel hot. If the rivers turned to ice, he would not feel cold. If violent thunder split the mountains, he would not be injured. If whirlwinds lashed the seas, he would not be frightened. Such being the case, he rides the clouds, mounts the sun and moon, and wanders beyond the four seas. Since not even life and death have any transforming effect upon him, how much less do benefit and harm?"

12

"I have heard from Confucius," said Master Timid Magpie, inquiring of Master Tall Tree, "that the sage does not involve himself in worldly affairs. He does not go after gain, nor does he avoid harm. He does not take pleasure in seeking, nor does he get bogged down in formalistic ways. He speaks without saying anything; he says something without speaking. Instead, he wanders beyond the dust of the mundane world. Confucius thinks this is a vague description of the sage, but I think that it is the working of the wondrous Way. What do you think of it, my master?"

"Even the Yellow Emperor would be perplexed by hearing these things," said Master Tall Tree. "How is Hillock capable of understanding them? It seems that you, too, are overly hasty in forming an estimate. You're counting your chickens before they're hatched, drooling over roast owl at the sight of a crossbow pellet.

"Let me say a few careless words to you and you listen carelessly, all right? The sage can lean against the sun and moon and tuck the universe under his arm because he melds things into a whole,

> Sets aside obfuscation,
> And is indifferent to baseness and honor.
> The mass of men are all hustle-bustle;
> The sage is slow and simple.
> He combines myriad years
> Into a single purity.
> Thus does he treat the myriad things,
> And thereby gathers them together.

"How do I know that love of life is not a delusion? How do I know that fear of death is not like being a homeless waif who does not know the way home? When the state of Chin first got Pretty Li, the daughter of the border warden of Ai, she wept till her robe was soaked with tears. But after she arrived at the king's residence, shared his fine bed, and could eat the tender meats of his table, she regretted that she had ever wept. How do I know that the dead may not regret their former lust for life?

"Someone who dreams of drinking wine at a cheerful banquet may wake up crying the next morning. Someone who dreams of crying may go off the next morning to enjoy the sport of the hunt. When we are in the midst of a dream, we do not know it's a dream. Sometimes we may even try to interpret our dreams while we are dreaming, but then we awake and realize it was a dream. Only after one is greatly awakened does one realize that it was all a great dream, while the fool thinks that he is awake and presumptuously aware. 'My excellent lord!' 'Oh, thou humble shepherd!' How perverse they are!

"Both Confucius and you are dreaming, and I too am dreaming when I say that you are dreaming. This sort of language may be called enigmatic, but after myriad generations there may appear a great sage who will know how to explain it and he will appear as though overnight.

"Suppose that you and I have a dispute. If you beat me and I lose to you, does that mean you're really right and I'm really wrong? If I beat you and you lose to me, does that mean I'm really right and you're really wrong? Is one of us right and the other wrong? Or are both of us right and both of us wrong? Neither you nor I can know, and others are even more in the dark. Whom shall we have decide the matter? Shall we have someone who agrees with you decide it? Since he agrees with you, how can he decide fairly? Shall we have someone who agrees with me decide it? Since he agrees with me, how can he decide fairly? Shall we have someone who differs with both of us decide it? Since he differs with both of us, how can he make a decision? Shall we have someone who agrees with both of us decide it? Since he agrees with both of us, how can he make a decision? Given that neither you nor I, nor another person, can know how to decide, shall we wait for still another?

"Whether the alternating voices of disputation are relative to each other or not, they may be harmonized within the framework of nature and allowed to follow their own effusive elaboration so they may live out their years. What does 'harmonized within the framework of nature' mean? I would say, 'Right may be not right, so may be not so. If right were really right, then right would be distinct from not right, and there would be no dispute. If so were really so, then so would be distinct from not so and there would be no dispute. Forget how many years there are in a lifespan, forget righteousness. If you ramble in the realm of infinity, you will reside in the realm of infinity.'"

13

Penumbra inquired of Shadow, saying, "One moment you move and the next moment you stand still; one moment you're seated and the next moment you get up. Why are you so lacking in constancy?"

Shadow said, "Must I depend on something else to be what I am? If so, must what I depend upon in turn depend upon something else to be what it is? Must I depend upon the scales of a snake's belly or the forewings of a cicada? How can I tell why I am what I am? How can I tell why I'm not what I'm not?"

14

Once upon a time Chuang Chou dreamed that he was a butterfly, a butterfly flitting about happily enjoying himself. He didn't know that he was Chou. Suddenly he awoke and was palpably Chou. He did not know whether he was Chou who had dreamed of being a butterfly or a butterfly dreaming that he was Chou. Now, there must be a difference between Chou and the butterfly. This is called the transformation of things.

3

ESSENTIALS FOR NURTURING LIFE

Through a series of exquisite fables, the secret of conserving life is conveyed: follow nature.

1

Our lives are limited,
But knowledge is limitless.
To pursue the limitless
With the limited
Is dangerous.

Such being the case, if one still goes after knowledge,

One's life will definitely be in danger.
In doing good, approach not fame;
In doing bad, approach not punishment.
Follow the central artery as conduit,

And you can preserve your body,
Maintain your life,
Nourish your inmost viscera,
And complete your allotted years.

2

A cook was cutting up an ox for Lord Wenhui.

Wherever
His hand touched,
His shoulder leaned,
His foot stepped,
His knee nudged,

the flesh would fall away with a swishing sound. Each slice of the cleaver was right in tune, zip zap! He danced in rhythm to "The Mulberry Grove," moved in concert with the strains of "The Managing Chief."

"Ah, wonderful!" said Lord Wenhui, "that skill can attain such heights!"

The cook put down his cleaver and responded, "What your servant loves is the Way, which goes beyond mere skill. When I first began to cut oxen, what I saw was nothing but whole oxen. After three years, I no longer saw whole oxen. Today, I meet the ox with my spirit rather than looking at it with my eyes. My sense organs stop functioning and my spirit moves as it pleases. In accord with the natural grain, I slice at the great crevices, lead the blade through the great cavities. Following its inherent structure, I never encounter the slightest obstacle even where the veins and arteries come together or where the ligaments and tendons join, much less from obvious big bones. A good cook changes his cleaver once a year because he chops. An ordinary cook changes his cleaver once a month because he hacks. Now

I've been using my cleaver for nineteen years and have cut up thousands of oxen with it, but the blade is still as fresh as though it had just come from the grindstone. Between the joints there are spaces, but the edge of the blade has no thickness. Since I am inserting something without any thickness into an empty space, there will certainly be lots of room for the blade to play around in. That's why the blade is still as fresh as though it had just come from the grindstone. Nonetheless, whenever I come to a complicated spot and see that it will be difficult to handle, I cautiously restrain myself, focus my vision, and slow my motion. With an imperceptible movement of the cleaver, plop! and the flesh is already separated, like a clump of earth collapsing to the ground. I stand there holding the cleaver in my hand, look all around me with complacent satisfaction, then I wipe off the cleaver and store it away."

"Wonderful!" said Lord Wenhui. "From hearing the words of the cook, I have learned how to nourish life."

3

When His Honor Decorated Chariot saw the Right Instructor he was startled and said, "Who is that man? Why is he so odd? Is it due to nature or to man?"

Someone said, "Nature made him this way, not man. Nature's engenderment causes things to be unique. Human appearances are endowed. That's how I know it's due to nature, not man."

4

The marsh pheasant has to take ten steps before it finds something to pick at and has to take a hundred steps before it gets a drink. But the pheasant would prefer not to be raised in a cage where, though you treat it like a king, its spirit would not thrive.

5

When Old Longears died, Idle Intruder went to mourn over him. He wailed three times and left.

"Weren't you a friend of the master?" a disciple asked him.

"Yes."

"Well, is it proper to mourn him like this?"

"Yes. At first, I used to think of him as a man, but now I no longer do. Just now when I went in to mourn him, there were old people crying over him as though they were crying for one of their own sons. There were youngsters crying over him as though they were crying for their own mother. Among those whom he had brought together, surely there were some who wished not to speak but spoke anyway, who wished not to cry but cried anyway. This is to flee from nature while redoubling human emotion, thus forgetting what we have received from nature. This was what the ancients called 'the punishment of fleeing from nature.' By chance the master's coming was timely, and by chance his going was favorable. One who is situated in timeliness and who dwells in favorableness cannot be affected by joy or sorrow. This is what the ancients called 'the emancipation of the gods.' "

6

Resins may be consumed when they are used for fuel, but the fire they transmit knows no end.

4

THE HUMAN WORLD

A wiser Confucius discusses the fine points of human relations with his favorite disciple and another diplomat, and then is reprimanded by the madman of Ch'u for his officiousness. Recognition of the usefulness of uselessness is advocated.

1

Yen Hui went to see Confucius and requested permission to take a trip.

"Where are you going?" asked Confucius.

"I'm going to the state of Wey."

"What will you do there?"

"I have heard that the Lord of Wey is behaving dictatorially in the vigor of his youth. He is frivolous in exercising his state prerogatives and is blind to his own faults. He looks lightly upon the death of his people, and those who die for the state fill the swamps like so many withered weeds. The people have no place to turn. Master, I have heard you say that one may leave a well-ordered state and go to one that is in chaos. 'There are many sick people at the gate of a physician.' In conformity with what you told me, I wish to think of a plan whereby perhaps I may cure the sickness of the state of Wey."

"Alas," said Confucius, "I'm afraid you'll end up in trouble if you go there. The Way should not be adulterated. Adulteration leads to multiplicity, multiplicity to confusion, confusion to worry. When one is worried, one cannot be saved. The ultimate men of the past first sought to preserve it in themselves and only after that to preserve it in others. Before one has settled what one seeks to preserve in oneself, where is there any leisure to attend to the behavior of a tyrant?

"Furthermore, do you know wherein integrity is dissipated and wherein knowledge is elicited? Integrity is dissipated through fame and knowledge is elicited by contention. Fame implies mutual conflict; knowledge is an instrument of contention. Both are instruments of evil and not something for which one should strive.

"Besides, a person of substantial integrity and solid trust may still not gain the approval of others; a person who does not contend for name and fame may still not gain the acquiescence of others. In such circumstances, forcibly to flaunt talk about humaneness, righteousness, and codes of conduct before a tyrant would be to glorify oneself at the expense of another's failings. This is called 'hurting others.' Those who hurt others will certainly be hurt by others in return. I'm afraid that you'll be hurt by others!

"What's more, if the lord appreciates the worthy and despises the unworthy, what need is there for you to try to be different? If you do not offer your views, the prince will certainly take advantage to display his own eloquence. Your eyes will be dazzled, your face fall flat, your mouth mutter diffidently, your expression embody your submissiveness, and your mind will confirm it. This is to fight fire with fire, drain water with water. We may call it 'excess.' If you are compliant from the start, there will be no end to it. But I fear that if you speak honestly to someone who does not trust you, you will certainly die at the hands of the tyrant.

"Of old, Kuan Lungp'ang was executed by Chieh and Prince Pikan was executed by Chow. Both had cultivated themselves as inferiors out of solicitude for their rulers' subjects. As inferiors, they ran afoul of their superiors, consequently their lords pushed them aside. This was due to their love of fame. Also, of old, Yao attacked Ts'ungchih and Hsü'ao, and Yü attacked the freehold at Hu. These countries were reduced to haunted wastelands and their rulers put to death. They were constantly engaged in war and always on the lookout for gain. These are all examples of individuals who sought fame or gain. Haven't you heard of them? Even the sage could not conquer the attractions of fame and gain. Can you? Nonetheless you must have a plan in mind. Let us hear what it is."

"Dignified and dispassionate, energetic and focused," said Yen Hui. "Will that work?"

"Oh, no! That won't work. The Lord of Wey is overflowing with pride and his moods are unstable. Ordinarily people do not oppose him. As a result, he suppresses the persuasions of others in order to gratify his own intentions. It is obvious that a small daily dose of integrity would have no effect on him, not to mention a grand dose all at once! He will stubbornly refuse your attempts to transform him. Outwardly he may agree with you, but inwardly he will remain unreflective. How could that possibly work?"

"Well, then, I will be inwardly direct but outwardly flexible and will complete myself through comparison to antiquity. He who is inwardly direct is a disciple of heaven. The disciple of heaven realizes that the son of heaven and himself are both born of heaven. So why should he expect that others will either approve or disapprove of his words? One who is like this will be viewed by others as an innocent child. This is what I mean by being a disciple of heaven. He who is outwardly flexible is a disciple of man. Saluting, kneeling, bowing, and scraping—these are the etiquette of a ruler's subject. Everyone else does them, so why shouldn't I? Doing what others do will not invite criticism from others. This is what I mean by being a disciple of man. Completing myself through comparison to antiquity, I shall be a disciple of the ancients. Although the substance of such words will be didactic and reproachful, they belong to the ancients, not to me. If I can be like this, although I am direct, I will be beyond reproach. This is what I mean by being a disciple of antiquity. If I can do this, will it work?"

"Oh, no!" said Confucius. "That won't work. You're glibly setting up too many orthodox laws. Although this is a crude approach, it may save you from blame. Yet that's about all it's good for; how could it result in anyone's transformation? You're still taking the mind as your model."

"I have nothing further to propose," said Yen Hui. "I venture to ask you for a method."

"Fasting," said Confucius. "I shall explain it for you. If you do things with your mind, do you think it will be easy? Bright heaven will not approve one who thinks it will be easy."

"My family is poor," said Yen Hui, "and it's been several months since I've drunk wine or tasted meat. May this be considered fasting?"

"This is fasting suitable for sacrifices, but it is not fasting of the mind."

"I venture to ask what 'fasting of the mind' is," said Hui.

"Maintaining the unity of your will," said Confucius, "listen not with your ears but with your mind. Listen not with your mind but with your primal breath. The ears are limited to listening, the mind is limited to tallying. The primal breath, however, awaits things emptily. It is only through the Way that one can gather emptiness, and emptiness is the fasting of the mind."

"Before I am able to exercise fasting of the mind," said Yen Hui, "I truly have an identity. But after I am able to exercise it, I will no longer have an identity. Can this be called emptiness?"

"Precisely," said Confucius. "Now I shall explain it for you. You may enter his realm as a wandering persuader, but don't be attracted by fame. If he accepts you, present your views; if he rejects you, cease. When there is neither gate nor opening, if you can dwell in unity and lodge in necessity, you're close to it.

"To eliminate one's footsteps by not walking is easy, but to walk without touching the ground is hard. If you are impelled by human feelings, it is easy to be false; if you are impelled by nature, it is hard to be false. I've only heard of creatures that fly with wings, never of creatures that fly with nonwings. I've only heard of people knowing things through awareness, never of people knowing things through unawareness. Observe the void—the empty room emits a pure light. Good fortune lies in stopping when it is time to stop. If you do not stop, this is called 'galloping while sitting.' Let your senses communicate within and rid yourself of the machinations of the mind. Then even ghosts and spirits will take shelter with you, not to mention men. This is how the myriad things are transformed. It is that to which Yao and Shun bound themselves, and that which Fuhsi and Chich'ü exercised all their lives. All the more is it suited for the masses."

2

When Sir High, Duke of She, was about to depart on a mission to Ch'i, he inquired of Confucius, saying, "The mission entrusted to me by the king is a very weighty one, but I expect that as ambassador the treatment given to me by Ch'i, though quite respectful, will not be attentive. One cannot push even a common man, how much less a head of state! This makes me very anxious. You have often told me, 'Only through the Way can one reach a happy conclusion in any affair, whether large or small. If one does not succeed in an affair, then there will surely be trouble from the way men react. If one does succeed, there will surely be trouble due to a dislocation of yin and yang. Only a person of integrity can escape trouble whether he succeeds or not.' I stick to plain fare and eschew fine cuisine, so that my kitchen boys never feel as though they have to cool themselves off. Yet, this morning I received my commission and in the evening I'm drinking ice water. I feel like I'm burning up inside! I haven't even been exposed to the actual circumstances of the affair and already I'm suffering from a dislocation of yin and yang. And if I do not succeed in this affair, there will surely be trouble from the way men will react. Faced with both of these troubles, it is more than I as minister can bear. Tell me, sir, what I should do."

"For all under heaven," said Confucius, "there are two great precepts: one is destiny and the other is duty. A child's love of her parents is destiny and is inseparable from her heart. A subject's service to his lord is duty. No matter where one goes, there is always a lord from whom one cannot escape in heaven or on earth. This is what I mean by 'great precepts.' Accordingly, one who serves one's parents and makes them secure regardless of the situation has attained the ultimate in filialness. One who serves one's lord and makes him secure regardless of the conditions has achieved the fullness of loyalty. One who attends to one's own mind and who is not easily diverted by sorrow and joy, realizing their inevitability and accepting them as if they were destiny, has attained the ultimate of integrity. One who is a subject or a son indeed sometimes has no alternatives. Then he must carry out his affairs according to circumstances and forget about his own person. What leisure has he for loving life and despising death? Thus, sir, you may proceed on your mission.

"Allow me to report what I have heard: in diplomacy, states that are near must rely on trust to maintain their ties, while those that are distant must resort to words to show their sincerity and words must be conveyed by someone. Now, one of the most difficult things in the world is to convey the pleasure or displeasure of two parties to each other. If both parties are pleased, their words will surely be full of exaggerated promise. If both parties are displeased, their words will surely be full of exaggerated insult. Any sort of exaggeration is false. Where there is falseness, trust is missing. And when trust is missing, the one who conveys the message is in danger. Therefore, in the *Legal Counsels* it is said, 'Transmit the gist of their sentiments, not their exaggerated words, and you may perhaps preserve yourself whole.'

"Moreover, those who contest for supremacy with cleverness begin openly but invariably end up in deception. In their excesses, they are full of chicanery. Those who drink according to etiquette begin politely but invariably end up disorderly. In their excesses, they are full of debauchery. It's the same with all affairs. They may begin with consideration, but invariably end up in prevarication. Their inception may be simple, but as they approach their conclusion they become enormously complex.

"Words are like the wind and the waves, deeds verify or invalidate them. Wind and waves are easily stirred up, verification and invalidation easily end perilously. Therefore, rage often results from no other reason than clever words and intemperate phrases. When an animal is threatened with death, it cries out involuntarily. Gasping wildly for breath, it gives vent to all the viciousness it can muster. When people are pressed too far, they will inevitably respond with evil intentions, not even knowing why they do so. If even they themselves do not know why they do so, who knows how it will all end? Therefore, in the *Legal Counsels* it is said, 'Do not deviate from your orders. Do not force a settlement. Immoderation is provocative overstatement.' To deviate from one's orders or to force a settlement endangers one's undertaking. An excellent settlement takes time; an unsatisfactory settlement, once made, is irrevocable. One cannot be too careful!

"Just ride along with things as you let your mind wander. Entrust yourself to inevitability and thereby nourish what is central. That's the ultimate course. What have you to do with the response of Ch'i? Nothing is better than to fulfill your destiny, but that's the hardest of all."

3

Yen Ho, about to become the tutor of the eldest son of Duke Ling of the state of Wey, inquired of Ch'ü Poyü, "Here is a man of a naturally cruel disposition. If I permit him to act without constraint, he will bring harm to our state. If I insist that he act with constraint, he will bring harm to my own person. He is just intelligent enough to recognize the faults of others, but not to recognize his own. This being the case, what am I to do?"

"An excellent question!" said Ch'ü Poyü. "Be restrained and cautious. Set yourself aright. Your bearing should be cordial, your attitude should be agreeable. Still, trouble may result even from these two approaches. While cordial, do not be overly intimate; while agreeable, do not be overly effusive. If your bearing is too intimate, everything will be ruined—a complete catastrophe. If you are too agreeable, you will be suspected of wanting reputation and fame—a life-threatening curse. If he acts like a baby, then you act like a baby along with him. If he acts unconventionally, then you act unconventionally along with him. If he acts without restraint, then you act without restraint along with him. Thus can you awaken him and lead him on to blamelessness.

"Don't you know about the praying mantis? Angrily waving its arms, it blocks the path of an onrushing chariot, not realizing that the task is far beyond it. This is because it puts a high premium on its own ability. Be restrained and cautious. If you put a high premium on always bragging about yourself and thereby offend him, you will be in jeopardy.

"And don't you know about the tiger keeper? He dares not give a live animal to his charges, for fear of stirring up their fury when they kill it, nor dares he give them a whole animal, for fear of stirring up their fury when they tear it apart. By gauging the times when the tigers are hungry or full, he can fathom their fury. Although the tigers are of a different species from man, they try to please their keeper because he goes along with them, whereas they kill those who go against them.

"He who loves horses catches their dung in baskets and receives their urine in giant clam shells. But if a mosquito or a snipefly should alight upon one of his horses and he slaps it at the wrong moment, the horse will chomp through its bit, break his head, and smash his chest. His intentions are the best, yet he may perish through his love. Can one afford not to be cautious?"

4

A carpenter named Shih, who was on his way to Ch'i, came to Bent Shaft. There he saw a chestnut-leaved oak that served as the local shrine. The tree was so big that several thousand head of cattle could take shade beneath it and it was a hundred spans in circumference. It was so tall that it surveyed the surrounding hills; only above eighty feet were there any branches shooting out from its trunk. It had ten or more limbs from each of which you could make a boat. Those who came to gaze upon it were as numerous as the crowds in a market. The master carpenter paid no attention to it, but kept walking without slowing his pace a bit. After his disciples had had their fill of gazing upon the great tree, they caught up with carpenter Shih and said, "Since we have taken up our axes to follow you, master, we have never seen such marvelous timber as this. Why, sir, were you unwilling to look at it, but kept on walking without even slowing down?"

"Enough! Don't talk about it! It's defective wood. A boat made from it would sink. A coffin made from it would rot right away. An implement made from it would break right away. A door made from it would exude resin. A pillar made from it would soon be grub-infested. This tree is worthless. There's nothing you can make from it. That's why it could grow to be so old."

After the carpenter had returned to his own country, the shrine oak appeared to him in a dream, saying, "With what trees will you compare me? Will you compare me with those that have fine-grained wood? As for the hawthorn, the pear, the orange, the pomelo, and other fructiferous trees, once their fruits are ripe, they are torn off, and the trees are thereby abused. The big branches are broken and the smaller branches are snapped. These are trees that make their own lives miserable because of their abilities. Therefore, they cannot finish out the years allotted to them by heaven but die midway. They are trees that bring upon themselves the assaults of the worldly. It's the same with all things. But I have sought for a long time to be useless. Now, on the verge of death, I have finally learned what uselessness really means and that it is of great use to me. If, after all, I had been useful, would I have been able to grow so big? Furthermore, you and I are both things, so why the deuce should you appraise another thing? You're a defective person on the verge of death. What do you know about 'defective wood'?"

When carpenter Shih awoke, he told the dream to his disciples. "If the oak's intention is to be useless, then why does it serve as the local shrine?" they asked.

"Silence! Don't say another word! The oak is merely assuming the guise of a shrine to ward off the curses of those who do not understand it. If it were not a shrine, it would still face the threat of being cut down. Moreover, what the oak is preserving is different from the masses of other trees. If we attempt to understand it on the basis of conventional morality, won't we be far from the point?"

5

Sir Motley of Southunc made an excursion to the Hillock of Shang. There he saw an unusual tree so big that a thousand four-horse chariots could be shaded by its leaves.

"Goodness! What tree is this?" asked Sir Motley. "It must have unusual timber." Looking upward at the smaller branches, however, he saw that they were all twisted and unfit to be beams.

Looking downward at the massive trunk, he saw that it was so gnarled as to be unfit for making coffins. If you lick one of its leaves, your mouth will develop ulcerous sores. If you smell its foliage, you fall into a drunken delirium that lasts for three days.

"This tree is truly worthless," said Sir Motley, "and that is why it has grown so large. Ah! The spiritual man is also worthless like this."

6

In the state of Sung, there is a place called Chingshih where catalpas, arborvitae, and mulberry trees thrive. Those that are more than a hand's breadth or two around are chopped down by people who are looking for tether posts for their monkeys. Those that are three or four spans in circumference are chopped down by people who are looking for lofty ridgepoles. Those that are seven or eight spans in circumference are chopped down by the families of aristocrats or wealthy merchants who are looking for coffin planks. Therefore, they do not live out the years allotted to them by heaven but die midway under the ax. This is the trouble brought about by having worth. Conversely, in carrying out an exorcistic sacrifice, one cannot present oxen with white foreheads, suckling pigs with upturned snouts, or people with hemorrhoids to the god of the river. All of this is known by the magus-priests, who consider these creatures to be inauspicious. For the same reasons, the spiritual person considers them to be greatly auspicious.

7

Scattered Apart's chin was buried in his bellybutton, his shoulders were higher than the crown of his head, his cervical vertebrae pointed toward the sky, the five dorsal inductories were all up on top, and his thighbones were positioned like a couple of extra ribs. By sewing and washing clothes, he earned enough to make ends meet. By sifting grain with a winnowing-fan, he could make enough to feed ten people. When the authorities came to conscript soldiers, Scattered would wander about among them flailing his arms. When the authorities organized a massive labor project, Scattered would be excused because of his congenital defects. When the authorities handed out grain to the sick, he would receive three bags plus ten bundles of firewood. Though his body was scattered, it was sufficient to enable him to support himself and to live out the years allotted to him by heaven. How much more could someone whose virtue is scattered!

8

When Confucius went to Ch'u, Chieh Yü, the madman of Ch'u, wandered about before his gate, saying:

"Phoenix! Oh, Phoenix!
How your virtue has declined!
The future you cannot wait for,
The past you cannot pursue.

When the Way prevails under heaven,
The Sage seeks for accomplishment;
When the Way is absent from the world,
The sage seeks but to preserve his life.
In an age like that of today,
All he can hope for is to avoid punishment.

Good fortune is lighter than a feather,
But no one knows how to carry it;
Misfortune is heavier than the earth,
But no one knows how to escape it.

Enough! Enough!
Stop confronting people with virtue;

Perilous! Perilous!
All this rushing about dividing up the earth.

Thorny dimwit,
Don't wound my shins!
Prickly scatterbrain,
Don't wound my feet!"

9

The mountain trees plunder themselves, the grease over a fire fries itself. Cinnamon can be eaten, therefore the trees that yield it are chopped down. Varnish can be used, therefore the trees that produce it are hacked. Everybody knows the utility of usefulness, but nobody knows the utility of uselessness.

5

SYMBOLS OF INTEGRITY FULFILLED

An individual may be physically mutilated and misshapen yet spiritually whole and attractive. The highest type of person is beyond all emotion.

1

There was a man of Lu, Princely Nag, who had been mutilated by having one of his feet cut off, yet those who followed him in his wanderings were as numerous as the followers of Confucius. Ch'ang Chi inquired of Confucius, "Princely Nag has had one of his feet cut off, yet those who follow him in his wanderings divide up half the state of Lu with you, master. He neither teaches when standing nor discourses when sitting. Yet those who go to him empty come back full. Is there truly a 'doctrine without words,' a formless mental accomplishment? What kind of person is he?"

"Sir," said Confucius, "he is a sage. It's simply because I'm a latecomer that I haven't yet gone over to him. I myself would take him as my teacher, so why shouldn't those who are unequal to me? Why stop with just the state of Lu? I would lead the whole of the empire to follow him."

"Though he has been mutilated," said Ch'ang Chi, "he lords it over you. How different he must be from the ordinary person. If this be so, what is special about the way he uses his mind?"

"Life and death are of great moment," said Confucius, "but he is able to avoid their transformations. Though heaven may collapse and earth overturn, he would not be lost in their wake. Settled in nonreliance, he is unmoved by the changes in things. He recognizes that evolution is the destiny of things and thereby maintains what is essential."

"What do you mean?" asked Ch'ang Chi.

"If one sees things from the viewpoint of the differences," said Confucius, "the liver and the gallbladder are as distant as Ch'u is from Viet. If one sees things from the viewpoint of their similarities, the myriad things are all one. He who realizes this is unaware of the attractions of the senses but lets his mind wander instead in the harmony of integrity. He sees what bespeaks the identity of things instead of what bespeaks their loss. He sees the loss of his foot as the sloughing off of a clump of earth."

"In his self-cultivation," said Ch'ang Chi, "through knowledge he attains mind, and through mind he attains eternal mind. Why, then, do things gather about him?"

"People cannot see their reflections in running water," said Confucius, "but in still water they can. Only stillness can still the hosts who seek stillness. Of those who receive their destiny from earth, only the pine and the arborvitae are correct—green summer and winter. Of those who received their destiny from heaven, only Yao and Shun were correct—at the head of the ten thousand things. Fortunately, they could correct their own lives and thereby correct a host of lives. The proof of the preservation of primal strength is realized in fearlessness. A single courageous warrior will heroically plunge into a mighty army. If a man who seeks fame can do this out of personal ambition, how much more so should one who takes heaven and earth as his palace and the myriad things as his treasury, his trunk and limbs as a mere lodging, his senses as phenomena; who treats as a whole all that knowledge knows; and whose mind never dies! He would simply pick a day and ascend to the heights. People may follow him, but how would he be willing to make such things his business?"

2

Shent'u Chia had been mutilated by having one of his feet cut off. He and Kungsun Sir Ch'an, prime minister of the state of Cheng, were studying together under Uncle Obscure Nobody. "Either I leave first and you stay here," Sir Ch'an said to Shent'u Chia, "or you leave first and I stay here." The next day they sat down together on the same mat in the hall. "Either I leave first and you stay here," Sir Ch'an said to Shent'u Chia, "or you leave first and I stay here. Now I am about to leave. Can you stay here for a while or not? Moreover, when you see a minister of state and do not step aside for him, do you consider yourself his equal?"

"Is there really a minister of state such as this studying in our master's school?" asked Shent'u Chia. "Are you so pleased with your prime ministership that you would look down on others? I have heard it said: 'If a mirror is bright, dust and dirt will not settle on it; if they settle on it, then the mirror is not bright. If one associates with wise men for long, he will be faultless.' Now, the great one with whom you have chosen to study is our master, and yet you utter words such as these. Isn't this a bit much?"

"In spite of the fact that you are like this," said Sir Ch'an, "you would still contest with Yao over who's the better man. If you take stock of your own virtue, shouldn't that be enough to prompt you to self-reflection?"

"Many are those who gloss over their own faults, believing they ought not to suffer," said Shent'u Chia. "Few are those who do not gloss over their own faults, believing they ought not to be spared. Only a person of integrity can recognize the inevitable and accept it as his destiny. It is only destiny that prevents someone who wanders within range of the archer's bow from being struck. . . . There are many people who laugh at me for having only one foot because they have both of their feet. It makes me boiling mad, but when I come here to the master's place, I return to my former placidity. Perhaps it's because the master purifies me with his goodness. I have wandered with him for nineteen years already, but he has never made me aware of my mutilation. Now you and I are wandering inside of the physical body, but you keep drawing me outside. Isn't that a bit much?"

Shuffling his feet with shame, Sir Ch'an changed his expression and said sedately, "Mention no more about it, sir."

3

In the state of Lu there was a mutilated man, Toeless Nuncle Hill, who went plodding along on his heels to see Confucius. "Because you weren't careful," said Confucius, "you have long since brought such a misfortune upon yourself. Although you've come to see me, it's already too late."

"It's only because I didn't know my duty and was heedless of my body that I lost the front of my feet," said Toeless. "In coming to you now, I am still possessed of something more precious than my feet and that's why I am striving to preserve it whole. There is nothing that heaven does not cover; there is nothing that earth does not support. I thought of you as heaven and earth, sir. How could I have expected that you would treat me like this?"

"That was uncouth of me," said Confucius. "Why don't you come in and allow me to explain for you what I have heard?"

Toeless left.

"Be diligent, my disciples!" said Confucius. "Toeless has been mutilated, and yet he conscientiously studies to make up for the error of his previous conduct. How much more should someone whose virtue is whole!"

Toeless went to see Old Longears and told him: "As for being an ultimate man, he hasn't made it yet, has he? So why does he imitate you so assiduously, sir? He probably hopes to become famous for his bizarre ideas and strange notions, but he doesn't realize that the ultimate man would consider himself to be shackled by them."

"Why not just have him consider life and death as a single cord and 'permissible' and 'impermissible' as a single strand?" asked Old Longears. "Wouldn't that free him of his shackles?"

"Heaven is punishing him," said Toeless. "How can he be freed?"

4

Duke Ai of Lu inquired of Confucius, saying, "In the state of Wey there was an ugly man called Nag the Hump. The men who lived with Nag doted on him so much that they could not stand to be away from him. Of the women who had seen him, more than ten petitioned their parents, saying, 'I would rather be his concubine than another man's wife.' No one had ever heard of him advocating anything; all he did was follow along with others. He did not occupy a lordly position whereby he could succor those in distress. He had no accumulated salary whereby he could fill people's stomachs. Furthermore, he was ugly enough to terrify all under heaven. He always followed along and never took the lead. And his knowledge did not extend beyond his immediate surroundings. Yet male and female alike congregated before him. Surely there must have been something that distinguished him from other men.

"I summoned him to me and saw that, indeed, he was ugly enough to terrify all under heaven. When he had lived with me for less than a month, I began to take notice of his personality. Before a full year had passed, I began to put my trust in him. As the state was without a prime minister, I offered the control of the country to him. After a while he responded inarticulately, as though he were vaguely declining. How embarrassed I was! Finally, I handed the state over to him. Before very long, however, he left me and went away. I was distressed and felt as though bereft, as though there was no one with whom to enjoy my state. What kind of person was he?"

"Once when I was on a mission to the state of Ch'u," said Confucius, "I happened to see some little pigs suckling at their dead mother. After a short while, they all abandoned her and ran away hastily. It was because they no longer saw themselves in her and because they no longer sensed her to be their kind. What they loved about their mother was not her physical form but that which animated her form. When men die in battle, they are buried without the feathered fans that normally adorn coffins. When a man's feet are amputated, he no longer has a reason to be fond of his shoes. In both cases, it's because there's no basis— coffins or feet—for the fans and the shoes.

"The palace ladies of the son of heaven do not trim their nails nor do they pierce their ears. Men who are newly married must stay outside of the court and may no longer perform their official duties. If the wholeness of physical form is sufficient to make the ruler be so finicky, how much more should he be attentive to people whose integrity is whole! Now, Nag the Hump spoke not but was trusted, accomplished nothing but was loved. He caused someone to hand over a state to him, fearing only that he wouldn't accept it. He must have been a person whose abilities were whole but whose integrity was not evident in his physical form."

"What do you mean by wholeness of abilities?" asked Duke Ai.

Confucius said: "Life and death, preservation and loss, fail- ure and success, poverty and wealth, worthiness and unworthi- ness, slander and praise, hunger and thirst, cold and heat—these are all the transformations of affairs and the operation of destiny. Day and night they alternate before us, but human knowledge is incapable of perceiving their source. Therefore, we should not let them disturb our equanimity, nor should we let them enter our numinous treasury. To make the mind placid and free-flowing without letting it be dissipated in gratification, causing it to have springtime with all things day and night uninterruptedly, this is to receive and engender the seasons in one's mind. This is what I mean by wholeness of one's abilities."

"What do you mean by integrity not being existent in physical form?"

"Levelness is the equilibrium of water at rest. We may use it as a standard, preserving it within so that without we are not ruffled. Integrity is the cultivation of complete harmony. We can tell that a person has integrity, even though it may not be evident in her physical form, because she is indispensable to all things."

On another day, Duke Ai related this conversation to Master Min, saying, "At first, I sat on my throne facing south and ruled over all under heaven. I held the reins of government and worried over the welfare of the people. I considered myself to be the ultimate enlightened ruler. But now I have heard this account of an ultimate man and am afraid that I lack substance. Heedless of my body, I may lose my state. The relationship between Confucius and me is not one of ruler and subject. We are simply friends in integrity."

5

Lipless Clubfoot Scattered offered his counsels to Duke Ling of Wey. The duke was so pleased with him that he looked upon people whose bodies were whole as having spindly shins. Jar Goiter offered his counsels to Duke Huan of Ch'i. The duke was so pleased with him that he looked upon people whose bodies were whole as having scraggy necks.

Thus, when one's integrity is outstanding, the physical form will be forgotten. If people do not forget what they usually forget, but instead forget what they usually do not forget, that may be called true forgetting.

Therefore, the sage has a place where he wanders, and considers knowledge as a curse, convention as glue, virtue as a social grace, and craft as commerce. The sage hatches no schemes, so what use has he for knowledge? He does no splitting, so what use has he for glue? He has no deficiency, so what use has he for virtue? He does no peddling, so what use has he for commerce? These four are the gruel of heaven. The gruel of heaven is sustenance from heaven. Since he receives sustenance from heaven, what use has he for man? He has a human form, but is without human emotions. Because he has a human form, he groups together with other men. Because he is without human emotions, "right" and "wrong" have no effect upon him. How insignificant and small is that part of him which belongs to humanity! How grand and great is his singular identification with heaven!

6

"Are there really men without emotions?" Master Hui asked Master Chuang.

"Yes," said Master Chuang.

"If a man has no emotions," asked Master Hui, "how can he be called a man?"

"The Way gives him an appearance," said Master Chuang, "and heaven gives him a form. How can he not be called a man?"

"Since he is called a man," said Master Hui, "how can it be that he has no emotions?"

"That is not what I mean by emotions," said Master Chuang. "What I mean by having no emotions is to say that a man should not inwardly harm his person with 'good' and 'bad,' but rather should accord with the spontaneous and not add to life."

"If he does not add to life," said Master Hui, "how can his person exist?"

"The Way gives him an appearance," said Master Chuang, "and heaven gives him a form. He does not inwardly harm his person with preferences and aversions. Now you, sir, dissipate your spirit and expend your essence by leaning against a tree while you mutter or by dozing over your study table. Heaven granted you a form, sir, but you go on babbling about 'hard' and 'white.' "

6

THE GREAT
ANCESTRAL TEACHER

A description of the true man (the Taoist ideal person) is followed by a meditation on life and death as natural transformations. After a brief discourse on the Way comes a series of stories about the acceptance of one's destiny, whatever it may be. In contrast, humaneness and righteousness, two virtues stressed by Confucians, are disparaged, as they are frequently elsewhere in the book.

1

To know the actions of heaven and to know the actions of man, that's the ultimate! She who knows the actions of heaven will live in accordance with heaven. She who knows the actions of men can nourish what is unknown to her intellect with what is known to her intellect. Thus she can live out the years allotted to her by heaven and not die midway. This is the height of knowledge.

However, there is still some difficulty. Namely, knowledge has to depend on something for its consequent accuracy, but that which it depends on is particularly unstable. How do we know that what we attribute to heaven may not be due to man, and that what we attribute to man may not be due to heaven?

Only when there is a true man is there true knowledge.

What is a true man? The true man of old did not oppose the minority, did not strive for heroic accomplishments, and did not scheme over affairs. Such being the case, he did not regret it when he made a mistake nor feel smug when he was right. Such being the case, he could climb high without trembling, enter water without getting soaked, and enter fire without feeling hot. Only one whose knowledge can ascend the heights of the Way can be like this.

The true man of old did not dream when he slept and did not worry when he was awake. His food was not savory, his breathing was deep. The breathing of the true man is from his heels, the breathing of the common man is from his throat. The words of those who unwillingly yield catch in their throats as though they were retching. Those whose desires are deep-seated will have shallow natural reserves.

The true man of old knew neither fondness for life nor aversion to death, was neither elated by going forth nor reluctant to return. Casually he went and casually he came. He neither forgot what his beginning had been nor sought what his end would be. Happily he received and forgetfully he returned. This is what is meant by not detracting from the Way with the mind, not assisting heaven with the human. This is what we call a true man.

Such being the case, his mind was forgetful, his visage calm, his forehead beamingly broad. Austere as autumn, warm as spring, his joy and anger were in touch with the four seasons. He was compatible with all things but no one knew his limits. . . .

The true man of old

Was towering in stature but never collapsed,
Seemed insufficient but accepted nothing;
Aloofly independent but not obstinate,

Amply empty but not ostentatious,
Merry, as though he were happy,
Demurring, as though he were compelled,
Suffused with an alluring charm,
Endowed with an arresting integrity,
Stern, as though he were worldly,
Arrogant, as though he were uncontrollable,
Reticent, as though he preferred to clam up,
Absent-minded, as though he forgot what to say. . . .

Thus his likes were reduced to one and his dislikes were also reduced to one. His "one" was one and his "not one" was also one. Being "one," he was a follower of heaven. Being "not one," he was a follower of man. He in whom neither heaven nor man is victorious over the other is called a true man.

2

Life and death are destined. Their constant alternation, like that of day and night, is due to heaven. What men are unable to interfere with are the attributes of all things. They particularly regard heaven as their father and love it with their very person. How much more should they love that which surpasses heaven! Men particularly regard their lord as superior to themselves and would sacrifice their very person for him. How much more should they be willing to do so for what is truer than any lord!

When springs dry up, fish huddle together on the land. They blow moisture on each other and keep each other wet with their slime. But it would be better if they could forget themselves in the rivers and lakes. Rather than praising Yao [sage] and condemning Chieh [tyrant], it would be better for people to forget both of them and assimilate their ways.

A boat may be hidden in a gully on a hill that, in turn, is hidden away in a marsh. We may think this is a secure arrangement, but someone strong might come in the middle of the night

and bear (both) the boat (and the hill) away, unbeknownst to the sleeping owner. The idea of hiding the smaller in the larger is appropriate, yet things may still disappear. But if we were to hide all under heaven inside of all under heaven, nothing would disappear. This is the great attribute of the eternality of things. We are especially happy when we chance to take on human form. What incalculable joy there is in these myriad transformations, such as human form, which never begin to reach a limit! Therefore, the sage wanders where things do not disappear and all are preserved. If people will emulate one who is good at being young and good at growing old, good at beginning and good at ending, how much more should they emulate that to which the myriad things are joined and upon which the unity of transformation depends!

3

The Way has attributes and evidence, but it has no action and no form. It may be transmitted but cannot be received. It may be apprehended but cannot be seen. From the root, from the stock, before there was heaven or earth, for all eternity truly has it existed. It inspirits demons and gods, gives birth to heaven and earth. It lies above the zenith but is not high; it lies beneath the nadir but is not deep. It is prior to heaven and earth, but it is not ancient; it is senior to high antiquity, but it is not old.

> The clansman Hsiwei attained it,
>> and thereby demarcated heaven and earth;
> The clansman Fuhsi attained it,
>> and thereby adjusted the breath of the mother.
> Polaris attained it,
>> and has not deviated throughout the ages;
> The sun and moon attained it,
>> and have never rested throughout the ages;
> K'anp'i attained it,
>> and thereby inherited Mount K'unlun;

P'ingyi attained it,
    and thereby wandered in the great rivers.
Chien Wu attained it,
    and thereby dwelled on supreme Mount T'ai;
The Yellow Emperor attained it,
    and thereby ascended to cloud-filled heaven.
Chuan Hsü attained it,
    and thereby dwelled in his dark palace.
Yüch'iang attained it,
    and stands at the north pole.
The Queen Mother of the West attained it,
    and sits at faraway Shaokuang;
        no one knows her beginning,
        no one knows her end.
Progenitor P'eng attained it,
    and lived from the time of Shun
    to the time of the five hegemons.
Fu Yüeh attained it,
    and thereby became minister of Wuting,
    grandly in possession of all under heaven;
        mounted upon Sagittarius,
        riding upon Scorpio,
            he joined the arrayed stars.

4

Sir Sunflower of Southunc inquired of Woman Hunchback, saying, "You are old in years, ma'am, but your complexion is like that of a child. How is this?"

"I have heard the Way."

"Can I learn the Way?" asked Sir Sunflower of Southunc.

"Oh, no! You can't. You're not the person for it. There was Lotbridge Learner who had the ability of a sage but not the Way of a sage. I have the Way of a sage but not the ability of a sage. I wanted to teach him, in hopes that he would truly become a sage, you see? In any event, it should have been easy to teach the Way of a sage to someone with the ability of a sage. Still, I had to instruct him and watch over him. After three days, he could put all under heaven beyond him. Once he was able to put all under heaven beyond him, I watched over him again. After seven days, he could put things beyond him. Once he was able to put things beyond him, I watched over him again. After nine days, he could put life beyond him. Once he was able to put life beyond him, he could then see with the clarity of morning light. Seeing with the clarity of morning light, he could envision uniqueness. Envisioning uniqueness, he could eliminate past and present. Eliminating past and present, he could enter the realm of lifelessness and deathlessness, where that which kills life does not die and that which engenders life does not live. As for what sort of thing it is, there's nothing that it doesn't send off, nothing that it doesn't welcome, nothing that it doesn't destroy, and nothing that it doesn't bring to completion. Its name is Tranquillity in Turmoil. Tranquillity in Turmoil may be defined as that which is brought to completion after passing through turmoil."

"Wherever did you learn all this?" asked Sir Sunflower of Southunc.

"I learned it from the son of Assistant Ink. Assistant Ink's son learned it from the grandson of Ready Reciter. Ready Reciter's grandson learned it from Bright Vision. Bright Vision learned it from Agreeable Whisper. Agreeable Whisper learned it from Earnest Service. Earnest Service learned it from Sighing Songster. Sighing Songster learned it from Murky Mystery. Murky Mystery learned it from Share Vacuity. Share Vacuity learned it from Would-be Beginning."

5

Sir Sacrifice, Sir Chariot, Sir Plow and Sir Come were all four talking together. "Whoever can take nonbeing as his head, life as his spine, and death as his buttocks, whoever knows the oneness of life and death, of existence and nonexistence, we shall be his friends." The four men looked at each other and smiled. Since there was no discord in their hearts, they became friends with each other.

Before long, Sir Chariot fell ill. When Sir Sacrifice went to call on him, Sir Chariot said, "Great is the Creator of Things! She's making me all crookedy like this!" His back was all hunched up. On top were his five dorsal inductories. His chin was buried in his bellybutton. His shoulders were higher than the crown of his head. His neck bones pointed toward the sky. His vital yin yang breaths were all out of kilter. Yet his mind was at ease, as though nothing were amiss. He hobbled over to a well and looked at his reflection in the water. "Alas!" he said. "The Creator of Things is making me all crookedy like this!"

"Do you resent it?" asked Sir Sacrifice.

"No, why should I resent it? Supposing that my left arm were transformed into a chicken, I would consequently go looking for a rooster that could call out the hours of the night. Supposing that my right arm were transformed into a crossbow, I would consequently go looking for an owl to roast. Supposing that my buttocks were transformed into wheels and my spirit into a horse, I would consequently mount upon them. What need would I have for any other conveyance?

"Furthermore, what we attain is due to timeliness and what we lose is the result of compliance. If we repose in timeliness and dwell in compliance, sorrow and joy cannot affect us. This is what the ancients called 'emancipation.' Those who are unable to win release for themselves are bound by things. Furthermore, long has it been that things do not win out against heaven. So why should I resent it?"

Before long, Sir Come fell ill. Gasping and on the verge of death, he was surrounded by his wife and children who were weeping. Sir Plow, who went to call on him, said to his family, "Shush! Go away! Do not disturb transformation!" Then, leaning against the door, he spoke to Sir Come: "Great is the Transforming Creator! What next will he make of you? Where will he send you? Will he turn you into a rat's liver? Will he turn you into a bug's leg?"

"The relationship of parents to a child," said Sir Come, "is such that he simply follows their commands, no matter which direction they may point him. The relationship of yin and yang to a man is no less important than that of parents to a child. If they urge me to die and I resist, that is my ill-temper. What fault of theirs is it? The Great Clod burdens me with form, toils me through life, eases me in old age, rests me in death. Thus, that which makes my life good is also that which makes my death good. Now, the Great Smelter casts his metal. If the metal were to jump up and say, 'You must make me into Excalibur!' the Great Smelter would certainly think that it was inauspicious metal. Now if I, who have chanced to take on human form, were to say, 'Man! I must remain a man!' the Great Transforming Creator would certainly think that I am an inauspicious man. Now, once I accept heaven and earth as the Great Forge, and the Transforming Creator as the Great Smelter, I'm willing to go wherever they send me."

Soundly he slept,
Suddenly he awoke.

6

Sir Mulberry Door, Meng Sir Opposite, and Sir Lute Stretch were all three talking together. "Who can associate in non-association and cooperate in noncooperation? Who can ascend to heaven and wander with the mists, bounding through infinity, forgetting themselves in life forever and ever without end?" The three men looked at each other and smiled. Since there was no discord in their hearts, they became friends with each other.

After an uneventful period of time, Sir Mulberry Door died. Before he was buried, Confucius heard about his death and sent Tzukung to participate in the funeral. When Tzukung arrived, he found one of them composing a tune and the other strumming on a lute. The song they sang along together went like this:

> Alas, Mulberry Door!
> Alas, Mulberry Door!
> You have already returned to the true,
> But we are still human, oh!

Tzukung hurried in and said, "I make bold to ask whether it is in accord with the rites to sing in the presence of the corpse."

The two men looked at each other and smiled, saying, "What does he know about the meaning of the rites?"

Tzukung went back and reported to Confucius, asking, "What kind of people are they? They cultivate nonbeing and put physical form beyond them. They sing in the presence of the corpse without the slightest change of expression. There's no way I can describe them. What kind of people are they?"

"They are people who wander beyond the spatial world," said Confucius, "while I wander within it. Beyond and within are incompatible. It was uncouth of me to have sent you to mourn him. They're about to become companions of the Creator of Things, and wander in the unity of the vital breath that joins heaven and earth. They consider life as an attached cyst, an appended tumor, and death as the bursting of a boil, the draining of an abscess. Such being the case, what do they care about the priority of life and death? They lodge in a common body composed of diverse elements. They forget their inner organs and are oblivious of the senses. Over and over turns the seamless cycle of beginning and ending. Faraway they are, roaming beyond the dust and dirt of the mundane world, carefree in the karma of nonaction. So how can they be bothered with worldly rites, merely to look good in the eyes of ordinary people!"

"Well, sir," asked Tzukung, "to which realm do you adhere?"

"I am one of heaven's condemned," said Confucius. "Nevertheless, this is something we share in common."

"I venture to ask their secret," said Tzukung.

"Fish delight in water," said Confucius, "and man delights in the Way. Delighting in water, fish find adequate nourishment just by passing through their ponds. Delighting in the Way, man's life is stabilized without ado. Therefore, it is said, 'Fish forget themselves in the rivers and lakes; men forget themselves in the arts of the Way.' "

"I venture to ask about the oddball," said Tzukung.

"The oddball may be odd to other men, but he is a pair with heaven. Therefore, it is said, 'The villain in heaven is a gentleman among men; the gentleman among men is a villain in heaven.' "

7

Yen Hui inquired of Confucius, saying, "When Mengsun Ts'ai's mother died, he cried without tears, his heart felt no distress, and during the period of mourning he felt no sorrow. Although lacking these three qualities, he was held to be the best mourner in the state of Lu. Can one really attain a name without the substance? I find this to be very strange."

"The clansman Mengsun was so thorough," said Confucius, "that he had advanced beyond knowledge. Although he may have wished to simplify mourning, but wasn't able to do so fully, still there is that which he did simplify. Mengsun didn't know why he lived and didn't know why he would die. He didn't know which came first, life or death, and which came last. You see, he just went along with the transformation of things, awaiting the unknown transformation that was in store for him. Moreover, as we are about to undergo transformation, how do we know that we aren't already transformed? As we are about to cease transformation, how do we know that we have already transformed? Perhaps you and I are in a dream from which we have not yet awakened. He, however, had a vulnerable physical body but no damage to his mind, a patched-together lodge but no expenditure of his essence. Mengsun was singularly awakened. When others cried, he cried too. That's why he behaved himself as he did.

"Moreover, people identify each other as 'I,' but how do we know that what we call 'I' may not really be 'I'? You may dream that you are a bird and streak across the sky, that you are a fish and descend to the depths. We cannot determine whether we who are speaking now are awake or dreaming. We may be so suddenly delighted that we don't have a chance to smile; we may break into a smile before we have a chance to arrange ourselves. Repose in what has been arranged for you and leave transformation behind, then you will be able to enter the unity of vast heaven."

8

Master Yierh went to see Hsü Yu. Hsü Yu asked him: "How has Yao aided you?"

"Yao told me," said Master Yierh, " 'You must dedicate yourself to humaneness and righteousness, and speak clearly about right and wrong.' "

"Then why have you come here?" asked Hsü Yu. "Yao has already tattooed you with humaneness and righteousness and lopped off your nose with right and wrong. How will you be able to wander on the path of untroubled and untrammeled evolution?"

"That may be," said Master Yierh, "but I'd like to wander along its borders."

"No," said Hsü Yu, "he who is blind has nothing to do with the charm of human features; he who is sightless has nothing to do with the attraction of colorfully embroidered garments."

"Unadorned's disregard of her beauty," said Master Yierh, "Bridge Support's disregard of his strength, and the Yellow Emperor's abandonment of his knowledge were all due to a process of remolding and reworking. How do you know that the Creator of Things may not erase my tattoo and restore my nose, enabling me to avail myself of wholeness so that I may become your disciple?"

"Ah!" said Hsü Yu. "That cannot yet be known. But I will tell you in general. My teacher, oh my teacher! She blends the myriad things, but is not righteous; her benefits reach to a myriad generations but she is not humane. She is senior to high antiquity but is not aged. She covers heaven, supports earth, and carves out a host of forms, but is not skillful. It is in this that one should roam."

9

"I'm making progress," said Yen Hui.

"What do you mean?" asked Confucius.

"I have forgotten rites and music."

"Not bad, but you still haven't got it."

Yen Hui saw Confucius again on another day and said, "I'm making progress."

"What do you mean?"

"I have forgotten humaneness and righteousness."

"Not bad, but you still haven't got it."

Yen Hui saw Confucius again on another day and said, "I'm making progress."

"What do you mean?"

"I sit and forget."

"What do you mean, 'sit and forget'?" Confucius asked with surprise.

"I slough off my limbs and trunk," said Yen Hui, "dim my intelligence, depart from my form, leave knowledge behind, and become identical with the Transformational Thoroughfare. This is what I mean by 'sit and forget.' "

"If you are identical," said Confucius, "then you have no preferences. If you are transformed, then you have no more constants. It's you who is really the worthy one! Please permit me to follow after you."

10

Sir Chariot and Sir Mulberry were friends. Once when it had rained continuously for ten days, Sir Chariot said to himself, "I'm afraid that Sir Mulberry may be in distress." So he wrapped up some food in a piece of cloth and went to feed him. When he reached Sir Mulberry's gate, he heard the strumming of a lute and a plaint that sounded as though it were between singing and crying:

> "Was it father?
> Was it mother?
> Heaven?
> Earth?"

The voice could barely sustain itself and the verses were uttered in haste.

Sir Chariot entered and asked, "Why is your song like this?"

"I am thinking about who might have brought me to this

extremity, but can't come up with an answer. Surely my father and mother would not wish for me to be so poor. And heaven shows no preference in whom it covers nor earth in whom it supports. How could they show preference in making me poor? I seek to find who might have done it, but can't succeed. Well, perhaps it was simply destiny that brought me to this extremity!"

7

RESPONSES FOR EMPERORS AND KINGS

After a look at virtue/integrity, the futility of inquiring about how to govern is pointed out. Instead, we are encouraged to wander in nonexistence. The ultimate Way is reflected in the stages of Yogic meditation displayed by a magus. Moralistic humaneness and righteousness are again belittled while the blessings of being empty and undifferentiated are upheld.

1

Gnaw Gap asked Princely Scion four questions, but he couldn't answer any of them. This made Gnaw Gap so happy that he jumped up and went off to tell Master Rushcoat.

"Did you only find that out now?" asked Master Rushcoat. "The clansman of the freehold at Yü was not up to the clansman T'ai. The clansman of the freehold at Yü treasured humaneness as a means of coercing humanity. While it may be that he did win over humanity, he never got out into nonhumanity. Clansman T'ai's dozing was so contented and his waking so peaceable that at one moment you might think he was a horse and at the next moment a cow. His knowledge was trustworthy, his integrity very true, but he never entered nonhumanity."

2

Chien Wu went to see Mad Chieh Yü. "What did Noonstart tell you?" asked Mad Chieh Yü.

"He told me," said Chien Wu, "that the ruler is one who issues canons, patterns, rules, and regulations on his own authority. What men would dare not obey them and be transformed by them?"

"That's deceptive virtue," said Mad Chieh Yü. "Using it to govern all under heaven is like trying to channel a river through the ocean or making a flea carry a mountain on its back. When the sage governs, does he govern externals? No, all he does is set things upright before acting and then make sure they do what they can. Birds fly high to escape harm from the hunter's dart. Mice burrow deep beneath the mound of the local god to avoid the threat of being smoked out or dug up. Don't you even know as much as these two tiny creatures?"

3

Skyroot was wandering south of Mount Abundance when he came to the edge of River Calm. There he happened to meet Anonymous, whom he asked, "May I ask how to govern all under heaven?"

"Go away!" said Anonymous. "You're a base fellow. Why ask such an unpleasant question? I'm about to become a companion of the Creator of Things. When I get tired, I'll mount upon a nebulous bird to go beyond the limits of the universe and wander in Never-never Land so that I may dwell in its wide open spaces. Why the dickens are you disturbing my mind with this talk of governing all under heaven?"

Skyroot persisted in his questioning.

"Let your mind wander in vapidity," said Anonymous, "blend your vital breath with immensity. Follow along with the nature of things and admit no personal preference. Then all under heaven will be well governed."

4

Sir Sunny Dweller went to see Old Longears and said, "Here is a man, alert and vigorous, perceptive and intelligent, and untiring in learning the Way. May such a man be compared with the enlightened kings?"

"Compared to the sages," said Old Longears, "he would be like a clerk at his labors or a craftsman tied to his work, toiling his body and vexing his mind. Furthermore, it is the patterned pelt of the tiger and the leopard that bring forth the hunter, it is the nimbleness of the gibbon and the monkey that bring forth the trainer with his leash. Can such as these be compared with enlightened kings?"

Surprised, Sunny Dweller said, "May I be so bold as to ask about the government of the enlightened king?"

"In the government of the enlightened king," said Old Longears, "his merit covers all under heaven, but it seems not to be his own. His transforming influence extends to the myriad things, but the people do not rely on him. Whatever he does, no one mentions his name, since he causes everything to enjoy itself. He stands in unfathomability and wanders in nonexistence."

5

In the state of Cheng, there was a magus of the spirits named Chi Hsien. He knew all about people's life and death, preservation and loss, misfortune and good fortune, longevity and mortality—predicting the year, month, week, and day as though he himself were a spirit. When the people of Cheng saw Chi Hsien coming, they would turn their backs on him and run away.

But when Master Lieh went to see him, he was utterly intoxicated. Upon his return, he related his encounter to Master Hu: "I used to think of your way as the ultimate one, but now I have discovered that there is one still more ultimate."

"What I have conveyed to you so far only deals with the surface," said Master Hu. "We haven't yet begun to deal with the substance. And you think you're already in possession of the Way? If you only have a bunch of hens and no rooster, what sort of eggs are you going to end up with? You take your way and go jostling with the world, assuming that people will believe you, but that's precisely why you let this fellow see through you. Try to bring him along with you next time and show me to him."

The next day, Master Lieh came with the magus to see Master Hu. As they were going out, the magus said to Master Lieh, "Ay! Your master is dying! He doesn't have much longer to live—less than ten days or so. I saw something strange about him. He looked like damp ashes."

Master Lieh went back in. His lapels soaked with tears and snivel, he related to Master Hu what the magus had said.

"Just now," said Master Hu, "I showed myself to him in the patterns of the earth. Unconscious, I was absolutely motionless. He probably saw me with the wellsprings of my integrity stopped up. Try bringing him around again sometime."

The next day, Master Lieh came again with the magus to see Master Hu. As they were going out, the magus said to Master Lieh, "Fortunately, your master met me. He has recovered and is fully alive. I have seen that his stoppage was only temporary."

Master Lieh went back in and related to Master Hu what the magus had said. "Just now," said Master Hu, "I showed myself to him in the appearance of heaven. I was affected neither by name nor by substance, and the wellsprings of my vitality issued from my heels. He probably saw me with my wellsprings in fine fettle. Try bringing him around again sometime."

The next day, Master Lieh came again with the magus to see Master Hu. As they were going out, the magus said to Master

Lieh, "Your master is unstable. There's nothing I can do to read his features. Let's wait till he stabilizes, then I'll read his features again."

Master Lieh went back in and related to Master Hu what the magus had said. "Just now," said Master Hu, "I showed myself to him in the neutrality of Great Nonvictory. He probably saw me with the wellsprings of my vital breath in balance. The depths of the whale's whirlpool are an abyss; the depths of blocked water are an abyss; the depths of flowing water are an abyss. There are nine types of abysses. Here I have shown three of them. Try bringing him around again sometime."

The next day, Master Lieh came again with the magus to see Master Hu. Before the magus had even come to a standstill, he lost his composure and ran away. "Pursue him!" said Master Hu. Master Lieh pursued the magus, but couldn't catch up with him. He returned and reported to Master Hu, "He's disappeared; he's lost. I couldn't catch up with him."

"Just now," said Master Hu, "I showed myself to him with my ancestry having not yet begun to appear. I was emptily intertwined with it so that one could not discern who was who. Thus did I bend with the wind and flow with the waves. Therefore he fled."

After this, Master Lieh came to believe that he had barely begun to learn. He returned home and did not go out for three years. He cooked for his wife and fed pigs as though he were feeding people. He took no sides in affairs and whittled himself back to the simplicity of the unhewn log. Clodlike, he stood alone in his physical form. Sealed off against perplexity, in this manner he remained whole to the end.

6

Do not be a corpse for fame,
Do not be a storehouse of schemes;

B. DALTON BOOKSELLER
STORE #467 ANNAPOLIS,MD (410)266-6370

REG#02   BOOKSELLER#011
RECEIPT#   8076   01/18/96   7:54 PM

S 0553374060   WANDERING ON THE WAY
                        1 @   11.95   11.95

SUBTOTAL   11.95
SALES TAX - 5%   .60
TOTAL   12.55
CASH PAYMENT   20.00
CHANGE   7.45

THANK YOU FOR SHOPPING AT B.DALTON!

Do not be responsible for affairs,
Do not be a proprietor of knowledge.

Thoroughly embody unendingness and wander in nonbeginning. Thoroughly experience what you receive from heaven but do not reveal what you attain. Just be empty, that's all. The mind of the ultimate man functions like a mirror. It neither sends off nor welcomes; it responds but does not retain. Therefore, he can triumph over things without injury.

7

The emperor of the Southern Sea was Lickety, the emperor of the Northern Sea was Split, and the emperor of the Center was Wonton. Lickety and Split often met each other in the land of Wonton, and Wonton treated them very well. Wanting to repay Wonton's kindness, Lickety and Split said, "All people have seven holes for seeing, hearing, eating, and breathing. Wonton alone lacks them. Let's try boring some holes for him." So every day they bored one hole, and on the seventh day Wonton died.

OUTER
CHAPTERS

8

WEBBED TOES

Metaphors of physical superfluity are used to criticize Confucian virtues and regulations. Keen vision and hearing are said to be maintained by paying attention to one's inner self instead of becoming subservient to external qualities.

1

Webbed toes and extra fingers may issue from one's nature, but they are superfluous to one's integrity. Attached cysts and appended tumors may issue from one's form, but they are superfluous to one's nature. Humaneness and righteousness may be arrayed among the five viscera of one who is meddlesome in their use, but they are not the correct approach according to the Way and its integrity. Thus a web between the toes is but the addition of a useless piece of flesh and an appendage on a hand is but the implanting of a useless finger. One who adds webs and appendages to the attributes of the five viscera, so that they are debauched and perverted by humane and righteous conduct, is to be meddlesome in the use of keen hearing and eyesight.

Thus, will not adding a web to one's eyesight bring chaos to the five colors, profligacy to patterned ornament, and dazzling resplendence to colorful brocades? This is what happened to Spidersight. Will not adding something extra to one's hearing bring chaos to the five sounds, profligacy to the six pitch-pipes and the tones of musical instruments made of metal, stone, silk, and bamboo, of the Yellow Bell and the Great Tube? This is what happened to Maestro K'uang. Will not the appendage of humaneness promote virtue and stopple one's nature, so as to receive name and fame, causing the emulation of an unattainable model to the raucous accompaniment of all the reeds and drums under heaven? This is what happened to Tseng Shen and Shih Ch'iu. Will not adding a web to one's disputation, piling up and knotting together forged phrases and hammered words, so as to let the mind wander amid "hard" and "white," "identical" and "different," merely lead to the waste of useless words for a temporary reputation? This was what happened to Yang Chu and Mo Ti. Therefore, these are all examples of the way of superfluous webs and extraneous branches, not of the ultimately correct way for all under heaven.

That which is ultimately correct does not lose the characteristics of its nature and destiny. Therefore, joining is accomplished without a web, branching is accomplished without extraneousness, lengthening is accomplished without a surplus, shortening is accomplished without inadequacy. Thus, although a duck's legs are short, if we extend them it will come to grief; although a crane's legs are long, if we cut them short, it will be tragic. Therefore, if what by nature is long is not cut short, and if what by nature is short is not extended, there will be no grief to dispense with. One suspects that humaneness and righteousness are not attributes of humanity! Otherwise, why would those humane men be so full of grief?

Furthermore, he whose big toe is joined to his second toe by a web would weep if it were torn apart; he whose hand has an extra finger would scream if it were bitten off. Of these two, in the one case there is a surplus in number and in the other there is a deficit, but the grief is the same. In today's world, the humane people grieve over the world's troubles with bleary eyes; the inhumane people cast aside the characteristics of nature and destiny in their greed for honor and wealth. Therefore, one suspects that humaneness and righteousness are not attributes of humanity. From the Three Dynasties on down, how much shrill contention there has been under heaven!

Furthermore, if we must depend upon the bevel, the ruler, the compass, and the L-square to make things correct, that would be to slice away their nature. If we must depend upon cords, twine, glue, and lacquer to make things solid, that would be to invade their integrity. Bowing and scraping to the rites and music, simpering and smirking with humaneness and righteousness to console the hearts of all under heaven, this is to forfeit constancy. Constancy implies the making of angles without a bevel, the making of straight lines without a ruler, the making of circles without a compass, the making of squares without an L-square, sticking things together without glue or lacquer, tying things together without cords or twine. Therefore, all under heaven are drawn into life but do not know why they are alive, and all are alike in attaining their ends without knowing why. Therefore, in ancient times and today, it has always been the same: imperishable. Then why should humaneness and righteousness wander incessantly amid the Way and its integrity like glue, lacquer, cords, and twine, causing confusion for all under heaven?

If there is but small confusion, there will be a change of direction; if there is great confusion, there will be a change of nature. How do we know this is so? The clansman of the freehold at Yü summoned humaneness and righteousness to vex all under heaven. When everyone under heaven goes rushing about at the behest of humaneness and righteousness, does this not change their nature through humaneness and righteousness? Therefore, I shall try to discuss this matter.

From the Three Dynasties on down, everyone has altered his nature for the sake of something. The petty man sacrifices himself for the sake of gain; the nobleman sacrifices himself for the sake of a name; the great officer sacrifices himself for the sake of his family; the sage sacrifices himself for the sake of all under heaven. Therefore, these various people, although of different occupations and dissimilar reputations, in damaging their nature through personal sacrifice are identical. A slave boy and a serf were out herding their sheep together and both lost their sheep. When the slave boy was asked how it happened, he said that he was holding his bamboo strips and reading. When the serf was asked how it happened, he admitted that he was playing at dice and making bets. Although the two of them were differently occupied, their loss of the sheep was equivalent. Poyi died for fame at the foot of Shouyang; Robber Footpad died for gain on top of Tungling. Although the two of them died for different reasons, the damage to their lives and the harm to their natures was equivalent. Why must we approve of Poyi and disapprove of Robber Footpad? Of all those under heaven who sacrifice themselves, those who do so for humaneness and righteousness are commonly called "superior men" while those who do so for goods and wealth are commonly called "petty men." Their sacrifice is the same, but one of them is accounted a superior man and the other a petty man. In regard to damaging life and injuring nature, Robber Footpad was just like Poyi. Why then should we choose a superior man and a petty man from between them?

Furthermore, he who subordinates his nature to humaneness and righteousness, although he may do so as thoroughly as Tseng Shen and Shih Ch'iu, is not what I would call "good." He who subordinates his nature to the five flavors, although he may do so as thoroughly as Shu'erh, is not what I would call "expert." He who subordinates his nature to the five sounds, although he may do so as thoroughly as Maestro K'uang, is not what I would call "keen of hearing." He who subordinates his nature to the five colors, although he may do so as thoroughly as Spidersight, is not what I would call "keen sighted." What I mean by calling a person "good" does not refer to her humaneness or righteousness, for such a person would be "good" only in her virtue. What I mean by calling a person "good" does not refer to so-called humaneness and righteousness, but simply to her acceptance of the characteristics of her nature and destiny. What I mean by calling a person "keen of hearing," does not refer to her hearing anything else, but only to her hearing herself. What I mean by calling a person "keen sighted" does not refer to her seeing anything else, but only to her seeing herself. He who does not see himself but only sees other things, and who does not realize himself but only realizes other things, is one who realizes what others realize but does not himself realize what he realizes. He strives to delight others but does nothing to delight himself. He who strives to delight others but does nothing to delight himself, though he be a Robber Footpad or a Poyi, is equally debauched and perverted. Because I feel shame before the Way and its integrity, I dare not engage in the elevated manipulation of humaneness and righteousness, nor in the debased conduct of debauchery and perversity.

9

HORSES' HOOVES

The sages (those honored by the Confucians) are rebuked for their pursuit of knowledge and interference with the innate characteristics of things. Left to their own devices, human beings and animals would form harmonious natural communities.

1

A horse's hooves can tread upon frost and snow, its hair can withstand the wind and the cold. It eats grass and drinks water; it prances about briskly. This is a horse's true nature. Though one might provide a horse with magnificent terraces and splendid bedrooms, they are of no use to it. But then came Poleh, who said, "I am skilled at training horses." And men began to singe them, clip their hair, trim their hooves, and brand them. They led them with bridles and hobbles, lined them up in stable and stall, resulting in the deaths of two or three out of ten. They made the horses go hungry and thirsty, raced them, and galloped them, arrayed them in rows and columns. In front were the tribulations of the bit and the ornamental halter, behind were the threats of the whip and the crop, resulting in the deaths of over half the horses.

The potter said, "I am skilled at working clay. My round pieces fit the compass and my square pieces fit the L-square." The carpenter said, "I am skilled at working wood. My angular pieces fit the bevel and my straight pieces match the ruler." Yet is it in the nature of clay and wood that they should fit the compass, the L-square, the bevel, and the ruler? Nonetheless, generation after generation extol them, saying, "Poleh was skilled at training horses; the carpenter and the potter are skilled at working clay and wood." This is also the error made by those who govern all under heaven.

I suspect, however, that those who are skilled at governing all under heaven would not do so. Their people, having a constant nature, would weave cloth to wear and plow the land in order to eat. This is called "common integrity." They would remain unified and not split into factions; this condition we may style "natural freedom." Therefore, in an age of ultimate integrity, they would walk with quiet confidence, look ahead with focused composure. In such an age, there would be no paths and tunnels through the mountains, no boats or bridges to cross the swamps. The myriad things would live in groups, their settlements lined up next to each other. Birds and beasts would form groups, the grasses and trees would thrive. Thus birds and beasts could be tamed but still wander about; one could climb up to the nests of magpies and peep in without disturbing them.

In a world of ultimate integrity, men would dwell together with the birds and the beasts. They would come together in tribes with the myriad things. What would they know of superior men and petty men? Equally without knowledge, they would not stray from their integrity. Equally without desire, this is called "the simplicity of the unhewn log." With the simplicity of the unhewn log, the people would attain their nature. Then along comes the sage, assiduous in his exercise of humaneness, plodding in his exercise of righteousness, and all under heaven begin to doubt. Music begins to multiply, rites begin to proliferate, and all under heaven begin to divide. Therefore, if the simple, unhewn log remained intact, who would carve a sacrificial vessel from it? If the white jade remained unimpaired, who would make scepters and tallies from it? If the Way and integrity were not discarded, who would choose humaneness and righteousness? If the attributes of our individual natures were not set aside, what use would there be for rites and music? If the five colors were not confused, who would make colorful patterns? If the five sounds were not confused, who would conform to the six pitch-pipes? The carving of the unhewn log into instruments is the fault of the craftsman; the impairment of the Way and integrity with humaneness and righteousness is the error of the sage.

Returning to the subject of horses, if they are allowed to live on the open land, they eat the grass and drink the water. When they are happy, they cross necks and rub against each other. When they are angry, they turn back to back and kick each other. The knowledge of horses amounts to this and no more. But if you put a yoke upon them and array them evenly with little moon-mirrors on their foreheads, all they know is to try to break the cross-bar, twist out of the yoke, smash the chariot cover, expel the bit, and bite through the reins. Therefore, to take the knowledge of a horse and make it behave like a brigand is the crime of Poleh.

In the time of the clansman Hohsü, when people stayed at home, they did not know what they were doing, and when they went outside, they did not know where they were going. They filled their mouths with food and were happy, strolling about with their bellies stuffed tight as a drum. The abilities of the people were this and no more. Then along came the sages to rectify the form of all under heaven with their bowing and scraping to the rites and music. They unveiled their humaneness and righteousness from on high to soothe the hearts of all under heaven, but the people began to be plodding in their fondness for knowledge. They ended up contending for profit and then they could not be stopped. This, too, is the error of the sages.

10

RANSACKING COFFERS

It is the (Confucian) sage, with all of his cleverness and virtuousness, who gives rise to robbers and thieves. Echoing the Tao Te Ching, *the author of this chapter longs for a time of primitive simplicity.*

1

In guarding against thieves who ransack coffers, search through bags, and break open cupboards, people are sure to bind them with ropes and cords, secure them with clasps and hasps. This is what common opinion calls being wise. But if a giant thief comes, he will put the cupboard on his back, pick up the coffer, carry the bag on a pole over his shoulder, and run away with them, fearing only that the ropes and cords, the clasps and hasps may not be secure enough. This being so, is not he whom I just referred to as wise merely collecting things for the great thief?

Therefore, let me try to explain. Is not he whom common opinion calls wise collecting things for the great thief? Is not the so-called sage a guardian for the great thief? How do we know this is so? Of old, in the state of Ch'i, neighboring villages gazed across at each other and could hear the sounds of each other's chickens and dogs. The area over which they spread their nets and which they plowed and cultivated was more than two thousand tricents square. Within their four boundaries, whenever they erected an ancestral temple or altar to the gods of the land and grain, and in carrying out the government of their villages, households, townships, neighborhoods, districts, and hamlets, they always modeled themselves after the sages. Of a sudden, however, Viscount Fieldborn murdered the ruler of Ch'i and stole his state. But was it only the state that he stole? Along with it he stole the laws of sagely wisdom. Therefore, while Viscount Fieldborn may have had the name of a robber and a thief, he was ensconced as firmly as Yao or Shun. The small states did not dare to find fault with him, the big states did not dare to punish him. For twelve generations, his family has possessed the state of Ch'i. Hence, not only did he steal the state of Ch'i, along with it he took the laws of sagely wisdom and used them to guard his robbing, thieving person.

Let me try to explain. Is not he whom common opinion calls ultimately wise collecting things for the great thief? Is not the so-called ultimate sage a guardian for the great thief? How do we know this is so? Long ago, Lungp'ang was beheaded, Pikan had his heart cut out, Ch'ang Hung was disemboweled, and Tzuhsü's corpse was left to putrefy. Therefore, even four worthies such as these could not escape such horrible deaths. Therefore, the followers of Footpad inquired of him, saying, "Do waylayers also have a way?"

"Wherever one goes," said Footpad, "there is always a way. By shrewdly surmising that valuables are stored in a room, the robber shows his sageness. By entering first, he shows his bravery. By going out last, he shows his righteousness. By knowing whether the robbery may be attempted or not, he shows his wisdom. By dividing the spoils equally, he shows his humaneness. There is no one under heaven who is not possessed of these five qualities that can become a great robber."

Viewed in this light, a good man who does not attain the

way of the sages cannot establish himself. And Footpad could not have pursued his course without the way of the sages. But the good men under heaven are few and the bad men are many. Thus the benefits of the sages to all under heaven are few and their harms to all under heaven are many. Therefore, we have the sayings: "When the lips are missing, the teeth will get cold"; "The diluted wine of Lu led to the siege of Hantan"; "When a sage is born, great robbers arise." If we were to assault the sages and release the robbers and thieves, all under heaven would begin to be governed. When the rivers run dry, the valleys are empty; when the hills are leveled, the chasms are filled in. When the sage dies, the great robbers do not arise. Then all under heaven will be at peace and without event.

If the sage does not die, there will be no end to great robbers. The more emphasis is placed on the sage in governing all under heaven, the greater the gain for Robber Footpad. If bushels and pecks are devised for measuring, then he will steal by the bushel and the peck. If weights and steelyards are devised for weighing, then he will steal by the weight and the steelyard. If tallies and seals are devised for verifying, then he will steal by the tally and the seal. If humaneness and righteousness are devised for reforming the world, he will steal by humaneness and righteousness. How do we know that this is so?

He who steals a belt buckle is executed;
He who steals a state becomes a feudal lord.
It is within the gates of the feudal lords
That humaneness and righteousness are preserved.

Is this not stealing humaneness and righteousness, sageness and wisdom? Thus those who follow after the great robbers and exalt the nobles, who steal humaneness and righteousness together with all the gains from bushels and pecks, weights and steelyards, tallies and seals—even the reward of carriage and crown will not dissuade them, even the threat of the executioner's ax will not constrain them. This increasing of the gain to Robber Footpad, making it impossible to constrain him, is the error of the sages.

Thus, there is the saying, "Fish cannot be removed from the watery depths; the profitable instruments of state cannot be shown to the people." The wisdom of the sage is the profitable instrument of all under heaven and is not something that should be revealed to all under heaven. Therefore, abolish sagehood and abandon wisdom, then the great robbers will be stopped. Throw away jade and smash pearls, then the petty robbers will not arise. Burn tallies and break seals, then the people will be simple and unsophisticated. Crush bushels and snap steelyards, then the people will not contend. Annihilate all the sagely laws under heaven, then it will be possible to begin to reason with the people. Confound the six pitch-pipes, melt down the mouth organ, and do away with the zither, stop up Maestro K'uang's ears, and all the people under heaven will begin to repossess their keenness of hearing. Eradicate patterned ornaments, disperse the five tints, glue shut the eyes of Spidersight, and all the people under heaven will begin to repossess their keenness of vision. Destroy bevel and ruler, abandon compass and L-square, crush the fingers of craftsman Ch'ui, and all the people under heaven will begin to repossess their cleverness. . . . Discard the conduct of Tseng Shen and Shih Ch'iu, clamp shut the mouths of Yang Chu and Mo Ti, cast aside humaneness and righteousness, and the integrity of all under heaven will begin to display its mysterious identity. When people repossess their keenness of eyesight, then all under heaven will no longer be glittery. When people repossess their keenness of hearing, then all under heaven will no longer be cacophonous. When people repossess their wisdom, then all under heaven will no longer be deluded. When people repossess their integrity, then all under heaven will no longer be perverse. Tseng Shen, Shih Ch'iu, Yang Chu, Mo Ti, Maestro K'uang, Craftsman Ch'ui, and Spidersight were all individuals who established their virtues outside of themselves and thereby disrupted all under heaven, useless to the law.

2

Do you, sir, not know of the age of ultimate integrity? Long ago, there were the clansmen Jungch'eng, Tat'ing, Pohuang, Chungyang, Lilu, Lihsü, Hsienyüan, Hohsü, Tsunlu, Chujung, Fuhsi, and Shennung. At that time, the people knotted ropes to keep records; they considered their food to be savory, their clothes to be beautiful, their customs to be pleasurable, their dwellings to be secure. They could gaze across at the neighboring state and hear the sounds of its dogs and chickens, but the people would never travel back and forth till they died of old age. Such a time as this was one of ultimate government. Now, however, we have arrived at a situation where people crane their necks and stand on tiptoe, saying, "There's a worthy man at such-and-such a place." And they rush off to him carrying whatever provisions they can muster. Thus, within the family they abandon their parents and outside they leave the service of the ruler. Their footsteps extend unbroken across the territories of the feudal lords, their chariot tracks criss-cross a thousand tricents away. This, then, results from the error of superiors who are overly fond of knowledge.

When superiors are genuinely fond of knowledge but lack the Way, all under heaven will be in great confusion. How do we know this is so? The more knowledge there is of bows, cross-bows, hand-nets, stringed arrows, and snares, the more the birds in the sky above are thrown into confusion. The more knowledge there is of hooks, bait, nets, throw-nets, pull-nets, and basket traps, the more the fish in the water below are thrown into confusion. The more knowledge there is of palings, pitfalls, rabbit nets, and gins, the more the animals in the marshes are thrown into confusion. The more varieties of cunning, deception, slipperiness, talk of "hard and white," prevarication, claims of "identical" and "different" there are, the more the common people will be deluded by disputation. Therefore, whenever all under heaven is in great confusion, the fault lies in fondness of knowledge. Thus, all men under heaven know how to seek what they do not know, but no one knows how to seek what he already knows. All men know how to condemn what they consider to be bad, but no one knows how to condemn what they consider to be good, and so there is great confusion. Thus, they rebel against the brightness of the sun and moon above, consume the essence of the mountains and rivers below, and disrupt the procession of the four seasons in between. From wriggling insects to the tiniest flying creatures, there are none that would not lose their natures. Great, indeed, is the confusion that is brought to all under heaven from fondness for knowledge! From the Three Dynasties on down, so it has been. The plain people are neglected, while the fussing flatterers find favor. The placidity of nonaction is rejected, while garrulously expressed ideas find favor. It is this garrulousness that has brought confusion to all under heaven.

11

PRESERVING AND ACCEPTING

The human mind is strengthened by letting it remain undisturbed. The second half of the chapter is a long exposition of the ultimate Way and the happy freedom that it affords.

1

I have heard of preserving and accepting all under heaven, but I have not heard of governing all under heaven. One "preserves" for fear that all under heaven will prostitute their nature; one "accepts" for fear that all under heaven will alter their integrity. If all under heaven do not prostitute their nature, and if all under heaven do not alter their integrity, what need would there be for someone to govern all under heaven? Long ago, when Yao governed all under heaven, he made everyone delightfully enjoy their nature, which means they were not placid. When Chieh governed all under heaven, he made everyone wearily feel the bitterness of their own nature, which means they were not content. To be neither placid nor content is a negation of integrity. There is no one under heaven who can long endure when her integrity is negated.

Is a man too happy?—he will have an excess of yang. Is a man too angry?—he will have an excess of yin. When there is an excess of yin and yang, the four seasons will not arrive on time, and the harmony of cold and heat will be incomplete. Would this not result in injury to the human body? If men are made to lose a proper perspective on happiness and anger, to dwell without constancy, to think without satisfaction, and to give up midway without completing what they have started, all under heaven will begin to be arrogantly perverse and fiercely proud, then there will be conduct like that of Robber Footpad, Tseng Shen, and Shih Ch'iu. Thus, the entirety of all under heaven would not be adequate to reward the good, nor would it be sufficient to punish the bad. Therefore, all under heaven, great as it is, is not adequate for rewards and punishments. From the Three Dynasties on down, people have all the while been boisterously occupied with rewards and punishments. What leisure have they for being secure in the attributes of their nature and destiny?

Furthermore, does he delight in keen eyesight?—he will be seduced by color. Does he delight in keen hearing?—he will be seduced by sound. Does he delight in humaneness?—he will be confused by virtue. Does he delight in righteousness?—he will be confounded by principle. Does he delight in rites?—he will encourage ingenuity. Does he delight in music?—he will encourage lasciviousness. Does he delight in sageness?—he will encourage artifice. Does he delight in knowledge?—he will encourage fussiness. If all under heaven are secure in the attributes of their nature and destiny, it would make no difference whether these eight delights are preserved or not. But if all under heaven are not secure in the attributes of their nature and destiny, these eight delights will begin to warp and ravish, bringing confusion to all under heaven. And if all under heaven begin to respect and cherish them, great indeed will be the delusion of all under heaven! These are not merely passing fancies that men will dispense with. Rather they fast before mentioning them, kneel as they present them, and dance before them with drum and song. And then what can we do about them?

Therefore, when the superior man has no choice but to oversee all under heaven, there is no better policy than nonaction. Having adopted a policy of nonaction, he can be secure in the attributes of his nature and destiny. Therefore it is said,

> When a man values his body so that he may
> manage all under heaven,
> then all under heaven can be entrusted to him.
> When a man is sparing of his body so that he may
> manage all under heaven,
> then all under heaven can be delivered to him.

Therefore, if the superior man can avoid dissipating his five viscera and overexerting his keen hearing and eyesight, remaining still as a corpse with a dragonish presence, silent in the depths with a thunderous voice, his spirit moving while heaven follows along with it, composed in nonaction while the myriad things are like so many motes of dust rising in the air, then what leisure will he have to govern all under heaven?

2

Ts'ui Chü inquired of Old Longears, saying, "If you do not govern all under heaven, how can you make men's minds good?"

"You must be careful not to disturb men's minds," said Old Longears. "When constrained, the human mind becomes depressed; when encouraged, it becomes elated. Whether through depression or through elation, the human mind may be imprisoned or killed. It is so soft that it can be worn down by what is hard and strong, yet its angles are sharp enough to chisel or carve. Its heat is like scorching fire, its cold is like solid ice. The mind may be so agitated that, in an instant, it has twice reached out beyond the four seas. At rest, it is deep-seated and calm. In action, it is remote as the sky. Ardently proud, it is not to be tied down. Such is the human mind!"

3

Long ago, the Yellow Emperor disturbed the minds of men with humaneness and righteousness. Consequently, Yao and Shun worked themselves to the bone, till there was not a hair left on their legs, toiling to nourish the bodies of all under heaven. They tormented their five viscera with the exercise of humaneness and righteousness; they depleted blood and vital breath to set up laws and regulations, but still there were some who would not submit. For this reason, Yao and Shun banished Huan Tou to Mount Ch'ung, expelled the Three Miao tribes to Sanwei, and exiled Kungkung to Yutu. This shows that they could not make all under heaven submit. Their ways were practiced down to the kings of the Three Dynasties, by which time all under heaven were in a great panic.

Of the lower type of character
   there were Chieh and Footpad;
Of the higher type of character
   there were Tseng Shen and Shih Ch'iu;
And finally the Confucians and the Mohists arose.

As a result,

The happy and the angry doubted each other,
The stupid and the wise cheated each other,
The good and the bad censured each other,
The boastful and the sincere jeered at each other,
So that all under heaven declined.

Great integrity became disparate, so that nature and destiny were dissipated. All under heaven were fond of knowledge, so that the hundred clans were bewildered. Thereupon,

> Axes and saws were used to control them,
> Ropes and cords to kill them,
> Hammers and chisels to execute them.

All under heaven were reduced to a riot of great confusion. The criminal cause of all this was the disturbing of men's minds. Therefore, worthy men hid themselves away at the foot of great mountains and rugged cliffs, while lords of ten thousand chariots trembled with anxiety in their ancestral halls.

In the present age, the bodies of those who have been executed lie pillowed upon each other, those who are forced to wear shackles and cangues bump into each other on the roads, and those who have been tortured and mutilated gaze upon each other in the markets, while the Confucians and Mohists begin to swagger and gesticulate among the fettered and manacled masses. Ai! This is too much! Their shamelessness and impudence are simply too much! Why haven't we realized that the knowledge of the sages may well be the bars of shackles and cangues, that humaneness and righteousness may well be the rivets of fetters and manacles? How do we know that Tseng Shen and Shih Ch'iu may not be whistling arrows that presage a tyrant like Chieh or a Robber Footpad? Therefore it is said, "Abolish sagehood and abandon knowledge, and all under heaven will be well governed."

4

The Yellow Emperor had been established as the Son of Heaven for nineteen years and his orders were carried out by all under heaven, when he heard that Master Broadly Complete was staying on Mount Emptysame, so he went to see him. "I have heard that you, sir, are accomplished in the ultimate Way," said the

Yellow Emperor. "I venture to ask what the essence of the ultimate Way is. I wish to take the essence of heaven and earth to assist the growth of the five grains for the nourishment of the people. I also wish to direct the yin and the yang to conform with the needs of all living beings. What should I do in order to accomplish this?"

"That which you wish to ask about," said Master Broadly Complete, "is the original substance of things. That which you wish to direct is the residue of things. Ever since you have governed all under heaven, the cloudy vapors have released their moisture before gathering, the trees and grasses have shed their leaves before turning yellow, and the light of the sun and moon have grown increasingly dim. You have the mind of a garrulous flatterer and are unfit to be told about the ultimate Way."

The Yellow Emperor retreated, gave up all under heaven, built himself an isolated hut, spread a mat made of white couch grass, and dwelt there unoccupied for three months. Then he went again to request instruction.

Master Broadly Complete was lying down with his head toward the south. With a deferential air, the Yellow Emperor crept forward on his knees. Bowing twice, he kowtowed and inquired of him, saying, "I've heard that you, sir, are accomplished in the ultimate Way. I venture to ask how I may govern my person so that I may long endure."

"An excellent question!" said Master Broadly Complete, getting up abruptly. "Come! I shall tell you about the ultimate Way.

> Cavernously dark
> Is the essence of the ultimate Way;
> Profoundly silent
> Is the extremity of the ultimate Way.

> There is neither sight nor hearing.
> When it embraces the spirit in stillness,

The form will correct itself.
You must be still—you must be pure.
Do not toil your physical form;
Do not stir up your essence.
Then you will be able to live long.

"If the eyes see nothing, the ears hear nothing, and the mind knows nothing,

Your spirit will guard your form,
And your form will live long.

Be careful of what is inside you
   and close yourself off to what is outside,
For much knowledge will defeat you.

"I will lead you to the height of great brightness, where we shall arrive at the source of ultimate yang. I will guide you through the gate of cavernous darkness, where we shall arrive at the source of ultimate yin. Heaven and earth have their directors; yin and yang have their treasuries. Carefully guard your body, and leave other things to prosper themselves. I guard the one so as to dwell in harmony. Thus have I cultivated my person for one thousand two hundred years and my physical form has still not decayed."

Bowing twice, the Yellow Emperor kowtowed and said, "Master Broadly Complete's instructions are from heaven."

"Come!" said Master Broadly Complete. "I shall tell you. The thing you seek is inexhaustible, but men all believe it has an end. The thing you seek is unfathomable, but men all believe it has a limit. He who attains my Way will be one of the august on high or a king below. He who loses my Way may see the light above but will remain as the soil below. Now,

All things that flourish
   are born of the soil
   and return to the soil.

Therefore,
>   I shall leave you

>   To enter the gate of inexhaustibility
>   And to roam in the fields of infinity.
>   I shall mingle my light
>   with that of the sun and moon,
>   And will become eternal
>   with heaven and earth.

>   I shall be unmindful
>   of what approaches me
>   And oblivious
>   of what distances itself from me.
>   Men may die altogether,
>   But I alone will survive!"

5

Cloud General was wandering in the east when he passed by an offshoot of a whirlwind and happened to meet with Vast Obscurity. Vast Obscurity was just at that moment enjoying himself by slapping his thighs and hopping about like a sparrow. Seeing him, Cloud General came to a sudden halt and stood there reverentially. "Who are you, old man?" he asked. "Why are you doing this?"

"I'm playing," replied Vast Obscurity to Cloud General as he kept on slapping his thighs and hopping like a sparrow.

"I would like to ask you a question," said Cloud General.

"Pshaw!" said Vast Obscurity as he looked up and saw Cloud General.

"The vital breath of heaven is in disharmony," said Cloud General. "The vital breath of earth is in disarray. The six vital breaths of transformation are in discord. The four seasons are out of rhythm. Now I would like to blend the essence of the six vital breaths to foster all living beings. How shall I do this?"

"I don't know!" said Vast Obscurity as he turned his head away, continuing to slap his thighs and hop like a sparrow. "I don't know!"

Cloud General was unable to ask any more questions. Three years later, when he was again wandering in the east, Cloud General was passing by the wilds of Sung when he happened to meet Vast Obscurity. Cloud General was greatly pleased and rushed forward to him, saying, "Have you forgotten me, oh heaven? Oh heaven, have you forgotten me?" Bowing twice, Cloud General kowtowed to show his willingness to listen to Vast Obscurity.

Vast Obscurity said,

"Wandering randomly,
I know not what I seek.
In my madness,
I know not where I go.
The wanderer, in his perplexity,
Observes the unexpected.

What more should I know?"

"I, too, consider myself mad," said Cloud General, "but the people follow me wherever I go. I have no choice but to be involved with the people, and now they emulate me. I would like a word of advice."

Vast Obscurity said,

"Whatever disorders the warp of heaven
Or goes against the circumstances of things,
Dark heaven will not bring it to completion.
Animal herds will be dispersed,
Birds will all begin to sing at night;

Disaster will strike grasses and trees,
Calamity will afflict reptiles and insects.

Ah! This is the error of governing men."

"Well, then," asked Cloud General, "what should I do?"

"Ah!" said Vast Obscurity. "Sheer perversity! Just return in transcendence."

"It has been hard for me to meet you, oh heaven," said Cloud General. "I would like one more word of advice."

"Ah!" said Vast Obscurity. "Nourish your mind.

Merely situate yourself in nonaction,
And things will evolve of themselves.

Slough off your bodily form,
Dim your intelligence.
Forget all relationships and things;
Join in the great commonality of boundlessness.

Release your mind,
Free your spirit;
Be impassively soulless.
The myriad things abound,
Yet each returns to its roots.

Each returns to its roots without being aware that it is doing so.

In a state of turbid chaos,
They do not leave it their whole life.
If they are aware of their return,
That means they have left it.

Do not ask its name;
Do not spy out its characteristics.
Things will assuredly come to life by themselves."

Cloud General said,

"Heaven, you have conferred your integrity upon me,
And have revealed to me its mystery;
Humbly and in person have I sought this teaching,
And today I have obtained it."

Bowing twice, he kowtowed, then arose and, saying goodbye, went away.

6

The common people of the world are all happy when others are like themselves, but are displeased when others are different from themselves. Both the desire for others to be like themselves and the desire that others not be different from themselves stem from their minds being set on distinguishing themselves from the crowd. But have those whose minds are set on distinguishing themselves from the crowd really done so? Better to go along with the crowd by being content with what one has learned, for it could never match the ingenuity of the crowd as a whole. Yet those who desire to administer the state of another only have their gaze set on the profits of the rulers of the three dynasties without seeing all of the troubles involved. This is to try one's luck with another's state. But how often can one try one's luck without bringing ruin to his state? The chances for the preservation of his state will not be one in ten thousand, while the chances that it will be ruined are more than ten thousand to one. How sad it is that those who possess the land are unaware of this!

The possessors of the land possess the greatest of all things. Possessing the greatest of all things, they should not be influenced by things. Having a thing but not being influenced by things, therefore they can treat things as things. He who perceives clearly how to treat things as things is himself not a thing. As such, he will not merely govern the hundred clans of all under heaven. He will pass in and out of the six reaches of the universe, he will wander through the nine regions. Alone he will come, alone he will go. This may be termed "possessing all alone." The man who possesses this all alone may be termed the noblest of all.

The teaching of the great man is like the shadow from a form, like the echo from a sound. When questioned, he replies, sharing his thoughts fully and serving as the companion of all under heaven. He dwells in Neverland and travels in Utopia. He leads all of you teeming masses back to where you belong, to wander in limitlessness. He passes in and out of nonattachment, beginningless as the sun. His discourse and corporeal form join in the great commonality. Having joined in the great commonality, he has no self. Having no self, how could he have being? If you look at those who had being, they were the superior men of old. If you look at those who had nonbeing, they were the friends of heaven and earth. . . .

12

HEAVEN AND EARTH

This is the first of three consecutive "heaven" chapters; it is significant that the syncretic, final chapter (33) is the fourth in the series. The authors of these four chapters were probably responsible for the original editing of the Chuang Tzu *anthology.*

Whereas Heaven was the favored cosmic concept of the Confucians, the Tao (Way) is obviously preferred by the Taoists and a nod is made in this chapter to the greatness of the Way. It is striking, however, that the author attempts to sanction virtue, the sage ruler, filial piety, and other Confucian concerns that Master Chuang ridiculed at every opportunity. We are thus confronted with the peculiar prospect of a superficial Taoist rhetoric being used to propagate a basically Confucian agenda.

1

Although heaven and earth are great, their evolution is uniform. Although the myriad things are numerous, their governance is unitary. Although the masses of men are multitudinous, their ruler is the one lord. The lord finds his source in virtue and his completion in heaven. Therefore it is said that the lords of dark antiquity ruled all under heaven through nonaction, through the virtue of heaven, and that is all.

If we observe words in the light of the Way, the names of all under heaven will be rectified. If we observe distinctions through the Way, the usages appropriate for ruler and subject will be clear. If we observe abilities through the Way, the officials of all under heaven will govern well. If we observe generally through the Way, the application of the myriad things will be total. Therefore, the Way is that which pervades heaven and earth, virtue is that which accords with the myriad things; administrative affairs are the means by which superiors govern the people; and skill is that which lends art to ability. Skill is linked to administrative affairs, administrative affairs are linked to righteousness, righteousness is linked to virtue, virtue is linked to the Way, and the Way is linked to heaven. Therefore, it is said, those among the ancients who reared all under heaven

> Were without desire,
> Yet all under heaven had enough.
> They did nothing,
> Yet the myriad things evolved.
> They were silent as the watery depths,
> Yet the hundred clans were settled.

A record says:

> Commune with the one,
> And the myriad affairs will be completed.

> Have no mind for achievement,
> And the ghosts and spirits will submit.

2

The master said, "The Way is that which covers and supports the myriad things. Oceanic is its greatness! The superior man must lay his mind bare to it. To act through nonaction is called heaven; to speak through nonaction is called virtue; to love men and benefit things is called humaneness; to make the dissimilar similar is called greatness; to conduct oneself without ostentation is generosity; to possess a myriad dissimilarities is wealth. Therefore, to maintain virtue is called the guideline; the completion of virtue is called establishment; to accord with the Way is called completion; not to allow things to distract the will is called fulfillment. When the superior man understands these ten qualities, how commodious will be the greatness of his mind, how copious will be his flowing with the myriad things! Such being the case, he lets the gold lie hidden in the mountains, the pearls in the depths. He does not profit from goods or property, does not associate with honor and wealth. He does not rejoice in longevity, is not saddened by premature death. He finds no glory in success, no shame in poverty. He would not grasp at the profit of the whole world to make it his private possession, nor would he rule all under heaven as his personal distinction. His distinction lies in understanding that the myriad things belong to a single treasury, and that life and death have the same appearance.

3

The master said, "How deep is the dwelling of the Way! How limpid its purity! Without it, metal and stone would have no means to sound. Thus, though metal and stone have a voice, if they are not struck they will not sound. Who can ascertain the myriad things?

"The man of kingly virtues proceeds in plainness and is ashamed to be involved with affairs. He establishes himself in the original source and his knowledge communicates with the spirits. Therefore, his virtue is broad and his mind goes forth when something stimulates it. Thus, without the Way, form would not be born. Without virtue, life would not be manifest. To preserve the bodily form and finish out one's life, to establish virtue and manifest the Way—is this not kingly virtue? Magnificent in his sudden going forth and in his quick movements, the myriad things follow him! This we call a man of kingly virtue.

"He sees into darkest darkness; he hears where there are no sounds. In the midst of darkest darkness, he alone sees a glimmer. In the midst of soundlessness, he alone hears harmony. Therefore, in the deepness of the deep, he can perceive things; in the spiritousness of the spirit, he can perceive essences. Thus, in his contacts with the myriad things, he provides for their needs through ultimate nothingness, gives them lodging through his timely diligence. . . ."

4

The Yellow Emperor was wandering north of Redwater when he ascended the heights of K'unlun and gazed toward the south. As he was returning home, he lost his pearl of mystery. Knowledge was sent to search for the pearl, but he couldn't find it. Spidersight was sent to search for the pearl, but he couldn't find it. Trenchancy was sent to search for the pearl, but he couldn't find it, whereupon Amorphous was sent and he found it. "Extraordinary!" said the Yellow Emperor. "In the end, it was Amorphous who was able to find it."

5

Yao's teacher was Hsü Yu; Hsü Yu's teacher was Gnaw Gap; Gnaw Gap's teacher was Princely Scion; and Princely Scion's teacher was Wearcoat.

Yao inquired of Hsü Yu, saying, "Can Gnaw Gap be the companion of heaven? If so, I could rely on Princely Scion to invite him to replace me on the throne."

"Perilous!" said Hsü Yu. "That would put all heaven in a precarious position. As a person, Gnaw Gap is intelligent, shrewd, quick-witted, and clever. His natural talents surpass those of other men and, furthermore, he is able to utilize his human abilities to receive the aid of heaven. He is cautious in preventing error, but he does not know whence errors arise. Let him be the companion of heaven? He would avail himself of his human abilities and neglect heaven. Then he would make his own person the basis of everything and alienate all other forms, would rush about furiously out of respect for knowledge, would be driven by trivialities, would be stymied by things, would react to things in whichever direction he glanced, would react to a host of opinions, would evolve along with things and thus would not begin to have any enduring principle of his own. How could he be fit to be the companion of heaven? Nevertheless, there are clans and there are ancestors. He could be the father of one group, but not the father of the fathers of many groups. This sort of government would lead to disorder. It would be a disaster for the north-facing ministers, a catastrophe for the south-facing ruler."

6

Yao was inspecting Hua when the border warden of the place said to him, "Aha! a sage! Allow me to ask blessings for the sage. Long live the sage!"

"I decline," said Yao.

"May the sage become wealthy!"

"I decline," said Yao.

"May the sage have many sons!"

"I decline," said Yao.

"Longevity, wealth, and many sons," said the border warden, "are what all men desire. Why do you alone not desire them?"

"Many sons," said Yao, "bring many fears. Wealth brings many affairs. Longevity brings many disgraces. These three blessings are of no use in nourishing virtue. Therefore, I decline them."

"At first," said the border warden, "I thought you were a sage.

But now I see that you are a superior man. In giving birth to the myriads of people, heaven is certain to assign them their duties. If you were to have many sons, you would assign them their duties, so what is there to fear? If you were wealthy, you could share with others, so what affairs would there be?

> The sage dwells like a quail
>   and is fed like a hatchling,
> Moves like a bird through the air
>   and leaves no traces.
> When the Way prevails under heaven,
> He enjoys prosperity along with all things;
> When the Way is absent under heaven,
> He cultivates his virtue in retirement.
> Tired of the world, after a thousand years
> He leaves it and ascends among the immortals.
> He mounts on the white clouds
> And arrives in the land of Deus.
> The three tribulations never affect him;
> His person is free from misfortune.

"So what disgrace would there be?"

As the border warden was leaving, Yao followed after him, saying, "May I ask about . . . ?"

"Away with you!" said the border warden.

7

When Yao was governing all under heaven, he appointed Uncle Complete Sir High as one of his feudal lords. Later, Yao passed the throne to Shun, and Shun passed it on to Yü, whereupon Uncle Complete Sir High resigned his position as feudal lord and became a plowman. Yü went to see him and found him plowing in the open fields. Scurrying downwind, Yao stood and questioned him, saying, "Long ago, when Yao was governing all under heaven, he appointed you, sir, as one of the feudal lords. Then Yao passed the throne to Shun, Shun passed it to me, whereupon you, sir, declined your position as feudal lord and became a plowman. I venture to ask what the reason for this is."

"Long ago," said Sir High, "when Yao was governing all under heaven, he made no rewards but the people were encouraged. He carried out no punishments, but the people were in awe. Now you, sir, use rewards and punishments, but the people are not humane. Consequently, virtue is on the wane and penalties are on the rise. The disorder of future ages begins with this. Why don't you just go away, sir, and not interrupt my work?" With that, he busily set to plowing again and paid no more attention to Yü.

8

In the grand beginning, there was only nonbeing,
But no being and no names.
Out of it arose the One;
There was One, but still no form.

From the One, things could be born, receiving what is called their virtue. That which still had no form was divided, yet there was no separation.

This is called destiny.

Through stasis and movement, things were born. As things were completed, various configurations were produced.

These are called forms.

The bodily form protects the spirit, the form and the spirit each having its own usages.

This we call nature.

Through cultivation of nature, it returns to virtue, and when virtue reaches its pinnacle, it is the same as at the beginning. Being the same, it is empty. Being empty, it is great. This is like joining in with the chirping of birds. Having joined in with the chirping of birds, one may join with heaven and earth.

> This joining is all blurry,
> As though one were stupid or muddled.
> This is called dark virtue,
> And is the same as the great confluence.

9

The master inquired of Old Longears, saying, "There are men who govern the Way as though they were banishing it. They affirm what is not affirmable, declare what is not so to be so. The sophists have a saying, 'One can distinguish "hard" and "white" as clearly as though they were suspended in space.' Can someone like this be called a sage?"

"Such a person," said Old Longears, "would be like a clerk at his labors or a craftsman tied to his work, toiling his body and vexing his mind. It is the hunting ability of the pointer and retriever that constrains them, it is the nimbleness of the gibbon and the monkey that brings them out of the mountain forests. Hillock, I will tell you what you cannot hear and what you cannot speak. Multitudinous are those who have heads and feet but no minds and no ears, while there is absolutely no one who has a physical form that can coexist with the formless and the shapeless. Their movement and cessation, life and death, rise and fall, moreover, are beyond their ken, yet their governance lies within man. To forget things and to forget heaven is called forgetting the self. The man who forgets himself may be said to have entered heaven."

10

At a meeting with Chi Ch'e, Chianglü Mien said to him, "The lord of Lu asked to receive my teachings, but I declined because I had not been given a command. In the end, however, I did tell him, but I don't know whether what I said was on the mark or not. Please let me repeat it to you. What I said to the lord of Lu was this: 'You must exercise respect and restraint, promote fairness and loyalty, and be without partiality. Who among the people, then, would dare to be uncooperative?' "

"Your words, sir," said Chi Ch'e with a chuckle, "insofar as they relate to the virtue of an emperor or a king, are like a mantis waving its arms angrily trying to stop a chariot in its tracks. Surely, they won't be up to the task. If he were to follow your recommendations, he would situate himself precariously among his observatories and terraces with their numerous objects, while opportunists would rush about in droves."

"I am bewildered by your words, sir," said Chianglü Mien, his eyes bulging with amazement. "Nevertheless, I hope you will explain the general drift."

"In governing all under heaven," said Chi Ch'e, "the great sage gives free rein to the people's minds. He lets them have their own ready-made doctrines and simple customs. Totally eradicating their thievish intentions, he would encourage their singular ambitions, as though they were doing it of their own nature, but the people would not know why they did so. Such being the case, would he treat Yao and Shun as his older brothers in teaching the people? Or would he unconsciously treat them as younger brothers? His only desire would be for the people to agree with virtue and rest peacefully in it."

11

Tzukung had wandered south to Ch'u and was returning through Chin. As he was passing along the south bank of the Han River, he saw an elderly man who was working in his vegetable garden. He had dug a channel to bring water from the well and was carrying jars to pour on the garden. He exerted a tremendous amount of energy, but with little result.

Tzukung said to him, "There are machines for this purpose that can irrigate a hundred plots in one day. They use very little energy but their results are great. Don't you want one, sir?"

The gardener looked up at him and asked, "How does it work?"

"It is a device fashioned from wood that is heavy in back and light in front. It picks up the water like a ladle, as fast as though it were boiling over. It's called a wellsweep."

The gardener made an angry grimace and said with a laugh, "I have heard from my teacher that where there are ingenious contraptions, there are sure to be ingenious affairs, and where there are ingenious affairs, there are sure to be ingenious minds. When one harbors an ingenious mind in one's breast, its pure simplicity will be impaired. When pure simplicity is impaired, the spiritual nature will be unstable. He whose spiritual nature is unsettled will not be supported by the Way. It's not that I am unaware of such things, rather that I would be ashamed to do them."

Flushing with embarrassment, Tzukung kept his head down and made no reply.

After a short interval, the gardener asked, "What do you do?"

"I'm a disciple of Confucius."

"Aren't you one of those," asked the gardener, "who rely on their wide learning to imitate the sages, who engage in trumpery to surpass the masses, and who sing their sad solos to buy a reputation under heaven? If you would just forget the vital breath of your spirit and slough off your physical form, you'd be close to it. You can't even govern yourself, so what leisure do you have to govern the world? Begone, sir, and do not interfere with my work."

Abashed, Tzukung turned pale. Anxious and ill at ease, only after he had walked thirty tricents did he recover.

"Who was that man just now?" asked his disciples. "And why, sir, have you changed your appearance and become pale, so that you have not returned to yourself the whole day?"

"At first, I thought that there was only one enlightened man under heaven, and did not realize that there was also this man. I have heard from the master that the Way of the sages is to seek success in one's affairs and completion of one's undertakings, to use a small amount of energy yet see great results. Now I realize that it is not so. The virtue of those who cleave to the Way is whole. He whose virtue is whole will be whole in form; he whose form is whole will be whole in spirit. Being whole in spirit is the Way of the sages. He entrusts his life to the people and travels along with them, without knowing where he is going. Vast and unimpaired is his purity! Achievement, profit, ingenuity, and cleverness will certainly be forgotten in the mind of such a man. Such a man does not go where his will disallows, does not do what his mind disapproves. Although all under heaven might praise him and accede to what he says, he would be loftily unheedful. Though all under heaven might censure him and reject what he says, he would be absent-mindedly unaffected. The censure and praise of all under heaven will neither benefit nor harm him. He may be called a man whose virtue is whole, while I may be called a person who is 'blown by the wind and tossed by the waves.' "

Upon his return to Lu, Tzukung told Confucius about his encounter with the gardener. "He's a false practitioner of the arts of clansman Wonton," said Confucius. "He recognizes the one, but doesn't know anything about two. He governs what is inside, but not what is outside. If you were to meet someone who understands great plainness, who subscribes to nonaction and returns to the simplicity of the unhewn log, who embodies his nature and embraces his spirit, so as to wander through the common world, you would really be surprised! As for the arts of clansman Wonton, what is there in them for you and me to learn?"

12

Zealot Vague was on his way east to the great gulf when he happened to meet Boreal Wind along the shores of the Eastern Sea.

"Where are you going?" asked Boreal Wind.

"I'm going to the great gulf."

"What for?"

"The great gulf is something that never fills up no matter how much water pours into it, and is never exhausted no matter how much water is drawn from it. I'm going there to wander about."

"Sir," asked Boreal Wind, "don't you have any thoughts for level-eyed man? I would like to hear about the government of the sage."

"The government of the sage?" asked Zealot Vague. "He appoints officials to posts for which they are duly suited; he makes promotions with due regard for ability. He examines circumstances and affairs thoroughly before taking any action. His words and his deeds proceed naturally, so that all under heaven are transformed. Wherever his hand points or his gaze directs, the people from the four quarters will go there without exception. This is called the government of the sage."

"I would like to hear about the man of virtue."

"The virtuous man dwells in thoughtlessness and proceeds without concern. He does not treasure 'right' and 'wrong' or 'beauty' and 'ugliness.' He finds satisfaction in sharing benefits among all within the four seas and security in giving to all alike. He is timid as an infant who has lost his mother, apprehensive as a traveler who has lost his way. His wealth and utensils are more than enough, but he knows not where they come from; his food and drink are more than adequate, but he knows not how he gets them. This is the description of the man of virtue."

"I would like to hear about the man of spirit."

"His spirit rises, mounted on the light,
While his physical form vanishes.
This is called 'illumination of immensity.'
He fulfills his destiny and perfects his attributes.
Heaven and earth rejoice;
The myriad affairs dissolve;
And the myriad things are restored to truth.
This is called 'merging with darkness.' "

13

Ghostless Gate and Longbranch Redwand were observing the army of King Wu.

"It's because he's no match for the clansman of the freehold at Yü," said Longbranch Redwand, "that he's involved in this trouble."

"Was all under heaven already thoroughly well ordered when the clansman of the freehold at Yü took over the government?" asked Ghostless Gate. "Or was it disordered until he took over the government?"

"It is the wish of all under heaven to be thoroughly well ordered," said Longbranch Redwand, "so why count on the clansman of the freehold at Yü? His method was like healing a man with scabies by giving him false hair after he's gone bald. He waited for people to get sick and then went looking for medicine. He was like a filial son who picks herbs and who, full of distress, offers them to his kind father. A sage would be ashamed of this.

"In an age of ultimate virtue, men of worth are not exalted, and men of ability are not employed. Superiors are like the upper branches of a tree, the people are like the deer in the wilds. They are upright without considering themselves to be righteous; they love each other without considering themselves to be humane; they are honest without considering themselves to be loyal; they are reliable without considering themselves to be trustworthy. They move about spontaneously, assisting each other without considering themselves to be generous. For this reason, their actions leave no traces, their affairs leave no records."

14

The filial son who does not fawn upon his parents and the loyal subject who does not flatter his lord are the best kinds of sons and subjects. When a son assents to whatever his parents say and approves of whatever they do, it is the common opinion of the world that he is unworthy. When a subject assents to whatever his lord says and approves of whatever he does, it is the common opinion of the world that he is unworthy. But can we be sure that this is necessarily so? When someone assents to whatever common opinion assents to and approves of whatever common opinion approves, he is not declared to be a flatterer. Is common opinion, then, more stern than a parent and more respected than a lord?

If you call someone a sycophant, he will instantly change countenance; if you call someone a flatterer, he will angrily change countenance, though he be a lifelong sycophant and a lifelong flatterer. He brings together similes and dresses up his diction to attract the multitudes, but from beginning to end, from top to bottom, he'll never admit his guilt. He lets his robes hang down, displays their brilliant colors, posturing and putting on airs, so as to captivate the whole world, but he doesn't call himself a flatterer. He is just a follower of those others who goes along with what they hold to be right and wrong, but he himself doesn't admit to being one of the crowd. This is the ultimate folly. He who knows his folly is not the greatest fool; he who knows his delusion is not greatly deluded. He who is greatly deluded will not be released from delusion his whole life; he who is a great fool will not become smart his whole life. If three men are walking along and one of them is deluded, they will reach their destination because the deluded are in the minority. But if two of them are deluded, they will walk in vain without ever reaching their destination because the deluded are in the majority. Today, all under heaven are deluded. Though I pray for their guidance, it cannot be had. Is this not sad?

Great music will not have any effect on the ear of a villager, but he will laugh with glee when he hears "Breaking the Willow" or "The Bright Flowers." For this reason, lofty words do not remain in the minds of the masses. Refined words make no impression because vulgar words are in the majority. A couple of jugs will delude the bell-player, and his aims will not be achieved. Today, all under heaven are deluded. Though I pray for their guidance, how can it be had? Knowing that it cannot be had yet forcing it upon them is but another delusion. Therefore, it would be best just to let them go and not push myself on them. If I do not push, who among them will feel anxiety?

The leprous woman gives birth to her child in the middle of the night. Quickly she snatches a torch and looks at it with dread, fearing only that the child may resemble herself.

15

A century-old tree is broken up and made into a sacrificial vessel decorated with green and yellow, while the shavings are thrown into a ditch. If we compare the sacrificial vessel with the shavings in the ditch, there may be a difference in their esthetic appeal, but they are alike in having lost their original nature. Though there may be a difference in the exercise of righteousness by the tyrant Chieh and Robber Footpad on the one hand, and Tseng Shen and Shih Ch'iu on the other, they are alike in having lost their original nature.

Furthermore, there are five things that may lead to the loss of one's original nature.

First are the five colors which confuse the eye
And make it less keen.
Second are the five sounds which confuse the ear
And make it less sharp.
Third are the five odors which becloud the nose
And assail the sinuses.
Fourth are the five flavors which dull the mouth
And make it insensitive.
Fifth are preferences and aversions which unsettle the
     mind
And make one's nature flighty.

These five things are all injurious to life. Yet Yang Chu and Mo Ti swagger about self-complacently, thinking they have hit on the answer, but it's not what I would call the answer. When the answer they have hit on constrains them, can it be *the* answer? If so, then the dove or the owl in a cage may also be said to have hit on the answer. Furthermore, preferences and aversions, sounds and colors are like so much firewood piled up within; leather caps and hats with kingfisher feathers, and official tablets inserted in long sashes restrain them from without. Inside, they are stuffed full with barricades of firewood and outside they are bound with layers of rope. Looking around from inside their ropes with a gleam in their eye, they think they have hit on the answer. If that be so, then criminals with their arms tied together and their fingers in a press, and the tiger and the leopard in their sacks or cages may also be said to have hit on the answer.

13

THE WAY OF HEAVEN

*The author of this chapter goes so far as to annex Tao (the Way) to T'ien
(Heaven) in a brazen effort to subordinate Taoist metaphysics to Confucian
politics. He espouses conventional hierarchy, etiquette, and laws in a manner
that is quite alien to the Master Chuang of the Inner Chapters and many of the
Miscellaneous Chapters. With the appearance of Lao Tzu (the Old Master)
toward the end of the chapter, a more authentic voice is heard.*

1

The Way of heaven revolves ceaselessly, so that the myriad things
are brought to completion; the Way of the emperors revolves
ceaselessly, so that all under heaven return to them; the Way of
the sages revolves ceaselessly, so that all within the seas submit to
them. He who understands heaven, who is conversant with the
sages, and who comprehends the virtue of emperors and kings
throughout the six directions of the universe and the four
regions, acts spontaneously but is always obliviously still. The
stillness of the sage is not because stillness is said to be good and
therefore he is still. It is because the myriad things are unable to
disturb his mind that he is still. When water is still, it clearly

reflects whiskers and brows. It is so accurate that the great craftsman takes his standard from it. If still water has such clarity, how much more so pure spirit! The stillness of the mind of the sage is the mirror of heaven and earth, the looking glass of the myriad things.

Emptiness, stillness, placidity, mildness, quietude, indifference, nonaction—these are the root of heaven and earth, the substance of the Way and virtue. Therefore, emperors, kings, and sages rest in them. Resting, they are empty; empty, they are full; full, they are prepared. Empty, they are still; still, they begin to move; moving, they attain. Still, they are nonactive; nonactive, they entrust the responsibility for affairs to others. Nonactive, they are content; content, anxiety, and trouble cannot discomfit them; so their longevity will be great.

Emptiness, stillness, placidity, mildness, quietude, indifference, nonaction—these are the root of the myriad things. Understanding this as the south-facing ruler, Yao was lord; understanding this as the north-facing minister, Shun was his subject. Occupying a superior position with this understanding is the virtue of emperors, kings, and the son of heaven; occupying an inferior position with this understanding is the Way of dark sages and plain kings. Those who withdraw into retirement with this understanding and wander at leisure will win the admiration of recluses from the rivers, lakes, mountains, and forests. Those who come forward into active life and succor the world with this understanding will achieve great accomplishments and brilliant fame by uniting all under heaven. Still, they are sages; moving, they are kings. Nonactive, they are respected; simple as an uncarved block, no one under heaven can contest with them for excellence.

The clear understanding of the virtue of heaven and earth is called the "great root" and "the great ancestor." It is that whereby one is in harmony with heaven. Evenly adjusting all under heaven with it, one may be in harmony with men. Being in harmony with men is called "human joy." Being in harmony with heaven is called "heavenly joy."

Master Chuang said, "My teacher, oh my teacher! He blends the myriad things, but is not righteous; his benefits reach to a myriad generations, but he is not humane. He is senior to high antiquity, but is not aged. He covers heaven, supports earth, and carves out a host of forms, but is not skillful. This is what I mean by heavenly joy. Therefore, it is said, 'He who knows heavenly joy walks with heaven in life and evolves with things in death. In stillness, he shares the same virtue as yin; in movement, he shares the same current as yang.' Thus, he who knows heavenly joy will find no complaint from heaven, no censure from men, no encumbrance from things, and no reproach from ghosts. Therefore, it is said, 'His movement is heaven; his stillness is earth. Once his mind is fixed, heaven and earth are rectified. His animus does not tire; his anima does not weary. Once his mind is fixed, the myriad things submit.' In other words, extending his emptiness and stillness to heaven and earth, conversant with the myriad things, this is called heavenly joy. Heavenly joy is the mind of the sage whereby he rears all under heaven."

2

The virtue of emperors and kings is to take heaven and earth as their ancestor, to take the Way and its virtue as their ruler, and to take nonaction as their constant. Through nonaction, one may use all under heaven and still have a surplus. Through action, one will be used by all under heaven but will be insufficient. Therefore, the ancients valued nonaction. When superiors and inferiors both subscribe to nonaction, this means that they share the same virtue. But when inferiors share the same virtue as superiors, this means that there are no subjects. When inferiors and superiors both subscribe to action, this means that they share the same way. But when superiors share the same way as inferiors, this means that there is no ruler. The superior must subscribe to nonaction and use all under heaven; inferiors must subscribe to action and be used by all under heaven. This is the unchanging Way. Therefore, those in antiquity who were kings of all under heaven, although their knowledge embraced heaven and earth, did not themselves formulate plans; although their eloquence encompassed the myriad things, they did not themselves propound theories; although their ability reached to the ends of the seas, they did not themselves act. Heaven produces not, yet the myriad things evolve; earth grows not, but the myriad things are nurtured; emperors and kings act not, but all under heaven is accomplished. Therefore, it is said, "Nothing is more spiritual than heaven, nothing is richer than earth, and nothing is greater than the emperors and kings." Thus, it is said, "The virtue of kings and emperors is a match for heaven and earth." This is the way to mount on heaven and earth, to ride the myriad things, and use the masses of men.

The root lies with superiors; the particulars lie with inferiors. The essentials lie with the ruler; the details lie with the subjects. The operations of the three armies with their five categories of weapons are the particulars of virtue; rewards and penalties, profit and loss, the application of the five types of punishment—these are the particulars of instruction. Ceremonies, laws, regulations, computations, usages, taboos, examinations, investigations—these are the particulars of government. The sounds of bells and drums, the appearance of plumes and banners—these are the particulars of music. Weeping, crying, coarse garments, hempen headbands and armbands, the various gradations of funeral services—these are the particulars of mourning. These five kinds of particulars require the operation of the essential spirit and the exercise of the arts of the mind before they can be put into effect.

The men of old did study particulars, but did not give them precedence. The lord precedes and his subjects follow; the father precedes and his sons follow; the older brother precedes and his younger brothers follow; the elder precedes and the youths follow; the man precedes and the woman follows; the husband precedes and the wife follows. The precedence of the honored and the coming behind of the lowly are the course of heaven and earth. Therefore, the sage adopts them as his symbols. Heaven is more honored and earth more lowly—such are their positions as gods. Spring and summer precede, autumn and winter come after—such is the sequence of the four seasons. The myriad things evolve and develop; even twisted little shoots have their own special shapes—such are the gradations of fullness and decline, the flow of transformation and evolution.

If even heaven and earth, which are of ultimate spirituality, have a sequence of more honored and more lowly, of that which precedes and that which comes behind, how much more so must the ways of men! In the ancestral temple, we venerate our relatives; at court, we venerate the honored; in the villages, we venerate our seniors; in the conduct of affairs, we venerate those who are worthy. This is the sequence of the great Way. If we speak of the Way but negate its sequence, we negate the Way itself. How can he who speaks of the Way, yet negates the Way, adopt the Way?

For this reason, those in the past who clarified the great Way first clarified heaven, and the Way and its virtue were next. Having clarified the Way and its virtue, humaneness and righteousness were next. Having clarified humaneness and righteousness, the observance of duties was next. Having clarified the observance of duties, forms and names were next. Having clarified forms and names, appointments according to qualification were next. Having clarified appointments according to qualification, inquests and interrogations were next. Having clarified inquests and interrogations, right and wrong were next. Having clarified right and wrong, rewards and penalties were next. Having clarified rewards and penalties, folly and knowledge occupied their rightful places, honor and meanness took their proper positions. The humane and the worthy as well as the unworthy were employed in conformity with their attributes. It was necessary to distinguish their abilities and accord with their names. Thus did they serve their superiors and rear their inferiors, govern things and cultivate their persons. They made no use of knowledge and schemes, turning only to heaven. This was called the great peace, the ultimate government.

Therefore, the book says: "There are forms and there are names." The ancients did have the concept of forms and names, but it is not what they put first. When the ancients discussed the great Way, it was only after four steps that they mentioned forms and names, and only after eight steps that they spoke of rewards and penalties. If they had spoken of forms and names right from the start, it would have shown that they did not know what is fundamental. If they had spoken of rewards and punishments right from the start, it would have shown that they did not know what is primary. He whose words invert the Way or run counter to it is to be governed by others. How could he govern others? To speak of forms and names and of rewards and penalties right from the start shows only that one knows the tools of government, not the Way of government. Such a person can be used by all under heaven, but is incapable of using all under heaven. He is what may be called a sophist, a person of one narrow skill. The ancients did have ceremonies, laws, regulations, computations, and the detailed comparison of form and name, but these are what inferiors use to serve their superiors, not what superiors use to rear inferiors.

3

Long ago, Shun inquired of Yao, saying, "As king appointed by heaven, how do you use your mind?"

"I am not arrogant toward those who have no one to whom they appeal; I do not abandon the poor people," said Yao. "I grieve for those who die, commend young children, and sympathize with women. This is how I use my mind."

"This is fine, all right," said Shun, "but it's not great."

"Well, then," said Yao, "what would you have me do?"

"Heaven ascends, earth is calm; the sun and moon shine, and the four seasons proceed," said Shun. "Be regular as the alternation of day and night, beneficent as the clouds that march through the sky and dispense their rain."

"How majestic and grand!" said Yao. "You, sir, are a match for heaven; I am but a match for man."

Heaven and earth are what the ancients hold to be great, and what the Yellow Emperor, Yao, and Shun join in admiring. Therefore, what did the ancients who were kings of all under heaven do? They conformed to heaven and earth, and that is all.

4

Confucius went west to deposit some books in the royal library of the Chou dynasty. Tzulu [one of his disciples] counseled him, saying, "I have heard that there was a librarian of the Chou named Old Longears. He has given up his post and returned to live in his own house. If you wish to deposit some books, sir, you might try going to see him for advice [on this important matter of state]."

"Good idea," said Confucius. So he went to see Old Longears, but the latter did not accede to his request. Whereupon Confucius launched into an exposition of the twelve classics to convince him.

Old Longears interrupted his speech, saying, "You're being too verbose. I just want to hear the gist of it."

"The gist lies in humaneness and righteousness," said Confucius.

"May I ask," said Old Longears, "whether humaneness and righteousness are human nature?"

"Of course," said Confucius. "If the superior man is not humane, he will be incomplete. If he is not righteous, he will lack vitality. Humaneness and righteousness are truly the nature of man. What more need he concern himself with?"

"May I ask," said Old Longears, "what is the meaning of humaneness and righteousness?"

"To have a loyal heart and be without conflict, to show

universal love and be without partiality—these are the charac-teristics of humaneness and righteousness," said Confucius.

"Ai!" said Old Longears, "these last words of yours are dangerous! Isn't the doctrine of universal love impractical? And being without partiality to others is being partial to oneself. If, sir, you wish to cause all under heaven not to lose that which shepherds them, then consider heaven and earth which assuredly have constancy; the sun and the moon which assuredly have brightness; the stars and the constellations which assuredly are arrayed; the birds and the beasts which assuredly group together; the trees and bushes which assuredly stand tall. Merely liberate your integrity as you walk along and comply with the Way as you hurry on, sir, and you will get where you're going. Why must you promote humaneness and righteousness so energetically as though you were beating a drum in search of a lost son? Ai! sir, you are bringing confusion to the nature of man!"

5

Fancypants Scholar went to see the Old Master and inquired of him, saying, "I have heard, sir, that you are a sage. By no means would I shirk the long journey, so I have come here wishing to see you. Though I developed thick calluses during the hundred stages of my trip, I dared not rest. Now that I have observed you, I find you're not a sage. There is leftover grain beside the rat holes, but he who throws things away carelessly is inhumane. Raw and cooked food that you haven't consumed piles up in front of you limitlessly."

Indifferent, the Old Master did not reply.

Fancypants Scholar went back to see him again the next day and said, "Yesterday I criticized you, but today I'm feeling really disheartened. Why is this?"

"I believe," said the Old Master, "that I have freed myself of wanting to be a person of clever knowledge and spiritual sagacity. Yesterday, if you had called me an ox, I would have agreed with you and, if you had called me a horse, I would have agreed with you too. If there is a fact and someone gives it a name that I refuse to accept, I'll be in double jeopardy. I acceded because I always accede, not for the sake of acceding itself."

Fancypants Scholar waddled backward out of the Old Master's shadow, then gingerly stepped forward and asked him, "How should I cultivate my person?"

The Old Master said, "Your appearance is haughty; your look is aggressive; your forehead is protruding; your mouth is snarly; your demeanor is self-righteous. You are like a horse restrained by its tether. You wish to move but are held back. You are set to release like the trigger of a crossbow. You are inquisitorial and judgmental. Your knowledge is cunning and your gaze is overbearing. All of this invites mistrust. If such a person were to be found on the borders, he would be labeled a brigand."

6

The master said, "The Way does not exhaust itself in what is great, nor does it absent itself from what is small. Therefore, the myriad things are realized in it. The Way is so broad that there is nothing it fails to accommodate, so deep that it is unfathomable. Form, virtue, humaneness, and righteousness are trifles of the spirit, but were it not for the ultimate man, who could determine them? The ultimate man holds the world—is this not a great responsibility? But it is not enough to burden him. All under heaven vie for the reins of power, but he does not accompany them. He examines flawlessness, but is unmoved by profit. He plumbs the truth of things and can guard what is fundamental. Therefore, he puts heaven and earth beyond him, leaves the myriad things behind, and so his spirit is never encumbered. He is conversant with the Way, joins with virtue, keeps humaneness and righteousness at a distance, and treats ceremonies and music as guests. Something there is that steadies the mind of the ultimate man."

7

Writing is that means by which the world values the Way, but writing is no more than words and words, too, have value. Meaning is what gives value to words, but meaning is dependent on something. What meaning depends on cannot be expressed in language, yet the world transmits writing because it values language. Although the world values writing, I, for my part, do not think it worthy of being valued, because what is valued is not what is really valuable. Thus, what can be seen when one looks are form and color; what can be heard when one listens are names and sounds. How sad it is that the people of the world feel that form, color, name, and sound are sufficient to grasp the reality of *that*! Now, since form, color, name, and sound are insufficient to grasp the reality of *that*,

One who knows does not speak,
One who speaks does not know.

But how could the world recognize this?

8

Duke Huan was reading in the upper part of his hall and Wheelwright Flat was hewing a wheel in the lower part. Setting aside his hammer and chisel, the wheelwright went to the upper part of the hall and inquired of Duke Huan, saying, "I venture to ask what words Your Highness is reading?"

"The words of the sages," said the duke.

"Are the sages still alive?"

"They're already dead," said the duke.

"Then what my lord is reading are merely the dregs of the ancients."

"How can you, a wheelwright, comment upon what I am

reading?" asked Duke Huan. "If you can explain yourself, all right. If you cannot explain yourself, you shall die."

"I look at it from my own occupation," said Wheelwright Flat. "If the spokes are loose, they'll fit sweet as a whistle but the wheel won't be solid. If they're too tight, you won't be able to insert them no matter how hard you try. To make them neither too loose nor too tight is something you sense in your hand and feel in your heart. There's a knack to it that can't be put in words. I haven't been able to teach it to my son, and my son hasn't been able to learn it from me. That's why I'm still hewing wheels after seventy years. When they died, the ancients took with them what they couldn't transmit. So what you are reading are the dregs of the ancients."

14

HEAVENLY
REVOLUTIONS

The extraordinary opening of this chapter takes the form of an extended series of riddles like those posed by ancient Indo-European seers and magi. It temporarily returns to par with the other heaven chapters by having a pseudo Master Chuang discourse clumsily upon the relative merits of humaneness and filialness. The remainder of the chapter, however, includes the magnificent description of the Yellow Emperor's transcendental ritual music and a group of interesting colloquies between Confucius and Lao Tzu.

1

"Does heaven revolve?
Does earth stand still?
Do the sun and moon jockey for position?
Who controls all of this?
Who unfolds all of this?
Who ties it all together?
Who dwells in inactivity,
Yet impels things on their course?

May it be that there are levers and threads
That drive them inexorably?
Or may it be that they just keep turning
And are unable to stop by themselves?

Do the clouds make the rain?
Or does the rain make the clouds?
Who bestows them so generously?
Who dwells in inactivity,
Yet urges things on to all this lusty joy?

The winds arise in the north
And, first to the east, then to the west,
They drift back and forth above us.
Who breathes them?
Who dwells in inactivity,
Yet does this fanning?

I venture to ask the reasons for all this."

"Come, and I shall tell you," said the Magus Hsien while beckoning. "Heaven has six poles and five constants. If emperors and kings conform to them, there will be good government, but if they go against them, there will be evil consequences. Tending to the affairs of the nine regions, government will be complete and virtue realized. Overseeing and illuminating the earth below, they will be supported by all under heaven. Thus they are called the August on High."

2

Tang, the Grand Steward of Shang, asked Master Chuang about humaneness.

"Tigers and wolves are humane," said Master Chuang.

"What do you mean?"

"Fathers and cubs are partial to each other," said Master Chuang. "How can we consider them inhumane?"

"May I ask about ultimate humaneness?"

"Ultimate humaneness is impartial," said Master Chuang.

"I have heard," said the Grand Steward, "that to be impartial is to be without love and that to be without love is to be unfilial. May we say that ultimate humaneness implies unfilialness?"

"Not so," said Master Chuang. "Ultimate humaneness is exalted, so of course filialness is inadequate to describe it. This is not to say that humaneness surpasses filialness, rather that it does not affect filialness. If someone journeys south until reaching Ying and then faces north, he won't be able to see Dark Mountain. Why is this? It's because he's so far away from it. Therefore, it is said, to be filial out of respect is easy, but to be filial out of love is difficult. To be filial out of love is easy, but to forget one's parents is difficult. To forget one's parents is easy, but to cause one's parents to forget themselves is difficult. To cause one's parents to forget themselves is easy, but to forget all under heaven is difficult. To forget all under heaven is easy, but to cause all under heaven to forget themselves is difficult. Virtue that leaves behind Yao and Shun and does not act will bestow benefit and nurture to a myriad generations, without all under heaven knowing. How can one merely heave a deep sigh and talk about humaneness and filialness? Filialness, brotherliness, humaneness, righteousness, loyalty, trustworthiness, honor, and incorruptibility—these all enslave virtue through self-constraint, but they are not worth putting a premium on. Therefore, it is said, ultimate nobility would discard the dignities of a state; ultimate wealth would discard the riches of a state; ultimate eminence would discard fame and praise. Thus, the Way never alters."

3

Complete Northgate inquired of the Yellow Emperor, saying, "When I heard the first part of the music of 'The Pond of

Totality' that you organized in the cavernous wilds, oh emperor, I was frightened. When I heard the second part, I became weary. And, when I heard the last part, I felt confused. Dumbstruck and disturbed, I couldn't get hold of myself."

"Your reaction is about what I would have expected," said the emperor. "I had it performed by men, directed by heaven, presented with ceremony and righteousness, and established in great purity. . . . It showed

> The four seasons arising in succession,
> The myriad things being born in sequence.
> In fullness and decline,
> Civil and military alternated with each other.

Now clear, now turbid, it harmoniously blended yin and yang,

> The notes flowing away in the light.

Then, as when hibernating insects begin to stir in spring,

> We startled the audience with the crash of thunder.
> There was no conclusion at the end,
> And no prelude at the beginning.
> It would die away for a while, then come back to life;
> Rise for a moment, then collapse.
> Its constancy was inexhaustible,
> Yet entirely unpredictable.

That's why you were afraid.
 "I had the second part

> Performed with the harmony of yin and yang,
> Illumined with the brightness of the sun and moon.

The notes
    Could be short or long,
    Could be soft or hard;
    While all the modulations were evenly uniform,
    They were not dominated by stale regularity.

They
    Filled every valley,
    Filled every ravine.
    Though one might block all openings
        and guard the spirit within,
    They permeated everything.
    The notes were lilting,
    The cadences lofty.

Consequently,
    Ghosts and spirits
        kept to their seclusion;
    The sun, moon, stars, and constellations
        stayed on their courses.
    I stopped the notes in finitude,
    Then let them flow into infinity.

You pondered over the music, but could not understand it; you gazed at it, but could not see it; you followed it, but could not catch it. Uncertain, you stood in the way with emptiness all around. Then you leaned against a withered parasol tree and moaned. Your mind was exhausted by wanting to understand; your eyes were exhausted by wanting to see; your strength was expended by wanting to pursue it, but even I could not catch up with it! Your form was brimming with emptiness, to the point that you became indifferent. That's why you felt weary.

"I had the third part

Performed with notes that would not weary
And that were tuned to a scale of spontaneity.

Thus
   They were born in clusters that came
       tumbling after each other,
   A forest of music
       without form.
   They were spread around
       without being dragged out,
   Subtly somber
       and soundless.

   Their movement came from nowhere,
   They dwelt in cavernous darkness.

   One might say they were dead,
   Another might say they were alive;
   One might say they were fruit,
   Another might say they were flower.

   Coursing and flowing, scattering and shifting,
   They were not dominated by constant sounds.

The world may doubt them and have them inspected by the sage,
for the sage is one who comprehends circumstances and follows
destiny. Though the heavenly mechanism is not set, the five
regulators are all prepared. To please the heart without any
words, this is called the music of heaven. Thus did the clansman
of the freehold at Yen eulogize it, saying:

You listen for it, but do not hear its sounds,
You look for it, but do not see its form;
It fills heaven and earth to the brim,
It envelops the six poles of the universe.

You wished to hear the music, but could not absorb it. That's why you felt confused.

"The music began by frightening you and, being frightened, you were spooked. Next, I had it played with wearisomeness and, being wearied, you would have withdrawn. I concluded it with confusion and, being confused, you felt stupid. Feeling stupid, you experienced the Way, the Way that can support you and make you whole."

4

When Confucius was wandering westward in Wey, Yen Yüan inquired of Maestro Chin, saying, "What do you think of the master's behavior?"

"It's a pity!" said Maestro Chin. "Your master's end is imminent!"

"Why?" asked Yen Yüan.

"Before straw dogs are displayed at a sacrifice," said Maestro Chin, "they are packed in bamboo containers wrapped with patterned embroideries. The impersonator of the dead fasts before taking them out. After they have been displayed, passers-by trample their heads and spines, grasscutters gather them for lighting cooking fires. That's all they're good for. If someone were to gather them up and pack them back into their bamboo containers covered with patterned embroideries, keeping them next to his side when he wandered abroad, stayed at home, and slept, he would certainly have bad dreams or repeated nightmares. Now, your master has likewise gathered up the straw dogs displayed by previous kings and keeps them next to his side while he wanders abroad, stays at home, and sleeps with his assembled disciples. Consequently, they had a tree they were resting under chopped down in the state of Sung and their traces obliterated in Wey, and they were impoverished in the capitals of the old Shang duchy and the Chou kingdom. Weren't these his bad dreams? When they were in the area of Ch'en and Ts'ai, Confucius and his disciples were besieged and went without cooked food for seven days, till they were on the verge of death. Wasn't this his nightmare?

"For traveling on water, nothing is better than a boat, and for traveling on land, nothing is better than a cart. A boat can travel on water, but if on that account you try to push it along the land, you wouldn't travel more than a few yards in a whole generation. Aren't antiquity and the present like water and land? Aren't the Chou dynasty and the state of Lu like the boat and the cart? Now, if one were to aspire to practice the ancient ways of Chou in Lu, this would be like pushing a boat on land; it would be all toil and no accomplishment. The person who tried it would certainly meet with misfortune. He has yet to learn the random rotation that responds to things inexhaustibly.

"Haven't you seen a wellsweep? When you pull on it, it goes down, and when you let go of it, it comes up. Because it is pulled by men and does not pull men around, it can go up and down without committing an offense against men. Therefore, the decorum and regulations of the three august sovereigns and five emperors were not prized because they preserved the status quo, but because they could bring good government. Thus we may compare the decorum and regulations of the three august sovereigns and five emperors to the hawthorn, the pear, the orange, and the pomelo. Although their flavors are quite different, they all taste good.

"Therefore, decorum and regulations should change with the times. Now, you may take a monkey and dress him up in the robes of the Duke of Chou, but he's certain to bite them and tear them, and he won't be satisfied until he's completely rid of them. If we observe the difference between antiquity and the present, it's like that between a monkey and the Duke of Chou. Likewise, when the beauteous Hsi Shih had heart pain, she would frown at her neighbors. An ugly woman of her village, seeing Hsi Shih do this, thought it made her look beautiful. So she went home and, pressing her hands over her heart, frowned at her neighbors. When the rich people of the village saw her, they would close their doors tightly and not go out. When the poor people saw her, they would grab their wives and children and run away. She knew that Hsi Shih's frowning was beautiful, but didn't know the reason why her frowning was beautiful. It's a pity! Your master's end is imminent!"

5

When Confucius was in his fifty-first year, he still had not heard the Way. He went south to P'ei to see Old Longears.

"Have you come, sir?" asked Old Longears. "I have heard, sir, that you are a worthy from the north. Have you also attained the Way?"

"I haven't attained it yet," said Confucius.

"How have you sought it?" asked the Old Master.

"I have sought for it in regulations and computations, but after five years I still haven't attained it."

"Then how did you seek it?" asked the Old Master.

"I sought for it in yin and yang, but after twelve years I still haven't attained it."

"So!" said the Old Master. "If the Way could be presented, then everyone would present it to his lord. If the Way could be offered, then everyone would offer it to his parents. If the Way could be told, then everyone would tell it to his brothers. If the Way could be given, then everyone would give it to his descendants. However, the reason why one cannot do these things is that if there is no host for it within, it will not stay, and if there is no sign of it without, it will not proceed. If that which goes forth from within is not received without, the sage will not let it go forth. If that which enters from without has no host to receive it within, the sage will not deposit it there. Fame is a public instrument upon which one may not draw too often. Humaneness and righteousness are the inns of the former kings in which one should not dwell for long, but stay only one night. . . .

"The ultimate men of the past borrowed a way through humaneness and lodged temporarily in righteousness, so that they could wander carefreely in emptiness, eat in the fields of plainness, stand in the garden of unindebtedness. Carefreeness implies nonaction, plainness implies easy nourishment, unindebtedness implies nonexpenditure. The ancients called this 'wandering about to pluck the truth.'

"He who considers wealth to be right will not part with his earnings. He who considers prominence to be right will not part with his fame. He who is partial to power will not share its handle with others. Grasping them, he trembles; letting go of them, he grieves. Yet he has not the slightest introspection to perceive that which he ceaselessly pursues. He is one of heaven's condemned.

"Resentment and kindness, taking and giving, admonition and instruction, sparing and killing—these eight are the instruments of rectification, but only she who complies with the great transformation without impediment can make use of them. Thus it is said, 'Rectitude is rectification.' The gate of heaven will not open for she whose mind does not believe this to be so."

6

When Confucius met Old Longears, he told him about humaneness and righteousness.

"In winnowing," said Old Longears, "the chaff can get in your eyes and blind you so that heaven, earth, and the four directions will all change their places. If mosquitoes and snipeflies pierce your skin, you won't be able to sleep the whole night long. But there is no greater confusion than that caused by humaneness and righteousness which maliciously muddle one's mind. If, sir, you were to cause all under heaven not to lose the simplicity of the unhewn log, you too could move with the abandon of the wind and stand forth in the wholeness of integrity. Instead, why must you overexert yourself as though you were carrying a bass drum and looking for a lost son? The swan does not bathe every day, yet it is white; the crow does not smudge itself every day, yet it is black. The natural simplicity of black and white is not worth disputing over; the spectacle of fame and praise is not worth bragging about."

Confucius did not speak for three days after returning from this meeting with Old Longears. "When you met Old Longears, oh master," asked his disciples, "how did you admonish him, as you surely must have?"

"Now, in him I have finally seen a dragon!" said Confucius. "Coiled up, his body is complete; extended, his scaly patterns are whole. He rides on the cloudy vapors and is nourished by yin and yang. My mouth fell open and I couldn't close it; my tongue arched upward so I couldn't even utter a halting word. How could I have admonished Old Longears?"

"So," asked Tzukung, "then can this man really remain still as a corpse with a dragonish presence, silent in the depths with a thunderous voice, setting forth in movement like heaven and earth? May I also have the opportunity to observe him?" Whereupon he went to see Old Longears with an introduction from Confucius.

Old Longears was just on the verge of squatting reposefully in his hall when he received Tzukung. "I'm getting on in years," he said softly. "What are you going to caution me about?"

"The government of all under heaven by the three august sovereigns and the five emperors was dissimilar," said Tzukung, "but the fame that accrued to them was the same. How is it that you alone consider them not to have been sages?"

"Come forward a little, young man," said Old Longears. "Why do you say that their government was dissimilar?"

"Yao passed the throne to Shun, and Shun passed it to Yü," was the answer. "Yü relied on his strength and T'ang on his troops. King Wen went along with the tyrant Chow and dared not go against him. King Wu went against Chow and dared not go along with him. That's why I said they were dissimilar."

"Come forward a little bit more, young man," said Old Longears. "I will tell you about the government of all under heaven by the three august sovereigns and the five emperors. When the Yellow Emperor governed all under heaven, he made the people of one mind. If someone's parent died and he did not weep, no one would blame him. When Yao governed all under heaven, he made the minds of the people biased. If someone disregarded the norm in the mourning garments he wore for his own parent, no one would blame him. When Shun governed all under heaven, he made the minds of the people competitive. Pregnant women still gave birth after ten months, but their children could talk five months after they were born, and they began to recognize people before they were toddlers. Consequently, people began to die prematurely. When Yü governed all under heaven, he made the minds of the people deviant. Men began to scheme and routinely resorted to force of arms. Claiming that they were killing robbers, not people, they considered themselves a breed apart, as did all under heaven. Hence, all under heaven were in a great panic, and the Confucians and the Mohists arose. It was because of their doing that there first came to be morality, but what can you say of the way things have ended up now?

"I tell you, we may speak of the three august sovereigns 'governing' all under heaven, but it is governing in name only, for there is no greater disorder than that which they caused. The knowledge of the three august sovereigns rebelled against the brightness of the sun and moon, conflicted with the essence of the mountains and rivers below, and disrupted the procession of the four seasons in between. Their knowledge was more fatal than the sting of a scorpion or the bite of a pit viper. Insecure in the reality of their nature and destiny, they still considered themselves sages. Is this not shameful?"

Tzukung stood there disconcerted and ill at ease.

7

Confucius said to Old Longears, "I have been studying the six classics—the *Odes, Documents, Ritual, Music, Changes,* and *Spring and Autumn Annals*—for what I myself would consider a long time and I know their contents thoroughly. I have discussed the ways of the former kings with seventy-two villainous rulers and have explained the achievements of dukes Chou and Shao, but not a single ruler has employed me. How very difficult it is to convince men and to explain the Way!"

"It's fortunate, sir, that you didn't encounter a ruler who could govern the world!" said the Old Master. "The six classics are the stale traces of the former kings, but they do not tell what created the traces! Now, sir, what you talk about are traces. Traces, however, are produced by shoes; they're not the shoes themselves!

"A pair of white egrets look at each other with motionless pupils and fertilization takes place. A male insect chirps from an air current above, a female answers from below, and fertilization takes place. The hermaphrodite is both male and female, hence fertilization takes place by itself. One's nature cannot be changed; destiny cannot be altered; time cannot be stopped; the Way cannot be blocked. If one attains the Way, there's nothing one cannot achieve. If one loses the Way, there's nothing one can achieve."

Confucius did not go outside for three months after this until he went to see Old Longears again and said, "I've finally got it! Birds brood, fish milt, the solitary wasp transmutes, and when a new baby boy is born the older brother cries because he can no longer share the teat. I have long been a man who has not shared in evolution. But how can a man who does not share in evolution help other men to evolve?"

"All right, Hillock," said the Old Master. "You've finally got it!"

15

INGRAINED OPINIONS

Censuring all disciplines and dogmas, ascetic or otherwise, the author propounds instead mere quietude and clarity. Here we see the outlines of an indigenous Taoist ethos of simplicity quite apart from any Yogic praxis.

1

Having ingrained opinions and a high estimate of one's own conduct, leaving the world behind and being different from common society, engaging in lofty discussions and resentfully slandering others—all this is merely indicative of arrogance. But it is favored by the scholars of mountain and valley, men who censure the world and throw themselves with withered visage into the watery depths. Discoursing on humaneness, righteousness, loyalty, and trustworthiness, being reverent, frugal, deferential, and yielding—all this is merely indicative of self-cultivation. But it is favored by the scholars who wish to bring peace to the world, men who teach and instruct, who pursue learning at home and abroad. Discoursing on great merit and establishing great fame, observing the ceremonies for lord and subject, and rectifying those on high and those below—all this is merely indicative of governing. But it is favored by the scholars of court, men who honor their ruler and strengthen his state, who devote themselves to incorporating other states. Retiring to bogs and marshes, dwelling in the vacant wilderness, fishing and living leisurely—all this is merely indicative of nonaction. But it is favored by the scholars of rivers and lakes, men who flee from the world and wish to be idle. Blowing and breathing, exhaling and inhaling, expelling the old and taking in the new, bear strides and bird stretches—all this is merely indicative of the desire for longevity. But it is favored by scholars who channel the vital breath and flex the muscles and joints, men who nourish the physical form so as to emulate the hoary age of Progenitor P'eng.

If someone could be lofty without having ingrained opinions, cultivate himself without humaneness and righteousness, govern without merit or fame, be idle without rivers or lakes, and live long without channeling and flexions, he would forget everything, yet he would possess everything. His tranquillity would be unlimited, yet a multitude of excellences would follow in his wake. This is the Way of heaven and earth, the integrity of the sage.

Therefore, it is said, "placidity, mildness, quietude, indifference, emptiness, nonbeing, and nonaction—these are the root of heaven and earth, the substance of the Way and virtue." Thus the sage rests in them. Resting, he is peaceful and easeful; peaceful and easeful, he is placid and mild. Hence worries and troubles do not assail him, pernicious influences do not assault him. Consequently, his integrity is intact and his spirit is undiminished.

Therefore, it is said, the sage "walks with heaven in life and evolves with things in death. In stillness, he shares the same integrity as yin; in movement, he shares the same current as yang." He is not the founder of fortune, nor is he the initiator of misfortune. He responds when affected, moves when pressed, and arises only when he has no other choice. He rids himself of knowledge and precedent, conforming to the principle of heaven. Thus, there will be "no calamity from heaven, no encumbrance from things, no censure from men, and no reproach from ghosts." His life is like floating; his death is like resting. He does not have anxious thoughts; he does not make plans beforehand. He is "bright but not dazzling," trustworthy but not expectant. He "does not dream when he is asleep, does not worry when he is awake." His spirit is unadulterated; "his soul does not weary." His emptiness, nonbeing, placidity, and mildness are a match for the integrity of heaven.

Therefore, it is said, sorrow and joy are perversions of integrity; happiness and anger are transgressions of the Way; likes and dislikes are failings of the mind. Thus, when the mind is free from anxiety and joy, that is the ultimate of integrity. When it is unified and unchanging, that is the ultimate of stillness. When there is nothing that irritates it, that is the ultimate of emptiness. When it has no dealings with other things, that is the ultimate of mildness. When there is nothing that runs counter to it, that is the ultimate of purity.

Therefore, it is said, when the physical form is toiled without rest it will become fatigued; when the spiritual essence is used without end it will be exhausted. . . . The nature of water is to be clear when unadulterated, to be level when undisturbed. But if it is blocked and not allowed to flow, it cannot retain its clearness. This is a symbol for the integrity of heaven. Hence, it is said, to be pure and unadulterated, to be still and unchanging, to be mild and nonactive, to walk with heaven when one moves—this is the Way to nourish the spirit. Now, he who owns a fine sword from the southeast stores it in a scabbard, not daring to use it lightly—this is the pinnacle of preciousness. But the spiritual essence flows forth in all directions, never reaching a limit. It borders heaven above, encircles the earth below, transforming and nurturing the myriad things. It cannot be symbolized, but its name is "With Deus."

The Way of purity and plainness lies only in guarding the spirit. Guard and do not lose it, becoming one with the spirit.

The essence of oneness will pervade and join with the order of heaven. There is a proverb that says, "The masses of men emphasize profit; the incorruptible scholars emphasize fame; wise men esteem will; the sage values essence." Hence plainness may be defined as what is unalloyed, and purity as keeping the spirit undiminished. One who can embody purity and plainness may be called a "true man."

16

MENDING NATURE

The author continues with his espousal of pureness and placidity as the best means for restoring one's original nature. A person's primary purpose should be the preservation of self by keeping things joyfully plain. Do not, says the author, strive to accumulate knowledge and do not engage in philosophical arguments— which is precisely what most of the Warring States thinkers did.

1

Those who would mend their nature through vulgar learning, seeking to restore its original condition, and those who would polish their desires through vulgar thinking, seeking to perfect their intelligence, may be called deluded persons.

The ancients who practiced the Way nourished knowledge with placidity. Understanding life, they did not use their knowledge to engage in action. This may be called nourishing placidity with knowledge. When knowledge and placidity nourish each other, then harmony and principle emerge from one's nature.

Now, virtue is harmony and the Way is principle. When there is nothing virtue does not accommodate, that is humaneness; when there is nothing the Way does not arrange, that is righteousness; when righteousness is manifest and things feel affection, that is loyalty. When the center is genuine and that is reflected in the emotions, there is music; when trustworthy conduct is accommodating and conforms to an elegant pattern, there is ceremony. But if ceremony and music are deviantly performed, all under heaven will be in disorder.

Correcting others yet concealing one's own virtue results in virtue remaining unexposed. But if it is exposed, things will lose their nature.

2

The ancients, in the midst of chaos, were tranquil together with the whole world. At that time, yin and yang were harmoniously still, ghosts and spirits caused no disturbances; the four seasons came in good time; the myriad things went unharmed; the host of living creatures escaped premature death. Although men had knowledge, there was no use for it. This was called ultimate unity. At that time, there was no action but only constant spontaneity.

This condition persisted until integrity deteriorated to the point that Torchman and Fuhsi arose to manage all under heaven, whereupon there was accord, but no longer unity. Integrity further declined until the Divine Farmer and the Yellow Emperor arose to manage all under heaven, whereupon there was repose, but no longer accord. Integrity declined still further until T'ang and Yü arose to manage all under heaven. They initiated the fashion of governing by transformation, whereby purity was diluted and simplicity dissipated. In their action, they parted from the Way; in their behavior, they endangered integrity. After that they deserted their nature and followed their mind. One mind recognized the knowledge of another mind, but it was not sufficient to bring stability to all under heaven. After that, they appended culture and added erudition. Culture destroyed substance, and erudition drowned mind. After that, the people began to be confused and disordered, without any means to return to their natural emotions or to revert to their origins.

Viewed from this vantage, when the world forsook the Way, the Way forsook the world. The world and the Way having mutually forsaken each other, there was no wherewithal for the man of the Way to have an impact upon the world, nor for the world to have an impact upon the Way. When there are no means for the Way to have an impact on the world, nor for the world to have an impact on the Way, even though the sage does not stay among mountains and forests, his integrity will remain hidden. . . .

Those whom the ancients called "hidden scholars" did not fail to reveal themselves by concealing their persons; did not fail to issue their ideas by refusing to speak; did not fail to present their knowledge by treasuring it away. It was because the mandate of the times was greatly out of kilter. If they had received the mandate of the times and been able to carry it out widely for all under heaven, they would have returned to the unity that leaves no traces. Not having received the mandate of the times and greatly stymied by all under heaven, they sunk their roots deep in utter tranquillity and waited. That is the Way they preserved in their persons.

Those ancients who preserved their persons did not decorate their knowledge with disputation. They did not impoverish all under heaven with their knowledge, nor did they impoverish integrity with their knowledge. They stayed aloof in their own place and returned to their own nature, doing nothing whatsoever. Indeed, the Way does not consist of petty behavior, nor does integrity consist of petty recognition. Petty recognition harms integrity; petty behavior harms the Way. . . .

Complete joy may be called attainment of the will. In ancient times, what was called "attainment of the will" did not mean getting carriages and crowns. It simply meant there was nothing that could be added to one's joy. What is nowadays called "attainment of the will" means getting carriages and crowns. But carriages and crowns pertain to the body, having nothing to do with one's nature and destiny. Things that come unexpectedly remain with us only temporarily. Being temporary, their coming cannot be controlled, and their going cannot be stopped. Hence, do not gratify the will with carriages and crowns; do not indulge in vulgarity because of impoverishment and privation—the joys of the former are similar to those of the latter. Thus, simply do not worry. If what is temporarily with us now leaves us and our joy is lost, then although it brought joy, it must have been false. Therefore it is said, "Those who forsake themselves for things, who lose their nature for vulgarity, are called topsy-turvy people."

17

AUTUMN FLOODS

The most powerful and expressive narrative in the entire book, the first half of the chapter presents the evocative dialogue between the Earl of the Yellow River and the Overlord of the Northern Sea. The remainder is occupied by half a dozen other short parables and allegories illuminating the essential spirit of Master Chuang.

1

When the time of the autumn floods arrived, the hundred tributaries poured into the Yellow River. Its onrushing current was so huge that one could not discern an ox or a horse on the opposite side or on the banks of its islets. Thereupon the Earl of the River delightedly congratulated himself at having complete and sole possession of all excellences under heaven. Following along with the current, he went east until he reached the Northern Sea. There he looked eastward but could not see the water's end, whereupon he crestfallenly gazed across the surface of the sea and said with a sigh to its overlord, "There is a proverb that says, 'He who has heard the Way a hundred times believes no one may be compared with himself!' This applies to me. Furthermore, when I first heard those who belittle the learning of Confucius and disparage the righteousness of Poyi, I did not believe them. But now that I behold your boundlessness, I realize that, had I not come to your gate, I would have been in danger, and would have been ridiculed forever by the practitioners of the great method."

The Overlord of the Northern Sea said, "You can't tell a frog at the bottom of a well about the sea because he's stuck in his little space. You can't tell a summer insect about ice because it is confined by its season. You can't tell a scholar of distorted views about the Way because he is bound by his doctrine. Now you have ventured forth from your banks to observe the great sea and have recognized your own insignificance, so that you can be told of the great principle.

"Of all the waters under heaven, none is greater than the sea. The myriad rivers return to it ceaselessly but it never fills up; the drain at its bottom endlessly discharges but it never empties. Spring and autumn it never varies, and it knows nothing of flood and drought. Its superiority to such streams as the Yangtze and the Yellow rivers cannot be measured in numbers. Yet the reason I have never made much of myself on this account is because I compare my own form to that of heaven and earth and recall that I received my vital breath from yin and yang. Amid heaven and earth, I am as a little pebble or tiny tree on a big mountain. Since I perceive of myself as small, how then can I make much of myself? May we not reckon that the four seas in the midst of heaven and earth resemble the cavity in a pile of stones lying in a huge marsh? May we not reckon that the Middle Kingdom in the midst of the sea is like a mustard seed in a huge granary? When we designate the number of things there are in existence, we refer to them in terms of myriads, but man occupies only one place among them. The masses of men occupy the nine regions, but wherever grain grows and wherever boats and carriages reach, the individual occupies only one place among them. In comparison with the myriad things, would he not resemble the tip of a downy hair on a horse's body? The succession of the five emperors, the contention of the three kings, the worries of humane men, the labors of the committed scholars, all amount to no more than this. Poyi declined it for the sake of fame. Confucius lectured on it for the sake of his erudition. This is because they made much of themselves. Is this not like you just now making much of yourself because of your flooding waters?"

"This being so," asked the Earl of the River, "may I take heaven and earth as the standard for what is large and the tip of a downy hair as the standard for what is small?"

"No," said the Overlord of the Northern Sea. "Things are limitless in their capacities, incessant in their occurrences, inconstant in their portions, uncertain in their beginning and ending. For this reason, great knowledge observes things at a relative distance, hence it does not belittle what is small nor make much of what is big, knowing that their capacities are limitless. It witnesses clearly the past and the present, hence it is not frustrated by what is far off nor attracted by what is close at hand, knowing that their occurrences are incessant. It examines fullness and emptiness, hence it is not pleased when it obtains nor worried when it loses, knowing that their portions are inconstant. It understands the level path, hence it is not enraptured by life nor perturbed by death, knowing that beginnings and endings are uncertain. We may reckon that what man knows is less than what he doesn't know; the time when he is alive is less than the time when he isn't alive. When he seeks to delimit the boundaries of the extremely large with what is extremely small, he becomes disoriented and can't get hold of himself. Viewed from this vantage, how do we know that the tip of a downy hair is adequate to determine the parameters of the extremely small? And how do we know that heaven and earth are adequate to delimit the boundaries of the extremely large?"

"The deliberators of the world," said the Earl of the Yellow River, "all say, 'That which is extremely minute has no form; that which is extremely large cannot be encompassed.' Is this true?"

"If we look at what is large from the viewpoint of what is minuscule," said the Overlord of the Northern Sea, "we won't see the whole. If we look at what is minuscule from the viewpoint of what is large, we won't see the details. Now, that which is minute is the smallest of the small; that which is enormous is the largest of the large. Hence, their differences are suitable and in accord with their circumstances. Yet, the minute and the coarse are both dependent upon their having a form. That which has no form is numerically indivisible; that which cannot be encompassed is numerically undelimitable. That which can be discussed in words is the coarseness of things; that which can be conceived of in thought is the minuteness of things. That which can neither be discussed in words nor conceived of in thought is independent of minuteness and coarseness. . . ."

"How, then," asked the Earl of the Yellow River, "are we to demarcate the value and magnitude of a thing, whether it be intrinsic or extrinsic?"

The Overlord of the Northern Sea said, "Observed in the light of the Way, things are neither prized nor despised; observed in the light of things, they prize themselves and despise others; observed in the light of the common lot, one's value is not determined by oneself. Observed in the light of gradations, if we consider to be large what is larger than something else, then the myriad things are without exception large; if we consider to be small what is smaller than something else, then all the myriad things are without exception small. If we regard heaven and earth as a mustard seed and the tip of a downy hair as a mountain, we can perceive the numerousness of their relative gradations. Observed in the light of merit, if we grant whatever merit they have, then the myriad things without exception have merit; if we point to whatever merit they lack, then the myriad things lack merit. If we recognize that east and west, though opposites, cannot be without each other, their shared merit will be fixed. Observed in the light of inclination, if we approve whatever they approve, then the myriad things without exception may be approved; if we condemn whatever they condemn, then the myriad things without exception may be condemned. If we recognize that Yao and Chieh approved of themselves but condemned each other, we can perceive their controlling inclinations.

"Long ago, Yao yielded his throne to Shun and the latter became emperor, but when K'uai yielded his throne to Tzu Chih, they were both cut down. T'ang and Wu became kings through contention, but the Duke of Po contended and was destroyed. Viewed in this light, the etiquette of contending and yielding, the conduct of Yao and Chieh, may be either prized or despised in accord with the times, but may not be taken as constants. A beam or a ridge-pole may be used to breach a city wall, but it cannot be used to plug a hole, which is to say that implements have specific purposes. A Ch'ichi or a Hualiu may gallop a thousand tricents in a day, but for catching rats they're not as good as a wild cat or a weasel, which is to say that creatures have different skills. An owl can catch fleas at night and can discern the tip of a downy hair, but when it comes out during the day it stares blankly and can't even see a hill or mountain, which is to say that beings have different natures. Therefore, when it is said, 'Make right your teacher, not wrong; make good government your teacher, not disorder,' this is to misunderstand the principle of heaven and earth and the attributes of the myriad things. It would be like making heaven your teacher and ignoring earth, like making yin your teacher and ignoring yang. The unworkability of this is clear. Still, if one goes on talking like this and does not give it up, one is either being stupid or deceptive. The emperors and kings of old had different modes of abdication, and the rulers of the three dynasties had different modes of succession. He who acts contrary to the times and contravenes custom is called a usurper; he who accords with the times and conforms to custom is called a disciple of righteousness. Keep silent, oh Earl of the Yellow River! How could you know about the gate of honor and baseness and about the practitioners of small and large?"

"Then what am I to do?" asked the Earl of the Yellow River, "and what am I not to do? With regard to rejecting and accepting, taking and giving, how should I behave?"

"Viewed in the light of the Way," said the Overlord of the Northern Sea,

"What is prized and what is despised
May be referred to as alternating developments of
      each other.
Do not persist in following the dictates of your will,
For it will bring you into great conflict with the Way.

What is few and what is many
May be referred to as reciprocal extensions of each
      other.
Do not be inflexibly monotonous in your behavior,
For it will put you at odds with the Way.

Be solemn as the lord of a state
    Whose integrity is impartial;
Be self-composed as the officiant of a sacrificial altar
    Whose blessings are impartial;
Be broad-minded as the immensity of the four directions
    Which have no borders.

Embosom all the myriad things,
Taking each one under your protective wings.
This may be referred to as universality.
The myriad things will be equally regarded,
There being no long or short among them.

The Way has neither beginning nor end,
But things have life and death.
Not being able to presume upon their completion,
They are now empty, now full,

Without stability in form.

The years cannot be advanced,
Nor can time be stayed.
Dissolution and generation, fullness and emptiness—
Whatever ends has a beginning.

Thus may we
　　Speak of the secret of the great purport,
　　Discuss the principle of the myriad things.

The life of things
Is like the cantering and galloping of a horse—
They are transformed with each movement,
They change with each moment.
What are you to do?
What are you not to do?
Just let things evolve by themselves."

"Then what is to be prized about the Way?" asked the Earl of the Yellow River.

The Overlord of the Northern Sea said, "She who knows the Way must apprehend principle; she who apprehends principle must be clear about contingency; she who is clear about contingency will not harm herself with things. She who has ultimate integrity will neither be burned by fire nor drowned in water, will neither be harmed by cold and heat nor injured by bird and beast. This does not mean that she belittles these things, but rather that she examines where she will be safe or in danger. She is tranquil in misfortune or in fortune; she is careful about her comings and goings, so that nothing can harm her. Therefore it is said, 'The heavenly is within, the human is without; integrity lies in heaven.' When you know the operation of the heavenly and the human, you will root yourself in heaven and position yourself in contentment. Then you will be hesitant and flexible, reverting to what is important and bespeaking perfection."

"What do you mean by heavenly and what do you mean by human?"

The Overlord of the Northern Sea said, "Oxen and horses having four feet is what is meant by 'heavenly.' Putting a halter over a horse's head or piercing an ox's nose is what is meant by 'human.' Therefore it is said,

'Do not destroy the heavenly with the human;
Do not destroy destiny with intentionality;
Do not sacrifice your good name for attainments.'
If you guard this carefully and do not lose it,
You may be said to have returned to the truth."

2

The unipede envies the millipede; the millipede envies the snake; the snake envies the wind; the wind envies the eye; the eye envies the mind.

The unipede said to the millipede, "I go hippity-hopping along on my one foot but barely manage. How is it, sir, that you can control myriad feet?"

"It's not so," said the millipede. "Haven't you seen a person spit? When he spews them forth, the big globs are like pearls, the droplets are like a mist. All mixed up together, the number that falls is immeasurable. Now, I just move by my natural inner workings but don't know why it is so."

The millipede said to the snake, "I go along on my multitudinous feet, but I'm not as fast as you who have no feet. How come?"

"How could we change the movements of our natural inner workings?" asked the snake. "What use do I have for feet?"

The snake said to the wind, "I go along by moving my spine

and ribs, thus I have a shape. But you, sir, who arise with a whoosh from the Northern Sea and alight with a whoosh in the Southern Sea, have no shape at all. How can this be?"

"It's true that I arise with a whoosh from the Northern Sea and alight in the Southern Sea," said the wind, "but whoever points at me vanquishes me and whoever treads upon me vanquishes me. Nonetheless, only I can snap big trees and blow down big houses. Therefore, the great vanquishing depends upon a host of minor defeats. It is only the sage who can be a great vanquisher."

3

When Confucius was traveling in K'uang, the local militia surrounded him several layers deep, but he kept right on singing and playing his lute. Tzulu went over to see him and said, "How can you be so cheerful, master?"

"Come!" said Confucius, "I shall tell you. Long have I shunned adversity, but have not been able to avoid it: that's my destiny. Long have I sought success, but have not been able to achieve it; that's the times. In the age of Yao and Shun, there was no one under heaven who met with adversity, but their achievements were not due to their knowledge. In the age of Chieh and Chow, there was no one under heaven who met with success, but their failures were not due to their lack of knowledge. It was because of the times and the circumstances they encountered.

"To travel on water yet not flee from crocodiles and dragons is the courage of the fisherman; to travel on land yet not flee from rhinoceroses and tigers is the courage of the hunter; to have naked blades cross before him yet view death as calmly as life is the courage of the ardent warrior; to know that adversity is due to destiny and that success is due to the times yet face great difficulty without fear is the courage of the sage. Just sit tight, Tzulu. I am under the control of my destiny."

Shortly afterward, the leader of the armed men came over

and apologized, saying, "We thought you were Tiger Yang and so we surrounded you. Now that we know you're not, please accept our apologies and we shall retreat."

4

Kungsun Lung inquired of Prince Mou of Wei, saying, "When I was young I studied the Way of the former kings, and when I grew up I understood the conduct of humaneness and righteousness. I joined sameness and difference, separated hardness from whiteness, asserted the unassertable, and affirmed the unaffirmable. I perplexed the thinkers of the hundred schools and refuted the disputers of the manifold persuasions. I considered myself to be ultimately accomplished. But now I have heard the words of Master Chuang and am bewildered by their oddity. I don't know whether it's because my powers of discussion are not up to his or because my knowledge is less than his. Now I feel that I can't even make a peep. I venture to ask what strategy I should adopt."

Prince Mou leaned against his table and heaved a great sigh. Then he looked up to heaven and, smiling, said, "Haven't you heard about the frog in the broken-down well? 'I really enjoy myself here!' it said to a turtle of the Eastern Sea. 'If I want to go out, I jump along the railing around the well, then I come back and rest where the brick lining is missing from the wall. I enter the water till it comes up to my armpits and supports my chin. When I slop through the mud, it covers my feet and buries my toes. Turning around, I see crayfish and tadpoles, but none of them is a match for me. Furthermore, I have sole possession of all the water in this hole and straddle all the joy in this broken-down well. This is the ultimate! Why don't you drop in some time, sir, and see for yourself?'

"But before the turtle of the Eastern Sea could get his left foot in, his right knee had already gotten stuck. After extricating himself, he withdrew a little and told the frog about the sea, saying, 'A distance of a thousand tricents is insufficient to span

its breadth; a height of a thousand fathoms is insufficient to plumb its depth. During Yü's time, there were floods nine years out of ten, but the water in it did not appreciably increase; during T'ang's time, there were droughts seven years out of eight, but the extent of its shores did not appreciably decrease. Hence, not to shift or change with time, not to advance or recede regardless of amount—this is the great joy of the Eastern Sea.' Upon hearing this, the frog in the broken-down well was so utterly startled that it lost itself in bewilderment.

"Furthermore, when you, whose knowledge is inadequate to understand the limits of 'right' and 'wrong,' still wish to see through the words of Master Chuang, it's like making a mosquito carry a mountain on its back or an inchworm race against the Yellow River—they won't be up to the task. Still further, aren't you, whose knowledge is inadequate to understand the words for discussing the uttermost mysteries and who satisfy yourself with a moment's profit, like the frog in the broken-down well?

"Master Chuang, however, marches through the Yellow Springs one moment and ascends to the empyrean the next.

> With him, there is neither north nor south,
> But only untrammeled release in all four directions
> And absorption in the unfathomable;
> There is neither east nor west,
> Beginning as he does in darkest obscurity
> And returning to grand perceptivity.

But you, sir, bewilderedly seek something with which to quiz him and grope for a means to dispute him. This is simply like peering at heaven through a tube or pointing at the earth with an awl—they're too small for the purpose. Begone, sir! Haven't you heard of the young lad from Shouling who tried to learn to walk the way people do in Hantan? Before he had acquired this new skill, he had forgotten how he used to walk, so all he could do was come crawling home on all fours. If you don't go away now, sir, you'll forget what you used to know and lose your profession."

Mouth agape and tongue-tied, Kungsun Lung fled in consternation.

5

Master Chuang was fishing in the P'u River. The king of Ch'u dispatched two high-ranking officials to go before him with this message: "I wish to encumber you with the administration of my realm."

Without turning around, Master Chuang just kept holding on to his fishing rod and said, "I have heard that in Ch'u there is a sacred tortoise that has already been dead for three thousand years. The king stores it in his ancestral temple inside of a hamper wrapped with cloth. Do you think this tortoise would rather be dead and have its bones preserved as objects of veneration, or be alive and dragging its tail through the mud?"

"It would rather be alive and dragging its tail through the mud," said the two officials.

"Begone!" said Master Chuang. "I'd rather be dragging my tail in the mud."

6

When Master Hui was serving as the prime minister of Liang, Master Chuang set off to visit him. Somebody said to Master Hui, "Master Chuang is coming and he wants to replace you as prime minister." Whereupon Master Hui became afraid and had the kingdom searched for three days and three nights.

After Master Chuang arrived, he went to see Master Hui and said, "In the south there is a bird. Its name is Yellow Phoenix. Have you ever heard of it? It takes off from the Southern Sea and flies to the Northern Sea. It won't stop on any other tree but the kolanut; won't eat anything but bamboo seeds; won't drink anything but sweet spring water. There was once an owl that, having got hold of a putrid rat, looked up at the Yellow Phoenix as it was passing by and shouted 'shoo!' Now, sir, do you wish to shoo me away from your kingdom of Liang?"

7

Master Chuang and Master Hui were strolling across the bridge over the Hao River. "The minnows have come out and are swimming so leisurely," said Master Chuang. "This is the joy of fishes."

"You're not a fish," said Master Hui. "How do you know what the joy of fishes is?"

"You're not me," said Master Chuang, "so how do you know that I don't know what the joy of fishes is?"

"I'm not you," said Master Hui, "so I certainly do not know what you do. But you're certainly not a fish, so it is irrefutable that you do not know what the joy of fishes is."

"Let's go back to where we started," said Master Chuang. "When you said, 'How do you know what the joy of fishes is?' you asked me because you already knew that I knew. I know it by strolling over the Hao."

18

ULTIMATE JOY

The author takes up one of the themes of Chapter 16—the wisdom of living simply. Perhaps the most touching tale in the book is related here: Master Chuang's acceptance of his wife's death as a natural transformation. A succession of weird encounters pursues the same thread—the advisability of accepting change as a natural process.

1

Is there ultimate joy anywhere under heaven? Is there a method for keeping the person alive? Now, if there is, what should one do and what should one rely upon? What should one avoid and what should one dwell in? What should one resort to and what should one leave behind? What should one enjoy and what should one detest?

That which all under heaven respect is wealth, honor, longevity, and a good name; that which they take joy in is security for their persons, rich flavors, beautiful clothes, pretty sights, and agreeable sounds; that which they look down on is poverty, meanness, premature death, and a bad name; that which they find distasteful is getting no ease for their persons, no rich flavors for their mouths, no beautiful clothes for their bodies, no pretty sights for their eyes, and no agreeable sounds for their ears. If they do not get these things, they become greatly troubled and frightened. Is it not foolish how this is all for the body?

The wealthy embitter themselves through frantic work. They accumulate more property than they can possibly use. Although they do this for the body, they actually alienate it. The honored worry day and night over whether they are being good. Although they do this for the body, they actually estrange it. The birth of men is also the birth of their anxieties. The greater their longevity the more addled they become and the longer they are anxious about not dying, a bitter fate indeed! Although they do this for the body, they actually distance it. The ardent warrior is viewed by all under heaven as good, but that is insufficient to keep his person alive. I do not know whether their goodness is truly good or not.

> If we consider it good,
> Still it is insufficient to keep their persons alive;
> If we consider it as not good,
> Still it is sufficient to keep others alive.

Therefore it is said,
> "If your loyal admonitions are not listened to,
> You should shrink back and not contend."

Hence,
> Tzuhsü's contention
>   led to the ruination of his body.
> Yet, had he not contended,
>   he would not have made a name for himself.

Was his goodness truly so or not?
> Now, as for what the common lot do and what they enjoy,

again I do not know whether their enjoyment is really joyful or not. I observe that what the common lot considers enjoyment is to rush headlong toward their goals in a flock as though they'd never stop. But I'm not sure whether what they all call enjoyment is enjoyable or not. Is there really enjoyment or not? I consider nonaction to be true enjoyment, but the common lot find it greatly distasteful. Therefore it is said, "The ultimate joy is to be without joy; the ultimate praise is to be without praise."

The right and wrong of all under heaven are really indeterminate. Nonetheless, nonaction can determine right and wrong. The ultimate joy is to keep the person alive, and only through nonaction do we come close to maintaining ultimate joy. Let me try to explain this.

> Through nonaction, heaven is pure,
> Through nonaction, earth is tranquil.

Thus, these two instances of nonaction join together and all the myriad things evolve.

> How nebulous and blurred!—
> They come from nowhere.
> How blurred and nebulous!—
> There are no images.

> The myriad things in their profusion
> Are all generated through nonaction.

Therefore it is said, "Heaven and earth are nonactive, yet there is no action left undone." Who among men can attain nonaction?

2

Master Chuang's wife died. When Master Hui went to offer his condolences, he found Master Chuang lolling on the floor with his legs sprawled out, beating a basin and singing.

"She lived together with you," said Master Hui, "raised your children, grew old, and died. It's enough that you do not wail for her, but isn't it a bit much for you to be beating on a basin and singing?"

"Not so," said Master Chuang. "When she first died, how could I of all people not be melancholy? But I reflected on her beginning and realized that originally she was unborn. Not only was she unborn, originally she had no form. Not only did she have no form, originally she had no vital breath. Intermingling with nebulousness and blurriness, a transformation occurred and there was vital breath; the vital breath was transformed and there was form; the form was transformed and there was birth; now there has been another transformation and she is dead. This is like the progression of the four seasons—from spring to autumn, from winter to summer. There she sleeps blissfully in an enormous chamber. If I were to have followed her weeping and wailing, I think it would have been out of keeping with destiny, so I stopped."

3

Nuncle Scattered and Nuncle Slippery were observing the mounds of the Earl of Darkness in the emptiness of K'unlun where the Yellow Emperor rested. Suddenly a willow began to sprout from Nuncle Slippery's left elbow. He looked startled, as though he resented it.

"Do you resent it?" asked Nuncle Scattered.

"No," said Nuncle Slippery. "Why should I resent it? Our lives are just a borrowed pretext. That which we borrow to maintain our lives is merely so much dust. Life and death alternate like day and night. As you and I were observing evolution, it caught up with me. So why should I resent it?"

4

When Master Chuang went to Ch'u, he saw an empty skull. Though brittle, it still retained its shape. Master Chuang tapped the skull with his riding crop and asked, "Did you end up like this because of greed for life and loss of reason? Or was it because you were involved in some treasonous affair and had your head chopped off by an ax? Or was it because you were involved in some unsavory conduct, shamefully disgracing your parents, wife, and children? Or was it because you starved or froze? Or was it simply because your time was up?"

When he had finished with his questions, Master Chuang picked up the skull and used it as a pillow when he went to sleep. At midnight, the skull appeared to him in a dream and said, "Your manner of talking makes you sound like a sophist. I perceive that what you mentioned are all the burdens of the living. When you're dead, there's none of that. Would you like to hear me tell you about death, sir?"

"Yes," said Master Chuang.

"When you're dead," said the skull, "there's no ruler above you and no subjects below you. There are no affairs of the four seasons; instead, time passes leisurely as it does for heaven and earth. Not even the joys of being a south-facing king can surpass those of death."

Not believing the skull, Master Chuang said, "If I were to have the Arbiter of Destiny restore life to your physical form, to give you back your flesh, bones, and skin, to return your parents, wife, children, and village acquaintances, would you like that?"

Frowning in deep consternation, the skull said, "How could I abandon 'the joys of a south-facing king' and return to the toils of mankind?"

5

When Yen Yüan went eastward to Ch'i, Confucius had a worried look. Tzukung stepped off his mat and inquired, saying, "Your humble disciple ventures to ask why you have such a worried look now that Yen Yüan is going eastward to Ch'i."

"You've asked a good question!" said Confucius. "Of old, Master Kuan had a saying of which I thoroughly approve. He said, 'A small bag cannot be made to contain something large; a short rope cannot be made to draw from a deep well.' Indeed, it is like this, there being that which is determined by our destiny and that which is suitable for our physical form. These can neither be augmented nor diminished. I'm afraid that Yüan will talk about the Way of Yao, Shun, and the Yellow Emperor with the Marquis of Ch'i, and that he'll go on to talk about Torchman and the Divine Farmer. The marquis will seek for correspondences in himself but will not find them. Not finding them, he will suspect the speaker and the one whom he suspects will be put to death.

"And haven't you heard about the seabird of old that alighted in the suburbs of Lu? The Marquis of Lu went out to welcome the seabird and held a banquet for it in his ancestral temple. For music, they performed 'The Ninefold Splendors,' and they offered it beef, mutton, and pork as sacrificial victuals. The bird's eyes, however, glazed over with sadness and it was unwilling to eat so much as a single sliver of flesh, nor drink a single cupful of wine; and in three days it died. The marquis was trying to nourish the bird as he would have nourished himself, and not with the nourishment suitable for a bird. Now, if we are to nourish birds as birds should be nourished, we ought to let them perch in the deep forests, wander over sandy islets, float on rivers and lakes, feed on loaches and minnows, follow along in rank till they stop, dwelling in self-contentment. The seabird disliked hearing human voices, so why go ahead and make all that hullabaloo? When the music of 'The Pond of Totality' and 'The

Ninefold Splendors' is performed in the cavernous wilds, birds fly away upon hearing it, beasts run away upon hearing it, and fish dive into the depths upon hearing it, but when the masses of men hear it, they circle around and look on. Fish dwell in the water and live; if men were to dwell in the water they would die. They are decidedly different from each other, so their likes and dislikes are different. Therefore the former sages did not insist that the abilities of all be identical nor that their affairs be similar. Their naming was limited by reality, and they established usages as appropriate. This is called 'holding on to blessings through orderly adaptation.' "

6

Master Lieh was on a journey and was having a meal by the side of the road. There he saw a hundred-year-old skull. He pulled away the weeds and pointed at it, saying, "Only you and I know that you have never died and that you have never lived. Are you truly distressed? Am I truly happy?"

7

In seeds there are germs. When they are found in water they become filaments. When they are found at the border of water and land they become algae. When they germinate in elevated places they become plantain. When the plantain is found in fertile soil it becomes crow's foot. The crow's foot's roots become scarab grubs and its leaves become butterflies. The butterflies soon evolve into insects that are born beneath the stove. They have the appearance of exuviae and are called "house crickets." After a thousand days the house crickets become birds called "dried surplus bones." The spittle of the dried surplus bones becomes a misty spray and the misty spray becomes mother of vinegar. Midges are born from mother of vinegar; yellow whirligigs are born from fetid wine; blindgnats are born from putrid slimebugs. When goat's-queue couples with bamboo that has not shooted for a long time, they produce greenies. The greenies produce panthers; panthers produce horses; horses produce men; and men return to enter the wellsprings of nature. The myriad things all come out from the wellsprings and all reenter the wellsprings.

19

UNDERSTANDING LIFE

By nourishing the vital breath, one can preserve the body, even under such extreme conditions as those to which Hindu fakirs subject themselves. Focusing on one's inner being, as opposed to external distractions, brings supreme skill and long-lasting life.

1

She who understands the attributes of life does not strive for what is not doable in life; she who understands the attributes of destiny does not strive for that which is not permitted by destiny. For the nourishment of the physical form, material things are a necessary prerequisite, but sometimes there is a surplus of things yet the physical form goes unnourished. For there to be life, a necessary prerequisite is that it not be separated from the physical form, but there are instances of nonseparation from the physical form yet life is lost. When life comes, it cannot be refused; when life goes, it cannot be stopped. How sad that the people of the world think that nourishing the physical form is sufficient to preserve life! But when it turns out that nourishing the physical form is insufficient for the preservation of life, what in the world can be done that is sufficient? Although doing things is insufficient, one cannot but do them unless one avoids doing altogether.

If one wishes to avoid doing things for the physical form, there is no better course than to abandon the world. Once one abandons the world, there are no entanglements. When there are no entanglements, there will be correct equanimity. When there is correct equanimity, one will be born again with that. Having been born again, one is close to it. But why is it sufficient to abandon affairs and to be lax about life? By abandoning affairs, the form is not toiled; by being lax about life, the essence is not diminished. When the form is complete and the essence is restored, you become one with heaven. Heaven and earth are the father and mother of the myriad things. When they join, the body is complete; when they disperse, completion begins anew. When the form and the essence are undiminished, this is called adaptability. With the essence of the essence, you return to become the assistant of heaven.

2

Sir Master Lieh inquired of Yin, the Director of the Pass, saying, "The ultimate man can walk under water without drowning, can tread upon fire without feeling hot, and can soar above the myriad things without fear. May I ask how he achieves this?"

"It's because he guards the purity of his vital breath," said Director Yin, "it's not a demonstration of his expertise or daring. Sit down, and I will tell you.

"Whatever has features, images, sound, and color is a thing. How, then, can one thing be distanced from another? And are there sufficient grounds for giving some precedence over others? They are merely forms and color, that is all. But a thing that is created from formlessness may end in nonevolution. How could other things impede someone who attains this in the highest degree? She will dwell in nonexcessiveness, hide in noncausability, and wander where the myriad things have their beginnings and ends. She will unify her nature, nurture her vital breath, and consolidate her integrity so as to communicate with that which creates things. Being like this, she will preserve the wholeness of her heavenly qualities and her spirituality will be flawless, so how could things enter and affect her?

"If a drunk falls from a carriage, even if it is going very fast, he will not die. His bones and joints are the same as those of other people, but the injuries he receives are different. It's because his spirit is whole. He was not aware of getting into the carriage, nor was he aware of falling out of it. Life and death, alarm and fear do not enter his breast. Therefore, he confronts things without apprehension. If someone who has gotten his wholeness from wine is like this, how much more so would one be who gets his wholeness from heaven! The sage hides within his heavenly qualities, thus nothing can harm him. . . ."

3

When Confucius was traveling in Ch'u, he passed through a woods and saw there a hunchback catching cicadas at the end of a long, sticky pole as easily as if he were gathering them up with his hands.

"That's quite a skill you have!" said Confucius. "Is there a special way to do it?"

"I have a way. For five or six months, I practice balancing two pellets at the end of my pole. When I can keep them from falling down, then I'll only lose a small fraction of the cicadas. When I can balance three balls and keep them from falling down, then I'll only lose one cicada in ten. When I can balance five balls and keep them from falling down, then I can gather up the cicadas as easily as if I were using my hands. I position my body as though it were an erect stump with twisted roots. I hold my arms as though they were the branches of a withered tree. The greatness of heaven and earth and the numerousness of the myriad things notwithstanding, I am aware only of the cicada's wings. I neither turn around nor to the side and wouldn't exchange the wings of a cicada for all the myriad things. How can I not succeed?"

Confucius turned to his disciples and said, "In exercising your will, do not let it be diverted; rather, concentrate your spirit. This is the lesson of the hunchback gentleman."

Yen Yüan inquired of Confucius, saying, "When I was crossing the gulf of Goblet Deep, the ferryman handled the boat like a spirit. I asked him about it, saying, 'Can handling a boat be learned?' 'Yes,' said he, 'good swimmers can learn quickly. As for divers, they can handle a boat right away without ever having seen one.' I asked him why this was so, but he didn't tell me. I venture to ask what you think he meant."

"A good swimmer can learn quickly because he forgets about the water," said Confucius. "As for a diver being able to handle a boat right away without ever having seen one, it's because he regards the watery depths as if they were a mound and the capsizing of a boat as if it were the rolling back of a carriage. Capsizing and rolling back could unfold a myriad times before him without affecting his heart, so he is relaxed wherever he goes. He who competes for a piece of tile displays all of his skill; he who competes for a belt buckle gets nervous; he who competes for gold gets flustered. His skill is still the same, but there is something that distracts him and causes him to focus on externals. Whoever focuses on externals will be clumsy inside."

4

T'ien K'aichih was having an interview with Duke Wei of Chou, who said to him, "I have heard that Worthy Invoker is a student of life. What have you heard from Worthy Invoker on the subject while you have wandered about with him?"

"What could I have heard from the master," said T'ien K'aichih, "while waiting upon him in the courtyard with my broom?"

"Do not be polite, Master T'ien," said Duke Wei. "I would like to hear what you have to say."

K'aichih said, "I have heard my master say, 'He who is good at nurturing life is like a shepherd. If he sees one of his sheep lagging behind, he whips it forward.' "

"What did he mean?" asked Duke Wei.

K'aichih said, "In Lu there was a man named Solitary Leopard who dwelled among the cliffs and drank only water. He did not vie with other people for profit. When he turned seventy, his complexion was still like that of an infant. Unfortunately, he encountered a hungry tiger who killed and ate him. There was also a certain Chang Yi who would rush about to call on all the high-ranking families in their houses with hanging door curtains. When he turned forty, he developed enteric fever and died. Leopard nourished his inner being and the tiger ate his outer person. Yi nourished his outer person and sickness attacked his inner being. Both of them failed to whip their laggards forward."

Confucius said,

"Do not withdraw and hide yourself away;
Do not go forth and flaunt yourself.
Stand stock still in the center.
If a person can meet these three conditions,
His fame will certainly be absolute."

As for the dangers of the road, where one person in ten is likely to be murdered, fathers will warn their sons and brothers will warn their brothers that they should venture forth only with a large group of armed retainers. Isn't this sensible? But there are dangers that men are exposed to on their sleeping-mats and while they are eating and drinking, yet no one knows enough to warn them. That is a mistake!

5

The invoker of the ancestors in his black square-cut robes approaches the pigpen and advises the porkers, saying, "Why are you afraid of dying? I will feed you with grain for three months, then I will practice austerities for ten days, fast for three days, spread white rushes on the ground, and place your shoulders and rumps on the carved sacrificial stand. You'll go along with that, won't you?" If he were planning for the porkers, he would say, "It would be better to feed you with chaff and dregs and leave you in your pigpen." Planning for himself, he would prefer to drag out his life with the carriage and cap due to his office and, when he dies, to be borne on an ornamented hearse among feathered wreaths. If he were planning for the porkers he would reject these, but planning for himself he would choose them. Why are his preferences so different from those of the porkers?

6

Duke Huan was hunting in the marshes with Kuan Chung as his charioteer when he saw a ghost. Grabbing hold of Kuan Chung's hand, he asked, "Did you see something, Father Chung?"

"Your servant saw nothing," was the reply.

After the duke returned he babbled incoherently and became ill, so that he did not go out for several days. There was a scholar of Ch'i named Master Leisurely Ramble who said to him, "Your Highness is harming yourself. How could a ghost harm you? If an embolism of vital breath caused by agitation disperses and does not return, what remains will be insufficient; if it rises and does not come back down, it will cause a person to be easily angered; if it descends and does not come back up, it will cause a person to forget easily; if it neither rises nor descends, it will stay in the center of a person's body, clogging his heart, and he will become ill."

"Yes," said Duke Huan, "but are there ghosts?"

"There are. In pits there are pacers; around stoves there are tufties. Fulgurlings frequent dust piles inside the door; croakers and twoads hop about in low-lying places to the northeast; spillsuns frequent low-lying places to the northwest. In water there are nonimagoes; on hills there are scrabblers; on mountains there are unipedes; in the wilds there are will-o'-the-wisps; and in marshes there are bendcrooks."

"May I ask what a bendcrook looks like?" said the duke.

"The bendcrook," said Master Ramble, "is as big around as the hub of a chariot wheel and as long as the shafts. It wears purple clothes and a red cap. This is a creature that hates to hear the sound of rumbling chariots. When it does, it stands up holding its head in its hands. He who sees it is likely to become hegemon."

Duke Huan erupted in laughter and said, "This was what I saw." Whereupon he adjusted his clothing and cap and had Master Ramble sit down with him. Before the day was over, his illness left him without his even being aware of it.

7

Master Recordo Reductio was rearing a gamecock for the king.

After ten days he was asked, "Is your cock ready to fight?"

"Not yet; he's just at the stage of being vainly arrogant and proud of his own vigor."

After ten days he was asked again and he said, "Not yet; he still responds to echoes and shadows."

After ten days he was asked again and he said, "Not yet; his gaze is still too tense and he's too full of energy."

After ten days he was asked again and he said, "Almost. Although another cock might crow, it would effect no change in him. When you look at him, he seems to be a cock made of wood. His integrity is complete. Other cocks dare not meet him, but turn around and run away."

8

Confucius was observing the cataract at Spinebridge where the water fell from a height of thirty fathoms and the mist swirled for forty tricents. No tortoise, alligator, fish, or turtle could swim there. Spotting an older man swimming in the water, Confucius thought that he must have suffered some misfortune and wished to die. So he had his disciples line up along the current to rescue the man. But after the man had gone several hundred yards he came out by himself. With disheveled hair, he was walking along singing and enjoying himself beneath the embankment.

Confucius followed after the man and inquired of him, saying, "I thought you were a ghost, but when I looked more closely I saw that you are a man. May I ask if you have a special way for treading the water?"

"No, I have no special way. I began with what was innate, grew up with my nature, and completed my destiny. I enter the very center of the whirlpools and emerge as a companion of the torrent. I follow along with the way of the water and do not impose myself on it. That's how I do my treading."

"What do you mean by 'began with what was innate, grew up with your nature, and completed your destiny'?" asked Confucius.

"I was born among these hills and feel secure among them—that's what's innate. I grew up in the water and feel secure in it—that's my nature. I do not know why I am like this, yet that's how I am—that's my destiny."

9

Woodworker Ch'ing was carving wood for a bellstand. When the bellstand was completed, all who saw it were as amazed as though they were seeing the work of a spiritual being. The

Marquis of Lu went to see it and inquired of the woodworker, saying, "With what art have you made this?"

"Your subject is merely a workman," was the reply. "What art could I possess? However, there is one thing. When I am getting ready to make a bellstand, I dare not waste any of my energy, so it is necessary to fast in order to calm my mind. After fasting for three days, I no longer presume to harbor any thoughts of congratulations and rewards, of rank and salary. After fasting for five days, I no longer presume to harbor any thoughts of censure or praise, of skill or clumsiness. After fasting for seven days, I abruptly forget that I have four limbs and a body. At that time, I have no thought of public affairs or the court. My skill is concentrated and all external distractions disappear. Only then do I enter the mountain forest and observe the heavenly nature of the trees till I find one of ultimate form. Only after the completed bellstand manifests itself to me do I set my hand to the work. Otherwise, I give up. Thus is heaven joined to heaven. This is what makes one suspect that my instruments were made by a spiritual being."

10

Wane Eastwild was showing off his chariotry to Duke Chuang. His horses went forward and backward as straight as a ruler, turned left and right as precisely as a compass. Duke Chuang thought that even a draftsman could not surpass him. He told him to do one hundred circuits and then return.

Yen Ho happened upon this scene and went in to see the duke, saying, "Wane's horses are going to jade." The duke kept silent and did not respond.

Soon thereafter, Wane's horses actually jaded and had to return early.

"How did you know that would happen?" the duke asked.

"His horses' strength was exhausted, but yet he kept demanding more of them. That's why I said they would jade."

11

Craftsman Ch'ui could draft as accurately freehand as if he were using compass and L-square because his fingers evolved with things and he did not calculate with his mind. Therefore, his numinous terrace remained unified and unfettered.

A shoe fits when you forget about your foot; a belt fits when you forget about your waist; the mind fits when you forget about right and wrong; opportunity fits when there is no internal transformation or external imitation. One who begins with what fits and never experiences what doesn't fit has the fitness that forgets about what fits. . . .

20

THE MOUNTAIN TREE

Master Chuang explains how to get beyond worthiness and worthlessness—abide by the Way and maintain integrity. This lesson is repeated in a succession of well-crafted tales. In current phraseology, we would be advised to "keep a low profile" and "mind your own business." The probable multiple authorship of even this one chapter is evident in the repetition, from three slightly different angles, of the story about Confucius being besieged between the statelets of Ch'en and Ts'ai.

1

Master Chuang was walking in the mountains when he saw a great tree with thick branches and luxuriant foliage. A lumberjack had stopped by its side but did not attempt to fell it. When Master Chuang asked him the reason, he said, "There's nothing that it can be used for."

"This tree has been able to live out the years allotted to it by heaven because it is worthless," said Master Chuang.

After he left the mountain, Master Chuang lodged in the home of an old friend. Delighted, the old friend ordered a boy to kill a goose and cook it. The boy asked for further instructions,

saying, "One of the geese can cackle and the other cannot. Which should I kill?"

"Kill the one that cannot cackle," said the host.

The next day, Master Chuang's disciples inquired of him, saying, "The tree we saw in the mountains yesterday was able to live out the years allotted to it by heaven because it is worthless, but today our host's goose will die because it is worthless. Which of these conditions would you rather be in, master?"

Master Chuang laughed and said, "I suppose I'd rather find myself somewhere between worthlessness and worthiness. But even finding oneself somewhere between worthlessness and worthiness, though it might seem like the right place to be, really isn't because it can't keep you out of trouble. That's not so, however, for someone who, mounted on the Way and integrity, drifts and wanders freely.

> Being neither praised nor rebuked,
> One moment a dragon and the next moment a serpent,
> He evolves together with the times
> And is unwilling to act for his own sake.
> One moment rising and the next moment descending,
> Taking harmony as his measure,

he drifts and wanders with the ancestor of the myriad things. He treats things as things but doesn't let them treat him as a thing. How, then, can he get in trouble? This was the method of the Divine Farmer and the Yellow Emperor. That's not so, however, for those who are concerned with the circumstances of the myriad things and the teachings on human relationships.

> No sooner do they join than they are sundered;
> No sooner do they succeed than they are ruined.
> If they are sharp, they are ground down;
> If they are honored, they are criticized.

Those who are active come up short;
Those who are wise are schemed against;
Those who are unworthy are cheated.

How can they be certain of what will happen to them? Alas! my disciples, remember this: abide only in the Way and integrity."

2

When Yiliao of Southmarket met the Marquis of Lu, the latter had a worried look.

"Why do you have such a worried look?" asked Master Southmarket.

"I have studied the Way of the former kings and have cultivated the inheritance of the former rulers of Lu," said the Marquis of Lu. "I respect the ghosts of the departed and honor men of worth. All this I attend to personally and without being idle for a moment, yet I cannot avoid calamity. That is why I am worried."

"Your techniques for ridding yourself of calamity are shallow," said Master Southmarket. "The thick-furred fox and the elegantly spotted leopard inhabit the mountain forest and lurk in cliffside caves—such is their stillness. At night they move around but during the day they stay at home—such is their caution. Though hungry and thirsty, they keep aloof, preferring instead to range far afield along lakes and rivers in search of food—such is their determination. Yet they cannot avoid the calamity of nets and snares. Where lies the blame? It's their pelts that bring them disaster. Now, is not the state of Lu your lordship's pelt? I would have you strip away your form and peel off your pelt, cleanse your mind and remove your desires, and go wandering in no-man's-land. In Namviet there is a fief called Country of Established Integrity. Its people are ignorant and simple, with little selfishness and few desires. They know how to make things but do not hoard them. They give but do not expect recompense. They know nothing about the application of righteousness and the operation of ceremony. Though they move about randomly as if they were mad, their footsteps follow the great method. Their births are celebrated with joy; their deaths are observed with funerals. I would have you leave your state and renounce common custom, and proceed there under the guidance of the Way."

"The way there must be distant and dangerous," said the lord. "Furthermore, there are rivers and mountains. Since I have no boat or carriage, what should I do?"

Master Southmarket said,

"Do not appear haughty;
Do not be obstinate—
That will be your carriage."

"The way there must be remote and isolated," said the lord. "Who will be my companion? I have no grain or other food. How can I obtain enough to reach there?"

Master Southmarket said, "Diminish your expenditures; decrease your desires—although you have no grain, it will be sufficient. Wade through the estuary and float on the sea, till no matter how hard you gaze you cannot see the shore and the farther your journey takes you the less you know where it will end. Those who escort your lordship to the shore will return. From that point on, you will be distant indeed!

"Thus he who possesses others is tied down with troubles and he who is possessed by others is beset by worries. Hence Yao neither possessed men nor was he possessed by them. I would have your lordship throw off the ties that trouble you, get rid of the worries that beset you, and wander alone with the Way in the land of great Nothingness.

"If someone is crossing a river in a double-hulled vessel and an empty boat comes and strikes against it, even though he may be a quick-tempered person, he will not be angry. But if there is a person in the boat he will shout to him to steer clear. If his first shout goes unheeded, he will shout again. If the second shout goes unheeded, he will shout a third time, and that will certainly be followed by a stream of abuse. In the previous instance he did not get angry but in the present instance he is angry, because the previous boat was empty but this one has a person in it. If a person can empty himself and go wandering in the world, who can harm him?"

3

Prodigal Northpalace was collecting contributions for Duke Ling of Wey to make a set of bells. He built an altar outside the gate of the outer city wall and, in three months, the set was complete even to the hanging of the upper and lower tiers.

Seeing this, Prince Ch'ingchi inquired of him, saying, "What arts did you employ?"

"In the midst of unity," said Prodigal, "I wouldn't dare to employ anything. I have heard it said,

'After all the carving and chiseling,
Return to the simplicity of the unhewn log.'

I was naively nescient,
Ingenuously indolent.
In droves and throngs,
I escorted those who were going,
    and welcomed those who were coming.
Those who wished to come
    were not prohibited;
Those who wished to go
    were not prevented.

I was indulgent with those who were strongly opposed, went along with those who were indecisive, relied on those who did their utmost. Thus I was able to collect contributions morning and evening without meeting with the slightest rebuff. How much more will this be true of one who follows the great path!"

4

When Confucius was besieged in the area between Ch'en and Ts'ai, he went without cooked food for seven days.

The old gentleman Jen went to console him, asking, "Were you close to death?"

"Yes."

"Do you dislike death?"

"Yes."

"Let me try to explain the Way to avoid death," said Jen. "In the Eastern Sea there is a bird named the lazybird. It flip-flops along as if it had no power. The lazybird will only fly when there are others to lead it on and will only roost when there are others that press close to its sides. When it goes forward it dares not take the lead; when it retreats it does not take the rear; when it eats it dares not take the first bite, always preferring to take the leftovers. Therefore, their ranks are seldom broken and outsiders rarely can harm them, hence they escape calamity.

The straight tree is the first to be felled;
The well with sweet water is the first to be exhausted.

You seem intent on ornamenting your knowledge to amaze those who are ignorant and on cultivating your person to highlight those who are vile. You are as ostentatious as if you were walking along holding the sun and moon above you. Hence you do not escape calamity. In the past, I heard a man of great accomplishment say,

'Who is self-assertive has no merit;
Merit that is complete will collapse;
Fame that is complete will decline.'

Who can get rid of merit and fame, and return to be with the masses of men?

He flows with the Way
    but does not rest in brilliance;
Walks with integrity
    but does not dwell in fame.
He is so plain and ordinary
That he may be compared to an imbecile.

He erases his traces and renounces his influence, doing nothing for merit or fame. For this reason he does not blame others, nor is he blamed by others. The ultimate man does not seek renown. Why, sir, do you like it so much?"

"Excellent!" said Confucius, whereupon he bid adieu to his associates, sent his disciples away, and retired to a great marsh. He dressed in skins and haircloth, and ate acorns and chestnuts. He went among animals without disturbing their herds, went among birds without disturbing their flocks. If even birds and animals were not afraid of him, how much less were men!

5

Confucius inquired of Sir Mulberry Thunderclap, saying, "I was twice driven out of Lu, had a tree I was resting under chopped down in Sung, had my traces obliterated in Wey, was impoverished in the capitals of the old Shang duchy and the Chou kingdom, and was besieged in the area between Ch'en and Ts'ai. I have encountered these numerous calamities, my close associates have become increasingly estranged, and my disciples and friends have scattered one after another. Why is this?"

"Haven't you heard about Lin Hui, the man who fled from the state of Chia?" asked Sir Mulberry Thunderclap. "He abandoned his jade disk of office that was worth a thousand pieces of gold and rushed away carrying his infant on his back. Someone asked him, 'Was it for money? But surely the money value of an infant is small. Was it because of the bother? But surely an infant is more bothersome. Why, then, did you abandon your jade disk and rush off carrying your infant on your back?' 'The union between the former and me is one of profit,' said Lin Hui, 'but the relationship between the latter and me is ordained by heaven.' When the union of things is determined by profit and they are pressed by impoverishment, misfortune, calamity, and harm, they will abandon each other; when the relationship of things is ordained by heaven and they are pressed by impoverishment, misfortune, calamity, and harm, they will stick together. Now, sticking together and abandoning each other are far apart indeed! Furthermore,

> The relationships of the gentleman
>   are as flavorless as water,
> While those of the petty person
>   are as sweet as new wine.

But the flavorlessness of the gentleman leads to closeness while the sweetness of the petty person leads to disaffection. A union that is without cause will result in separation without cause."

"I respectfully accept your instructions," said Confucius. Sauntering slowly, he went back to his own home. He cut short his studies and cast aside his books. Though his disciples no longer bowed before him, their love for him increased all the more.

On another day, Mulberry Thunderclap further said to Confucius, "When Shun was on the verge of death, he instructed Yü, saying, 'You must be cautious! For the physical form, nothing is better than compliance; for the emotions, nothing is better than complaisance. If you are compliant, there will be no separation; if you are complaisant, there will be no toil. When there is neither separation nor toil, you need not seek to embellish your physical form so that you may depend on it, and when you seek not to embellish your physical form so that you may depend on it, you will definitely not have to depend on things.' "

6

Master Chuang passed by the King of Wei wearing patched clothing made of coarse cloth and shoes tied together with twine. "How come you're so wretched, master?" asked the King of Wei.

"It's poverty," said Master Chuang, "not wretchedness. When a scholar possesses the Way and integrity but cannot put them into practice, he is wretched. When his clothing is tattered and his shoes have holes in them, he is poor, not wretched. This is called, 'not having met with the right time.' Has your majesty not seen the high-climbing gibbon? When it is on a nanmu, catalpa, or camphor tree, the gibbon grasps the branches with its hands and feet or wraps around them with its tail, moving nimbly among them. Even Yi and P'engmeng would not be able to take accurate aim at it. When, however, the gibbon is on a silkworm thorn, ramosissimus, thorny limebush, or matrimony vine, it moves furtively and glances sideways, shaking and trembling all the while. This is not because the gibbon's sinews and bones have become stiff and lost their suppleness, but because it finds itself in an inconvenient situation and cannot show off its ability. Now, if I am situated under a benighted ruler and confused ministers, and still wish not to be wretched, how could I be so? This is proof that a Pikan might have his heart cut out!"

7

When Confucius was isolated in the area between Ch'en and Ts'ai and had not eaten cooked food for seven days, he leaned against a withered tree with his left hand and, tapping it with a withered branch held in his right hand, sang the ode of the clansman Piao. Although he had an instrument, he couldn't keep the beat; although he had a voice, he couldn't carry the tune. The sound of the wood and the sound of his voice had a peculiarly plaintive effect upon the hearts of those who were listening.

Yen Hui stood respectfully with his hands folded on his chest and turned his eyes around to glance at him. Fearing that Yen Hui would succumb to delusions of grandeur through overesteem for himself and that he would succumb to sorrow through love of himself, Confucius said, "Hui, it is easy not to accept the afflictions of heaven, but it is difficult not to accept the favors of men. There is no beginning that is without an ending; in this the human and the heavenly are identical. Who, for example, was the one who was singing just now?"

"I venture to ask what you mean by 'it is easy not to accept the afflictions of heaven,' " said Hui.

Confucius said, "Hunger, thirst, cold, and heat, and having one's progress shackled—these are due to the operation of heaven and earth and to the discharge of things as they revolve. This is what is meant when we say that everything passes away together. He who is the subject of another man dare not ignore his wishes. If the way of maintaining the status of a subject is like this, how much more so is it true of he who waits upon heaven!"

"What do you mean by 'it is difficult not to accept the favors of men'?"

Confucius said, "When someone is initially employed, he achieves success in all directions. Rank and emoluments arrive together in an unending stream, but these material advantages do not belong to himself. They are what I style 'externals.' The gentleman does not thieve; the man of worth does not steal. If I were to take things, what would I be? Therefore, it is said, no bird is smarter than the swallow. When it spots a place that is unsuitable for it, the swallow does not give a second glance. Although it may drop the berry in its beak, the swallow will abandon it and hurry away. It is afraid of men, yet it finds its own niche among them and builds an altar there."

"What do you mean by 'there is no beginning that is without an ending'?"

Confucius said, "Of that which causes the evolution of the myriad things and the unknown one that brings about their succession, how can we know where they end? How can we know where they begin? We simply must wait for them, and that is all."

"What do you mean by 'the human and the heavenly are identical'?"

Confucius said, "That there is man is because of heaven, and that there is heaven is also because of heaven. That man cannot possess heaven is because of his nature. The body of the sage placidly passes away, and that is the end of it."

8

Chuang Chou was wandering in the park at Eagle Mound when he saw a strange magpie coming from the south. Its wingspan was seven feet and its eyes were one inch in diameter. It brushed against Chou's forehead and then alighted in a chestnut grove. "What kind of bird is this?" asked Chuang Chou. "Its wings are huge but it doesn't fly very far; its eyes are big but it doesn't see very clearly." He gathered up his skirts and strode over to it. Raising his pellet bow, he waited for the right moment. He saw a cicada that had just found a nice, shady spot and had forgotten all about protecting its own body. A praying mantis raised its forelegs and seized the cicada. Seeing only its prey, the mantis had forgotten to protect its own physical form. The strange magpie consequently took advantage of the situation. Seeing only its advantage, the magpie forgot its true being.

Startled, Chuang Chou said, "Ai! Things indeed bring trouble to each other, one creature inviting calamity from another." He cast aside his pellet bow and hurried back, a scolding park watchman in pursuit.

When Chuang Chou returned home, he went inside and stayed there unhappily for three days. In attendance upon him, Lin Chü asked, "Master, why have you been so unhappy recently?"

Chuang Chou said, "I have been guarding my physical form but forgotten about my body; I have been observing the turbid water but am oblivious to the clear depths. Furthermore, I have heard my master say, 'When in a place where certain customs prevail, follow the rules of that place.' Now, as I was wandering at Eagle Mound, I forgot about my body. A strange magpie brushed against my forehead and, wandering in the chestnut grove, forgot about its true being. The watchman of the chestnut grove considered me a poacher. That's why I am unhappy."

9

On his way to Sung, Master Yang spent a night at an inn. The innkeeper had two concubines, one beautiful and one ugly, but he prized the ugly one and despised the beautiful one. Master Yang asked the reason and was told by a little boy at the inn, "The beautiful one is so much aware of her own beauty that we ignore it; the ugly one is so much aware of her own ugliness that we ignore it."

Master Yang said, "Remember this, my disciples! If you behave worthily but put aside all thoughts of your own worthiness, where can you go that you will not be loved?"

21

SIR SQUARE FIELD

In this chapter, full of the insights of gurus and pandits revealed to supplicating students, Confucius is sometimes cast in the role of the former, sometimes in the role of the latter. The true wise man, unlike conventional literati, is not concerned about his external appearance, social etiquette, or eloquence. The ultimate man exists in another realm altogether.

1

Sir Square Field was sitting in attendance upon Marquis Wen of Wei. Several times he praised Gorge Worker.

"Is Gorge Worker your teacher?" asked Marquis Wen.

"No," said Sir Square, "he just lives in the same village with me. When he talks about the Way, he is often right on the mark, so I praised him."

"Then you don't have any teacher?" asked Marquis Wen.

"I have one," said Sir Square.

"Who's your teacher?"

"Sir Accord of Easturb," said Sir Square.

"Well, then," said Marquis Wen, "why haven't you praised him?"

"As a person," said Sir Square, "he is true. He has the appearance of a human but the emptiness of heaven. Through compliance he preserves the truth, through purity he accommodates things. Should things be without the Way, he rectifies his countenance to enlighten them, thereby causing human ideas to disappear. How could I be fit to praise him?"

After Sir Square went out, Marquis Wen spent the rest of the day in a state of dumb uncertainty. Then he summoned before him the officials who were standing on duty and said to them, "How far we are from the gentleman of complete integrity. At first I considered the words of the sages and the wise men, the practice of humaneness and righteousness to be the ultimate. But now that I have heard about Sir Square's teacher, my physical form is unstrung and I have no desire to move; my mouth is clamped shut and I have no desire to speak. What I have emulated is only an earthen image, and the state of Wei has truly been an encumbrance to me."

2

When Master Uncle Warmsnow was on a journey to Ch'i, he stopped off for a while in Lu. While there, a man of Lu requested an interview with him. "He cannot have one," said Master Uncle Warmsnow. "I've heard that the gentlemen of the Middle Kingdom are clear about ceremony and righteousness but that they are woefully ignorant of the human heart. I don't want to see him."

After he had gone to Ch'i, he stopped off in Lu on his way back, and the same man requested an interview again. Master Uncle Warmsnow said, "When I was on my way to Ch'i he sought an interview with me, and now he is seeking an interview with me again. He must have some means by which he thinks to rescue me."

He went out to see the guest and when he came back in he sighed. The next day when he came back in after seeing the guest he sighed again. "Why is it," asked his servant, "that every day after seeing this guest, you come back in and sigh?"

"As I told you before, 'the people of the Middle Kingdom are clear about ceremony and righteousness, but they are woefully ignorant of the human heart.' The man who has come to see me these past few days entered and withdrew as punctiliously as though he were completing a circle or a square. His demeanor was now like that of a dragon, now like that of a tiger. He remonstrated with me as though he were my son; he guided me as though he were my father. That's why I sighed."

When Confucius saw Warmsnow, he did not say a word. Tzulu said, "Master, you have long wanted to see Master Uncle Warmsnow, but now that you have seen him you didn't say a word. Why?"

"As soon as my eyes came in contact with that man," said Confucius, "I felt that I was in the presence of the Way. There was simply no room for me to make a sound."

3

Yen Yüan inquired of Confucius, saying, "When you pace, I also pace; when you rush, I also rush; when you race, I also race; but when you run so fast that you outstrip the dust, I am left behind staring at you blankly."

"Hui, what do you mean?" asked the master.

"By 'when you pace, I also pace,' I meant that when you speak, I also speak. By 'when you rush, I also rush,' I meant that when you dispute, I also dispute. By 'when you race, I also race,' I meant that when you speak of the Way, I also speak of the Way. And by 'when you run so fast that you outstrip the dust, I am left behind staring at you blankly,' I meant that you are believed even when you don't speak; that you encompass all without partiality; and that, although you do not possess the implements of state, the people throng before you—yet I do not know at all how this can be so."

"Ah!" said Confucius. "We'd better examine this more care-fully! Now, there is no greater sadness than the death of the mind—the death of the person is secondary. The sun comes up in the east and sets in the western extremities, all the myriad things orienting themselves accordingly. Those that have eyes and toes complete their tasks only after waiting upon it. When it comes out they are preserved; when it goes in they disappear. It's the same with the myriad things: there is that upon which they wait before dying and that upon which they wait before being born. Once I have received my complete physical form, I remain unchanged while I await extinction. I move in imitation of things day and night without a break, not knowing where it will end. From gathering wisps our physical form is completed and, though we may know destiny, we cannot perceive its antecedents. Thus do I pass on day after day.

"I have spent my whole life in bosom friendship with you, and yet you have missed this. Is it not sad? You have probably noted what I have noted, but that is already finished. Yet you go seeking for it as though it still existed, which is like seeking for a horse in a deserted marketplace. I have been quite forgetful in my service to you, and you have been quite forgetful in your service to me. Nevertheless, why should you be so troubled by this? Although you may forget the old me, there still exists something about me that cannot be forgotten."

4

Confucius went to see Old Longears, who had just finished shampooing and was disheveling his hair so it could dry. He was so absorbed that he seemed inhuman. Confucius waited on him off to the side for a while and then went over to introduce himself. "Were my eyes deceiving me? Or were you really like that? Just now your physical body was stiff as a withered tree, sir. You seemed to have left everything behind, parted company with humanity, and were standing there in solitude."

"I was letting my mind wander in the origin of things," said Old Longears.

"What do you mean?" asked Confucius.

"The mind is so confined that one cannot know it; the tongue is so tied that one cannot tell of it. But I shall try to describe it for you roughly.

"The ultimate yin is austere; the ultimate yang is dazzling. Austerity comes forth from earth and dazzlement issues from heaven. When these two are in communication, harmony is achieved and things are born. Perhaps there is something regulating this, but no one has seen its form. Dissolution and generation, fullness and emptiness, now dark, now bright; the sun shifts and the moon evolves—daily this process goes on, but no one sees its effect. Birth has that from which it sprouts; death has that to which it returns. Beginning and ending are opposed to each other in randomness, but no one knows where they conclude. If it is not like this, then who is the ancestor of it all?"

"May I ask how you let your mind wander in this realm?" said Confucius.

"The attainment of this," said Old Longears, "is the ultimate beauty and the ultimate joy. She who attains ultimate beauty and wanders in ultimate joy is called the ultimate woman."

"I would like to hear about your method," said Confucius.

"Herbivorous animals are not vexed by a change of pasture; aqueous insects are not vexed by a change of water. This is because a small transformation is carried out without the loss of a greater constant, so that pleasure, anger, sorrow, and joy will not enter the breast. It is under heaven that the myriad things are unified. When they achieve unity and share it equally, their four limbs and hundred members of the body become so much dust and dirt; death and life, ending and beginning become as day and night; none of this can confound them, and much less can the distinctions between gain and loss, between misfortune and fortune. Abandoning subject status is like abandoning a clump of mud, because one knows that one's person is more valued than the subject status. Value lies in oneself and is not lost by a change of status. Since there are myriad transformations that never begin to reach a limit, which of them is sufficient to trouble the mind? He who is already a doer of the Way comprehends this."

Confucius said, "Your integrity is a companion of heaven and earth, Master, yet you borrow ultimate words to cultivate the mind. Were there any gentlemen of antiquity who could get beyond this?"

"No," said Old Longears. "The babbling of water is its natural quality, not an intentional act. The relationship of the ultimate man to integrity is similar in that nothing can escape its influence though he does not cultivate it. He is like heaven which is naturally high; like earth which is naturally substantial; and like the sun and moon which are naturally bright. What need is there for him to cultivate it?"

Confucius went out and reported what he had heard to Yen Hui, saying, "Is not my relationship to the Way like that of a bug in a vat of vinegar? Had the master not lifted up the lid, I would not have known the great perfection of heaven and earth."

5

When Master Chuang had an interview with Duke Ai of Lu, the duke said, "There are many literati in Lu, but few of them practice your methods."

"There are few literati in Lu," said Master Chuang.

"Throughout the state of Lu there are people wearing literati garb," said Duke Ai. "What do you mean, 'there are few'?"

"I have heard," said Master Chuang, "that the literatus wears a round cap to signify that he knows the seasons of heaven; that he wears square sandals to signify that he knows the forms of earth; and that he ties at his waist a pendant shaped like a slotted ring to signify that he decisively handles affairs which come to him. But the gentleman who possesses a particular way does not necessarily wear a particular garb, and the person who wears a particular garb does not necessarily know a particular way. Since your highness obviously thinks this is not so, why don't you issue this proclamation throughout the land? 'Whoever wears a particular garb without possessing the particular way that it signifies will be guilty of a capital offense.' "

Thereupon Duke Ai issued the proclamation and, within five days, there were no more people who dared to wear literati garb, except for a single old man who stood at the duke's gate. The duke summoned him immediately and asked him about affairs of state. Although their conversation took a multitude of twists and turns, the duke could not exhaust his knowledge.

Master Chuang asked, "If there is only one person in the state of Lu who is a literatus, can we say that there are 'many'?"

6

Ranks and salaries did not enter the mind of Poli Hsi. Therefore, when he fed cattle, the cattle got fat, which caused Duke Mu of Ch'in to forget his lowly position and turn over the government to him. Life and death did not enter the mind of the clansman of the freehold at Yü, therefore he was able to move others.

7

Lord Yüan of Sung wished to have some charts drawn. A crowd of clerks arrived and, after receiving their instructions and bowing, they stood in line licking their brushes and mixing their ink. There were so many that half of them remained outside. There was one clerk who arrived late, casually and without hurrying. He received his instructions and bowed, but did not stand in line, returning instead to his dormitory. When the duke sent someone to look in on him, he was found half-naked, with his shirt off, sitting with his legs splayed out. "He will do," said the lord. "This is a true draftsman."

8

King Wen was sightseeing at Tsang when he spotted an old man fishing with a line, but the line had no hook. He was not one of those who insists that his fishing line has to have a fishhook, thus his was an eternal fishing.

King Wen wished to elevate him to office and hand over the government to him, but was afraid that his high officers and his seniors would be uneasy. Then he wished to stop thinking about the man and leave him alone, but he could not bear to let the hundred clans be without such a heaven-sent guardian. Therefore, the next morning he called together his great officers and said to them, "Last night I dreamed I saw a man with a swarthy complexion and a beard. He was riding a piebald horse whose hooves were crimson on one side. 'Entrust your government to the old man from Tsang,' he cried out, 'so that the people may be cured!' "

"It was your late father, the king," said the great officers in astonishment.

"If so, then let us divine the matter," said King Wen.

"Since it is the order of your late father," said the great officers, "you need not consider anything else. Why should you divine the matter?"

Whereupon the king welcomed the old man of Tsang to his court and handed over the government to him. The statutes and laws remained unchanged and no unjust directives were issued. After three years King Wen toured the country and found that the ranks of the officials had destroyed their factions and disbanded their cliques, that senior officers did not flaunt their virtue, and that no one dared to bring odd-sized measurements inside the four borders. When the ranks of the officials had destroyed their factions and disbanded their cliques, they began to emphasize cooperation; when the senior officers did not flaunt their virtue, they began to devote their attention to the common good; when no one dared to bring odd-sized measurements inside the four borders, the feudal lords began to cease their duplicity.

Thereupon King Wen appointed him Grand Preceptor. Facing north, he asked, "Can my government be extended to all under heaven?" The old man from Tsang was so oblivious that he did not respond except to decline vaguely. In the morning he was still in charge, but by nightfall he had vanished, never to be heard from for the rest of his life.

Yen Yüan inquired of Confucius, saying, "Was not even King Wen up to it? And why did he have to resort to a dream?"

"Be silent!" said Confucius. "Don't say a word! King Wen had reached perfection. How can you criticize him? He only used it as a momentary expedient."

9

Lieh Yük'ou was demonstrating his archery for Uncle Obscure Nobody. He drew the bow to its full extent, had someone place a cup of water on his elbow, and released the string. No sooner had he shot the first arrow than he nocked another, and as soon as he shot the second arrow another was lodged on the nocking point. All the while he stood like a statue.

Uncle Obscure Nobody said, "This is the archery of an archer, not the archery of a nonarcher. Let's climb a high mountain and clamber over steep rocks till we overlook a chasm one hundred fathoms deep. Will you be able to shoot then?"

Thereupon Nobody and Yük'ou climbed a high mountain and clambered over steep rocks until they were overlooking a chasm one hundred fathoms deep. Nobody inched out backward so that his feet were halfway over the edge. He bowed to Yük'ou and invited him to come forward, but Yük'ou had fallen prostrate on the ground, with sweat dripping down to his heels.

"The ultimate man," said Uncle Obscure Nobody, "peers into the cerulean sky above and descends into the Yellow Springs below. Though he roams to the eight ends of the universe, his

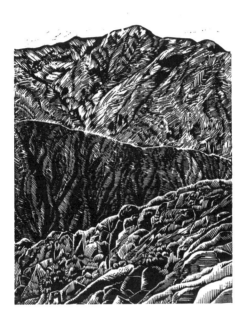

spirit and vitality undergo no transformation. But now the timorousness of your will shows in your dazed eyes. Your inner state of being is in peril!"

10

Chien Wu inquired of Sun Shu'ao, saying, "Three times you were made chief minister but didn't feel that it was glorious; three times you were dismissed but didn't appear dejected. At first I was suspicious of you, but now I see that the breath from your nostrils is relaxed. Just how is it that you apply your mind?"

"In what manner do I surpass other men?" asked Sun Shu'ao. "When the position came to me, I thought that I could not refuse it; when it was taken away from me, I thought that I could not prevent it. I believed that gaining or losing the position was not up to me, so I didn't appear dejected, that's all. In what manner do I surpass other men? Furthermore, I didn't know whether the honor had to do with the position or with me. If it had to do with the position, then it had nothing to do with me. If it had to do with me, then it had nothing to do with the position. I'm about to go sauntering off and gazing in the four directions; what leisure do I have to care whether people honor or despise me?"

Confucius heard of this and said, "The true man of old could not be persuaded by those who are cunning, could not be seduced by beautiful women, could not be plundered by robbers, could not be befriended by Fuhsi and the Yellow Emperor. Life and death are of great moment, but they could effect no transformation upon him, how much less rank and salary? This being so, his spirit might pass over a great mountain without impediment, enter a deep spring without getting wet, dwell in humble circumstances without feeling wretched. He was filled with heaven and earth, so that the more he gave to others, the more he had for himself."

11

The King of Ch'u was sitting with the Lord of Fan. After a short while, the attendants of the king repeated three times that Fan would be destroyed. "The destruction of Fan," said the Lord of Fan, "is not sufficient to destroy what I aim to preserve. Now, if 'the destruction of Fan is not sufficient to destroy what I aim to preserve,' then the preservation of Ch'u is not sufficient to preserve what it wishes to preserve. Viewed from this vantage, Fan has not begun to be destroyed and Ch'u has not begun to be preserved."

22

KNOWLEDGE WANDERS NORTH

Proceeding with the theme of the ineloquence, indeed ineffability, of true wisdom, the author of this long chapter emphasizes nonaction and unity with the vital breath of the universe. The omnipresent, eternal Way can only be hinted at; it cannot be encompassed by knowledge or defined by argument. The best way to experience it is just to go awandering.

1

Knowledge wandered north to the banks of the Dark Water, where he climbed the hill of Obscure Prominence and happened to meet Dumb Nonaction. Knowledge said to Dumb Nonaction, "I have some questions I wish to ask you. By what thought and what reflection may we know the Way? Where shall we dwell and how shall we serve so that we may be secure in the Way? From what point of departure and by what way may we attain the Way?" He asked three questions and still Dumb Nonaction did not answer. Not only did he not answer, he did not know how to answer.

Being unsuccessful with his questions, Knowledge went back south to White Water, where he climbed up Solitary Confine and caught sight of Mad Stammerer. Knowledge asked the same questions of Mad Stammerer. "Ah!" said Mad Stammerer. "I know the answers and will tell you." But right when he started to speak, he forgot what he wanted to say.

Being unsuccessful with his questions, Knowledge went back to the imperial palace where he saw the Yellow Emperor and asked him the questions.

The Yellow Emperor said, "Don't think and don't reflect—only then may you begin to know the Way. Don't dwell and don't serve—only then may you begin to be secure in the Way. Have no departure and no way—only then may you begin to attain the Way."

Knowledge asked the Yellow Emperor, saying, "You and I know the answers, but those two do not. Who's right?"

The Yellow Emperor said, "It's Dumb Nonaction who's truly right. Mad Stammerer seems like he is, but you and I come last and are not even close. Now,

> One who knows does not speak;
> One who speaks does not know.

Therefore, the sage practices a doctrine without words. The Way cannot be compelled and integrity cannot be forced. Humaneness may be practiced; righteousness may be slighted; but ceremony is for being false to one another. Therefore, it is said,

> 'When the Way is lost,
>   afterward comes integrity.
> When integrity is lost,
>   afterward comes humaneness.
> When humaneness is lost,
>   afterward comes righteousness.
> When righteousness is lost,
>   afterward comes ceremony.

> Ceremony is but the blossomy ornament of the Way,
> and the source of disorder.'

Therefore, it is said,
> 'The practice of the Way results in daily decrease.
> Decrease and again decrease,
> Until you reach nonaction.
> Through nonaction,
> No action is left undone.'

Now, is it not difficult for what has already become a thing to return to its roots? Could anyone but the great man find it easy?

"For life is the disciple of death and death is the beginning of life. Who knows their regulator? Human life is the coalescence of vital breath. When it coalesces there is life; when it dissipates there is death. Since life and death are disciples of each other, how should I be troubled by them? Thus the myriad things are a unity. What makes the one beautiful is its spirit and wonder; what makes the other loathsome is its stench and putrefaction. But stench and putrefaction evolve into spirit and wonder, and spirit and wonder evolve once again into stench and putrefaction. Therefore it is said, 'A unitary vital breath pervades all under heaven.' Hence the sage values unity."

Knowledge said to the Yellow Emperor, "When I asked Dumb Nonaction and he didn't respond, not only didn't he respond, he didn't know how to respond. When I asked Mad Stammerer and he didn't tell me just when he was starting to do so, not only didn't he tell me, he forgot the questions just when he was starting to do so. Now, when I asked you, you knew the answers. Why did you say you weren't even close?"

"The reason Dumb Nonaction was truly right," said the Yellow Emperor, "is because he didn't know. The reason Mad Stammerer seemed to be right is because he forgot. The reason you and I came last and were not even close is because we knew."

Mad Stammerer heard of this and considered the Yellow Emperor someone who knew how to speak.

2

Heaven and earth have great beauty but do not speak; the four seasons have a clear law but do not deliberate; the myriad things have a complete principle but do not explain. The sage is one who probes the beauties of heaven and earth and comprehends the principles of the myriad things. Hence the ultimate man does not act and the great sage makes nothing, which is to say that they observe heaven and earth.

Now, the spiritual intelligence of heaven and earth is the ultimate essence that undergoes hundreds of evolutions with things. Things in all of their dying and living, their squareness and roundness, know not their roots, yet surely they have existed for all eternity in their ubiquitousness. The six reaches of the universe are enormous, but they cannot get beyond the spirit of heaven and earth. A downy hair of autumn is small, but it depends on the spirit of heaven and earth for its embodiment. There is nothing under heaven that does not wax and wane and that remains immutable throughout its existence. Yin and yang and the four seasons revolve in their courses, each in its own proper order. Dully, the spirit of heaven and earth seems nonexistent yet it persists; smoothly it inspirits without assuming a form of its own. It rears the myriad things, but they are unaware. This is called the root and the source; through it we may observe heaven.

3

Gnaw Gap asked Wearcoat about the Way. Wearcoat said, "If you

> Rectify your physical form
>   and unify your vision,
> Heavenly harmony will arrive;
> Gather in your knowledge
>   and unify your consciousness,

The spirit will come to take up its abode.
Integrity will beautify you;
The Way will reside in you.
You will look at things with the eyes
                    of a newborn calf
    Who does not seek out their causes."

Before Wearcoat had finished speaking, Gnaw Gap had already fallen fast asleep. Wearcoat was greatly pleased and went away singing this song:

"His form is like a withered carcass,
His mind is like dead ashes;
He verifies his real knowledge,
But doesn't insist on his own reasoning.
Obscure and dim,
In his mindlessness, you can't consult with him.
What kind of man is he?"

4

Shun inquired of his aide, saying, "Can one obtain the Way and then possess it?"

"You don't even possess your own body. How could you obtain the Way and possess it?"

"If I do not possess my own body," asked Shun, "then who does possess it?"

"It is a form entrusted to you by heaven and earth. Nor do you possess your life which is a harmony entrusted to you by heaven and earth. Nor do you possess your nature and destiny which are entrusted to you by heaven and earth to follow. Nor do you possess your descendants who are cast-off skins entrusted to you by heaven and earth. Therefore, when you walk you don't know where you're going; when you stay in one place you don't know what you're clinging to; and when you eat you don't know what you're tasting. These are all due to the powerful vital breath of heaven and earth, so how could one obtain and possess them?"

5

Confucius inquired of Old Longears, saying, "Today we are at leisure, so I venture to ask about the ultimate Way."

Old Longears said, "You must fast so as to cleanse your mind, purify your spiritual essence, and purge your knowledge. The Way is profound and difficult to describe, but I shall give you a rough outline of it.

> Luminosity is produced from darkness,
> Differentiation is produced from formlessness,
> Essence is produced from the Way,
> Basic form is produced from essence,
> And the myriad things
>> produce each other through their forms.

Therefore,
> Those with nine orifices are womb-born,
> Those with eight orifices are egg-born.

The Way
> Comes without a trace,
> Goes without a horizon,
> Has neither gate nor house,
> Extends majestically
>> in all four directions.

Those who encounter it have
> Strong limbs,
> Expansive thoughts,
> Keen hearing,
>> and clear eyesight.
> Using their minds is not toilsome;

Without it,

> Heaven would not be high,
> Earth would not be broad,
> The sun and moon would not progress,
> The myriad things would not prosper.

Is this not the Way?

"Furthermore, erudition does not necessarily imply knowledge and disputation does not necessarily imply wisdom, so the sage severs himself from them. That which may be added to without increasing and subtracted from without decreasing is what the sage protects. Deep as the ocean, towering as a mountain, it comes to an end then starts all over again. In full measure, it conveys the myriad things without neglecting any of them. (The way of the superior man, however, has to do with externals, does it not?) The myriad things all go to it for their sustenance yet there is no deficiency. Is this not the Way?

"Here is a man of the Middle Kingdom who is neither yin nor yang and who dwells between heaven and earth. For the moment he is a man, but he will return to the source. Viewed from the root, life is a mere effervescence of things. Although one may have a long life or a premature death, there's not much difference between them. One might say that it is only a matter of moments, surely insufficient to determine whether Yao is right and Chieh is wrong.

"Fructiferous plants have their principles and human relationships, though difficult, have that whereby they mesh. When the sage encounters affairs, he does not go against them; when he passes beyond them, he does not maintain them. To respond to things through adjustment is integrity; to respond to things as a companion is the Way. It was thus that the emperors thrived and the kings arose.

"Man's life between heaven and earth is like a white colt passing a crack in the wall—suddenly it's finished. Rapidly surging, all things come forth; smoothly subsiding, all things reenter. Having evolved they are born, then they evolve again and are dead. Living things are sorrowed by it; mankind is saddened by it. But it's only the untying of a heavenly bow-case, the emptying of a heavenly book-bag. With a flurry and a flourish, the animus and the anima depart, and then the body follows. This is the great returning!

"From formlessness to form, from form to formlessness—this is known to all men in common, but not something to which one who will attain the Way attends. This is something which is discussed by the masses of men in common, but he who attains it does not discuss it, and those who discuss it do not attain it. Even the clear-sighted do not encounter it, so better to remain silent than dispute over it. The Way cannot be heard, so better to stop up your ears than listen for it. This is what is meant by the great obtainment."

6

Master Easturb inquired of Master Chuang, saying, "Where is the so-called Way present?"

"There's no place that it is not present," said Master Chuang.

"Give me an example so that I can get an idea," said Master Easturb.

"It's in ants," said Master Chuang.

"How can it be so low?"

"It's in panic grass."

"How can it be still lower?"

"It's in tiles and shards."

"How can it be still lower?"

"It's in shit and piss."

Master Easturb did not respond. "Your questions," said Master Chuang, "did not touch the substance of the matter. When the superintendent of markets asked the manager of a market why he stepped on hogs, he was told that the deeper the foot sinks the fatter they are. Just don't try to be so specific, because there's no escape from things. The ultimate Way is like this, as are great words. 'All-around,' 'everywhere,' and 'all-inclusive' are three different names for the same reality. They all indicate unity.

"Let's go wandering in the Never-never Palace where we'll join in mutual discussion that will be endless. Let's participate in nonaction—how placid and quiet we'd be! how still and pure! how in tune and at ease! How vacuous our wills would be! We'd go without knowing where we'd reach; we'd come without knowing where we'd stop. Then after we had gone and come, we wouldn't know where we'd end up. We'll go roaming in vacancy. Great knowledge would enter in without our knowing when it would be exhausted.

"That which makes things has no boundaries with things, but for things to have boundaries is what we mean by saying 'the boundaries between things.' The boundaryless boundary is the boundary without a boundary.

"We speak of fullness and emptiness, of decline and decay, but that which causes fullness and emptiness is neither full nor empty, and that which causes decline and decay neither declines nor decays. That which produces the roots and the tips is neither root nor tip, and that which causes things to accumulate and disperse neither accumulates nor disperses."

7

Pretty Lilysweet and the Divine Farmer were studying together under Old Lucky Dragon. The Divine Farmer had closed his door and was leaning against his low table taking a nap. At midday Pretty Lilysweet burst open the door and entered, saying, "Old Dragon is dead!" Leaning against his staff, the Divine Farmer got up and then, throwing away the staff with a clatter, he laughed and said, "Heaven knew how uncouth and brash I am, so he abandoned me and died. It's all over. The master did not leave behind any of his 'mad' words to inspire me before he died."

Hearing this, Covercrock Condole said, "All the gentlemen

under heaven attach themselves to one who embodies the Way. Now, even those who do not occupy so much as one ten thousandth of the tip of a downy hair at the end of autumn, when it comes to the Way, still know enough to hide their 'mad' words when they die. How much more so would one who embodies the Way! We look for it, but it is formless; we listen for it, but it is soundless. Those who discuss it for others say that it is darkest darkness, but the way that is discussed is not the Way."

Thereupon Exalted Purity inquired of Infinity, saying, "Do you know the Way?"

"I don't know it," said Infinity.

And he asked the same question of Nonaction.

"I know it," said Nonaction.

"Can you enumerate various points about the Way that you know?"

"I can."

"What are they?"

Nonaction said, "I know that the Way can be valued and that it can be despised, that it can be constrained and that it can be dispersed. These are the various points which I know about the Way."

Exalted Purity went with these words to Nonbeginning and inquired, saying, "This being so, between Infinity's not knowing and Nonaction's knowing, who was right and who was wrong?"

Nonbeginning said, "Not knowing is deep and knowing is shallow; not knowing has to do with what's intrinsic, knowing has to do with what's extrinsic."

Thereupon Exalted Purity looked up and sighed, saying, "Then not to know is to know? To know is not to know? Who knows the knowing of not knowing?"

Nonbeginning said, "The Way cannot be heard, for what is heard is not the Way; the Way cannot be seen, for what is seen is not the Way; the Way cannot be spoken, for what is spoken is not the Way. Do you know the formlessness of that which gives form to form? The Way does not correspond to any name."

Nonbeginning said, "He who responds when asked about the Way does not know the Way. Thus, although one may ask about the Way, he doesn't learn anything about it. For the Way is not to be asked about, and questions about the Way are not to be answered. If one asks what is not to be asked about, the question is futile. If one answers what is not to be answered, the answer is inane. In this fashion, those who counter futility with inanity are unobservant of the universe without and unaware of the great origin within. Thus they cannot pass over K'unlun and wander in grand emptiness."

8

Resplendent Light inquired of Nonexistent Existence, saying, "Master, do you exist or do you not exist?"

Not getting an answer to his question, Resplendent Light looked at the other's sunken, hollow appearance intently. For a whole day, he looked at him but couldn't see him, listened to him but couldn't hear him, groped for him but couldn't grasp him.

"The ultimate!" said Resplendent Light. "Who else could attain such a state? I can conceive of the existence of nonexistence, but not of the nonexistence of nonexistence. And when it comes to the nonexistence of existence, how could one attain such a state?"

9

The forger of hooks for the minister of war was already eighty years old, but he hadn't lost an ounce of his ability.

The minister of war asked him, "Is it because of your skill? Or do you have a way?"

"It's because of what your subject guards. When I was twenty, I already liked to forge hooks. I didn't look at anything else. If it wasn't a hook, I didn't pay any attention to it."

His competence at forging hooks was premised upon his

incompetence in other areas. Thus was he able to maintain his competence for such a long period of time. How much more so is this the case with someone who is not incompetent! All things will avail themselves of him.

10

Jan Ch'iu inquired of Confucius, saying, "Can we know what it was like before there were heaven and earth?"

"Yes," said Confucius, "it was the same in the past as it is in the present."

Jan Ch'iu lost the train of his question and withdrew. The next day he came to see Confucius again and said, "Yesterday I asked 'Can we know what it was like before there was heaven and earth?' and you said 'Yes, it was the same in the past as it is in the present.' Yesterday I thought I understood you clearly, but now I feel muddled. I venture to ask what you meant, master."

Confucius said, "Yesterday you thought you understood clearly because your spirit anticipated my reply. Today you feel muddled, however, because you are seeking to understand with your nonspiritual side. There is neither past nor present, neither beginning nor end. Is it conceivable that there could be one generation of descendants unless there were an earlier generation of descendants?"

Jan Ch'iu did not reply.

"Enough!" said Confucius. "You needn't respond. We cannot enliven death with life, we cannot deathify life with death. Are death and life counterposed? There is that which embodies both of them as a unity. Is there something that was born before heaven and earth? That which makes things things is not a thing. Things that are produced cannot be prior to all other things, for there is still that which makes them things; and this state of there still being that which makes them things is unending. The idea that the sage's love for man is forever unending is also modeled on this."

11

Yen Yüan inquired of Confucius, saying, "Master, I have heard you say, 'Do not give grounds for being sent off and do not give grounds for being welcomed.' I venture to ask what sort of wandering this is."

Confucius said, "The men of antiquity transformed outwardly but not inwardly. The men of today transform inwardly but not outwardly. He who transforms along with things has a unity that does not transform. Secure in transformation and in nontransformation, secure in mutual jostling with things, he will surely not turn away from them. The clansman Hsiwei's park, the Yellow Emperor's garden, the clansman of the freehold at Yü's palace, and the chambers of T'ang and Wu. The superior men of antiquity, such as the teachers of the literati and of the Mohists, obstinately pulverized each other over who was right and who wrong. How much more is this so of the men of today! The sage accommodates himself to things and does not injure them. He who does not injure things cannot be injured by things. Only he who is not injurable can send off and welcome others.

"Ah, the mountain forests and the hilly uplands! How happy and joyful they make me! But before my joy is finished, it is succeeded by sorrow. I cannot prevent the coming of sorrow and joy, nor can I stop their going. How sad that the people of the world are only inns for things! They understand what they meet, but they do not understand what they do not meet. They can do what they are capable of, but they cannot do what they are incapable of. Lack of understanding and lack of capability are indeed unavoidable for men. For them assiduously to avoid that which men cannot avoid, is this not also sad? Ultimate speech is to be rid of speech; ultimate action is to be rid of action. How shallow it is to equate all the understanding that can be understood!"

MISCELLANEOUS
CHAPTERS

23

KENGSANG CH'U

An unusual chapter in displaying great narrative unity despite considerable length and complexity of content, it strives to embrace the major concerns of the Outer Chapters while touching upon many of the subjects that will be treated more fully in succeeding chapters and even going back to some of the issues discussed in the Inner Chapters. It thus serves as a transitional springboard into the Miscellaneous Chapters and an encapsulation of the whole book.

1

Among the servants of Old Longears, there was a Kengsang Ch'u who had gotten a partial understanding of the Way of Old Longears. With it, he went north to dwell in the Jagged Mountains. He dismissed his attendants who were ostentatiously knowledgeable and distanced himself from his concubines who were insistently humane. He dwelled with rustics and made busy bees his servants. After he had dwelled there for three years, there was a great harvest at Jagged. The people of Jagged said to each other, "When Master Kengsang first came, we were startled by his strangeness. Now, when we estimated him by the day, he was inadequate, but when we estimate him by the year, he's more than enough. Indeed, he's virtually a sage! Why don't you invoke him as our impersonator of the dead and build an altar to him as our god of the land and grain?"

When Master Kengsang heard this, he sat facing south feeling preoccupied. Master Kengsang's disciples considered this strange, but he said to them, "Why, my disciples, should you consider this strange of me?

> The vital breath of spring arises
>> and the hundred grasses are born;
> The height of autumn arrives
>> and the myriad treasures ripen.

Are spring and autumn like this for no reason? It's because of the operation of the Way of heaven. I have heard that the ultimate man dwells quietly as a corpse within the surrounding walls of his room, while the common people rush about madly without knowing where they are going. Now the petty people of Jagged presumptuously wish to make offerings to me along with the wise men. Am I a man to be held up as such a paragon? That is why I am perplexed by the words of Old Longears."

"Not so," said his disciples. "Huge fish have no room to turn their bodies around in a ditch that is a few yards wide, but mud loaches can cut circles through it. Huge beasts have no place to hide their bulk on a hillock that is a few paces high, but the wily fox thinks it's just dandy. Furthermore, the wise should be honored and the capable should be rewarded, while precedence should be given to the good and the beneficial. From old, Yao and Shun behaved thus. How much more should the people of Jagged do so! You, too, should accede to them, oh master."

"Come closer, my little ones!" said Master Kengsang. "Supposing there were a beast so large that it could hold a chariot in its mouth. If it were to stray away from the hills, it would not escape being troubled by nets. Supposing there were a fish so large that it could swallow a boat. If it were to splash out of the water, it could be tormented by ants. Therefore, birds and beasts do not detest heights; fish and turtles do not detest depths. The man who would preserve his form and life intact hides his person and detests not depth and distance, that's all.

"Furthermore, how are those two worthy of your praise? In their disputations, it was as though they were recklessly boring through walls to plant bushes and brambles, selecting strands of hair to comb, counting grains of rice to cook. Being so presumptuous, how could they have been worthy of aiding the world? If you promote those who are wise, the people will compete with each other; if you appoint those who have knowledge, the people will rob from each other. Those who count things are not worthy of assisting the people. The people are so eager for profit that a son will kill his father and a subject will kill his lord. They will rob in broad daylight and tunnel through brick walls at noon. I tell you that, surely as the root of great disorder was born in the times of Yao and Shun, its branches will last for more than a thousand generations. After a thousand generations, there will surely still be people who eat each other."

Disconcerted, Rufus Southglory sat up straight and said, "What means can someone who is old like me rely upon to attain what you have spoken about?"

Master Kengsang said,

> "Preserve your form,
> Protect your life;
> Do not let your thoughts
>   be agitated.

If you do this for three years, you can attain what I have spoken about."

"In form," said Rufus Southglory, "I cannot tell the difference between eyes, yet the blind cannot see with theirs. In form, I cannot tell the difference between ears, yet the deaf cannot hear with theirs. In form, I cannot tell the difference between hearts, yet the mad are not in self-possession of theirs. One form may well be comparable to another form, yet perhaps things serve to distinguish them. I may desire to emulate another without being able to achieve what he has. Now, you have said to me,

> 'Preserve your form,
> Protect your life;
> Do not let your thoughts
>   be agitated.'

I strive to hear the Way but it only reaches my ears."

"My words are finished," said Kengsang Ch'u. "It is said, 'A wispy wasp cannot transform the bean caterpillar; Viet chickens cannot hatch swan eggs, but Lu chickens certainly can.' It's not that the quality of one chicken is dissimilar to that of the other chicken. The ability of the one and the disability of the other are certainly due to the magnitude of their talents. Now, I am of small talent that is insufficient to transform you, sir. Why don't you go south to see the Old Master?"

Carrying his provisions, Rufus Southglory arrived at the Old Master's place after seven days and seven nights.

"Have you come from Ch'u's place?" asked the Old Master.

"Yes," said Rufus Southglory.

"Why have you come with such a host of people accompanying you?" asked the Old Master. Rufus Southglory looked around behind himself fearfully.

"Do you not know what I am talking about?" asked the Old Master.

Abashed, Rufus Southglory lowered his head. Then he looked up and said with a sigh, "Now I have forgotten my answer, so I have lost my question."

"What do you mean?" asked the Old Master.

"If we suppose that I am without knowledge," said Rufus Southglory, "people will say that I am a cretin. If we suppose that

I am knowledgeable, on the contrary, I would be tormented about my individuality. If I were inhumane, I would harm others. If I were humane, on the contrary, I would be tormented about my person. If I were not righteous, then I would wound others. If I were righteous, on the contrary, I would be tormented about my self. How can I possibly escape from this predicament? It is these three watchwords that are troubling me. At Ch'u's suggestion, I would like to ask you about them."

"A moment ago," said the Old Master, "by looking you closely in the eyes, I could tell what was on your mind. Now what you have said only confirms it. You are bewildered, as though you had lost your parents and had picked up a pole to seek them in the sea. You are a man who is adrift and astray! You wish for recovery of your proper nature, but have not the wherewithal to embark upon it. How pathetic!"

Rufus Southglory requested that he be permitted to enter the Old Master's school and take up residence in its dormitory. There he summoned what he liked and dismissed what he disliked. For ten days he tormented himself, then went back to see the Old Master.

"If you are purging yourself," asked the Old Master, "why are you so melancholy? Instead, you are still overflowing with dislikes. When external distractions cannot be constrained and arrested, bar them from within; when internal distractions cannot be restrained and arrested, bar them from without. Even a man of the Way and integrity would not be able to maintain himself in the face of such internal and external distractions, how much less could someone whose practice is but an imitation of the Way!"

"When a villager gets sick," said Rufus Southglory, "and his fellow villagers ask about it, if the sick person can describe his sickness, then he's not really sick. In the case of my hearing about the Great Way, it's like drinking medicine that adds to my sickness. I would like to hear about the basic rules for guarding life, that's all."

"The basic rules for guarding life," said the Old Master, "are

Can you embrace unity?
Can you keep from losing it?
Can you know what is auspicious and inauspicious
    without oracle bones and divining stalks?

Can you stop when it's time to stop?
Can you cease when it's time to cease?
Can you give up looking for it in others
    and seek for it in yourself?

Can you be casual? Can you be naive? Can you be like a child? The child howls the whole day but its throat does not become hoarse—the height of harmony. It clasps its hands all day long, but they do not become cramped—it concentrates its integrity. It stares with its eyes the whole day, but they do not blink—it is not diverted by externals. It walks but knows not where; it remains stationary but knows not why. It is intertwined with things and ripples along together with them. These are the basic rules for guarding life."

"But is this then all there is to the integrity of the ultimate man?" asked Rufus Southglory.

"No. This is merely the so-called thawing of the ice and melting of the frost. As for the ultimate man, along with others he prays for food from earth and prays for joy from heaven. He does not come into conflict with men and things over advantage and disadvantage. He does not do strange things, make plans, or engage in affairs with others. Casually he goes; naively he comes. These are the basic rules for guarding life."

"But is this then the ultimate?"

"Not quite. I had originally asked you whether

You could be 'like a child.'
The child moves
    but does not know why,

Walks but does not know where.
Its body is like a branch of withered wood
   and its mind is like dead ashes.

Being like this,
   Misfortune does not arrive,
   Nor does fortune come.
   When there is neither fortune nor misfortune,
   How can there be human calamities?"

When space is serenely stabilized, it emits a heavenly light. When the heavenly light is emitted, humans reveal their humanity, things reveal their substantiality. When humans have cultivated themselves, they finally achieve constancy. When someone has constancy, humans will take shelter with him and heaven will help him. Those whom humans take shelter with are called people of heaven. Those whom heaven helps are called sons of heaven.

Learning is to learn what cannot be learned; action is to act out what cannot be acted; disputation is to dispute over what cannot be disputed. Knowledge that stops at what it cannot know is the ultimate. If someone does not subscribe to this, he will be worn down by the celestial potter's wheel.

Provided with things to succor the physical form, storing up unconcern to enliven the mind, respecting what lies within to communicate with what lies without—if one does this and still myriad evils arrive, it is all due to heaven and not to man. They will be insufficient to disturb completeness and incapable of admittance to the numinous terrace. The numinous terrace has a guardian, but unless it knows what is guarding it, it cannot be guarded.

If one sallies forth without realizing this sincerity, every sally will be improper. Affairs will enter into him, and he will not be able to get rid of them, so that he will invariably fail all the more.

He who ostentatiously does what is not good will be subject to the punishment of men; he who surreptitiously does what is not good will be subject to the punishment of ghosts. Only he who has a clear understanding of men and ghosts will be able to act independently.

He who attends to what is inside him acts without regard for fame; he who attends to what is outside himself has his will focused on the expectation of gain. He who acts without regard for fame, although ordinary, will be illuminated; he who had his will focused on the expectation of gain is but a merchant— people will observe his anxiety, even though he may appear to have imposing stature. He who is thoroughly conversant with things will have things enter into him; he who sets up barriers against things will not be able to admit them into his person— how will he be able to admit other people? He who is unable to admit other people will have no intimates—having no intimates, he will be cast off from people. No weapon is more lethal than the will—even Excalibur is inferior to it. No tyrant is greater than yin and yang, from which nothing can escape between heaven and earth. But it is not yin and yang who are the thieves—it is the mind that causes them to be so.

Through the Way, all things become one. To split something up is to create something else; to create something is to destroy something else. What is hateful about splitting is that it splits what is complete; what is hateful about completeness is that it takes something to be complete. Therefore, if a man goes forth but does not return, he will have revealed his ghost. If he goes forth and acquires, this is called "acquiring death." If he is extinguished yet a kernel remains, it is the unity of his ghost. By imaging the formless with the formed, he is stabilized.

He goes forth but has no root; he enters but has no opening. He has a kernel of reality, but it is not located in a place; he has duration, but no origin or conclusion. Having that whence he goes forth but being without an opening, he has a kernel of reality. Having a kernel of reality but not being located in a place is his spatial dimension. Having duration but being without an origin or a conclusion is his temporal dimension. [Space + Time = Universe.] He has life; he has death; he has a going forth; he has an entering. Entering and going forth without revealing his form, this is called "the gate of heaven." The gate of heaven is nonbeing. The myriad things come forth from nonbeing. Being cannot bring being into being; it must come forth from nonbeing, and nonbeing is singularly nonbeing. The sage hides himself in this.

The knowledge of the ancients attained the ultimate. What was the ultimacy that it attained? They realized that there was a stage before there were things. This is the ultimacy they had attained, the utmost to which nought can be added. Next, there were those who recognized that there were things yet considered that life was bereavement and death but a return. This was already a division. Next, there were those who said, "In the beginning was nonbeing. Subsequently, there was life, and once there was life, suddenly there was death. We consider nonbeing the head, life the body, and death the buttocks. Whoever knows that which guards over nonbeing, death, and life, we shall be friends with him." Although these three are different, they belong to a common clan, just as the Chaos and the Chings, who bear the surnames of their appointed offices, and the clansmen of Chia, who bear the surname of their fief, while not identical, all belong to Ch'u royalty.

The existence of life is fraught with obscurities. Expansively, we refer to these as mutable referents. We may attempt to speak of mutable referents, but they are not that which can be spoken of and, in any event, are not something that can be known. At the winter sacrifice, there are tripe and hoofs that can be thought of as separable but they are really inseparable parts of the sacrificial animal. When we examine a house we go all around its sleeping quarters and shrines and we even visit its toilet, all of which are mutable referents of the house as a whole.

Let me try to speak of mutable referents. People take life as their root and knowledge as their teacher, consequently they become attached to right and wrong. As a result, there are names and realities, consequently they take themselves as subjective substance and cause others to take them as their own paragon, consequently they would indemnify their paragonhood with death. Such being the case, they take employment as knowledge and unemployment as stupidity, they take success as fame and failure as disgrace. In their attachment to mutable referents, the people of today are the same as the cicada and the dovelet in being all alike.

If you step on somebody's foot in the marketplace, you apologize for your carelessness. If you step on your older brother's foot, you give him an affectionate pat. If you step on your parent's foot, you do nothing. Therefore, it is said, "Ultimate etiquette makes no distinction between self and others; ultimate righteousness makes no distinction between self and things; ultimate knowledge does not scheme; ultimate humaneness is impartial; ultimate trust spurns gold.

> Extirpate the perversities of the will;
> Eradicate the absurdities of the mind;
> Eliminate the complexities of virtue;
> Exterminate the perplexities of the Way.

Honor and wealth, prominence and majesty, fame and profit—these six are the perversities of the will. Appearance and gestures, beauty and elocution, attitudes and intentions—these six are the absurdities of the mind. Dislikes and desires, pleasure and anger, sorrow and joy—these six are the complexities of virtue. Renouncing and acceding, taking and giving, knowledge and ability—these six are the perplexities of the Way. When these four sets of six do not churn within your breast, then you will be correct; being correct, you will be still; being still, you will be lucid; being lucid, you will be empty; being empty, you will be nonactive, thus nothing will be left undone. The Way is the sovereign of virtue; life is the light of virtue; nature is the substance of life. The movement of nature is called action; the falsification of action is called failure. Knowledge is reception; knowledge is scheming. But knowledge which is unknowing is like a sideways glance. Movement in which one has no alternative is called virtue; movement in which there is nothing other than ego is called order. Although the names are opposite, the realities are in accord.

2

Yi was adept at hitting a tiny target but clumsy in causing others to praise him endlessly. The sage is adept in dealing with heaven but clumsy in dealing with humanity. It is only the complete man who can be adept in dealing with heaven and good in dealing with humanity. Only insects can be insects because only insects can accord with heaven. The complete man hates heaven because he hates the humanization of heaven. How much more so the self-appropriation of heaven and humanity!

Should a sparrow come within range of Yi, Yi would be certain to get hold of it—such was the majesty of his archery. If all under heaven were a cage, then sparrows would have nowhere to escape. For this reason, T'ang caged Yi Yin as his cook and Duke Mu of Ch'in caged Poli Hsi by ransoming him with five goatskins. For this reason, if you try to get hold of people by caging them with other than what they like, it will never happen.

A man who has had one of his feet chopped off throws away his fancy clothing because he is beyond praise or blame. A convicted criminal will climb to any height because he has left life and death behind him. He who has been so repeatedly intimidated that he no longer feels shame will be oblivious of others. Oblivious of others, he will consequently become a man of heaven. Therefore, only if a man is respected and it does not make him happy, or if he is insulted and it does not make him angry, can he be one who shares in the harmony of heaven. If someone who is not angry exhibits anger, his anger is an exhibition of nonanger; if someone who is not acting exhibits action, his action is an exhibition of nonaction. Desiring to be still, he calms his breath; desiring to be spiritous, he tames his mind. Should action be required of him, he desires that it be appropriate, and only as a result of there being no alternative. The type who act only when there is no alternative is on the Way of the sages.

24

GHOSTLESS HSÜ

A series of odd wisemen instruct rulers and others about where their real interests lie. People in general are too busy with their daily occupations and neglect what is genuinely important in their lives. Master Chuang has an anti-philosophical discussion with Master Hui and then mourns his passing.

Most of the episodes in this lengthy chapter are directed against clever, sophistical disputation, Confucian moralizing, and involvement with mundane affairs. The spiritual man (the Taoist true man) is not confused by such distractions because he has a more profound vision that sees things clearly.

1

Ghostless Hsü obtained through Nü Shang an introduction for an interview with Marquis Wu of Wei. Marquis Wu consoled him, saying, "You must be exhausted, sir! I suppose that you were willing to come see my humble self only because you have suffered so bitterly from your toils in the mountain forests."

"It is I who should console you, my lord," said Ghostless Hsü. "What is there for you to console me about? If you gratify your yearnings and desires and satisfy your likes and dislikes, then the condition of your nature and destiny will be diseased.

But if you suppress your yearnings and desires and repress your likes and dislikes, then your senses will be diseased. I shall console you, my lord. What is there for you to console me about?" Marquis Wu haughtily made no reply.

After a short while, Ghostless Hsü said, "Let me tell your lordship how I judge dogs. Those of inferior quality are content merely to seize their prey and fill their stomachs—they have the virtue of a wild cat. Those of middling quality seem to look up at the sun. Those of superior quality seem to have lost their own identity. But my judging of dogs is not up to my judging of horses. When I judge horses, if they make straight lines that would fit a ruler, angles that would fit a bevel, squares that would fit an L-square, circles that would fit a compass, they are horses for a kingdom, but they are not as good as horses that are suitable for all under heaven. The horse that is suitable for all under heaven has talents that are complete. He seems distressed and distracted, as though he had forfeited his own identity. A horse like this is so surpassing that he outstrips the dust, not knowing where he is." Marquis Wu laughed with great delight.

When Ghostless Hsü went out, Nü Shang asked him, "How was it, sir, that your persuasions had such a singular effect on my lord? In attempting to persuade him, my indirect persuasions are drawn from the *Odes, Documents, Ritual,* and *Music,* while my direct persuasions are drawn from the *Metal Tablets* and *Six Bow-cases.* The number of greatly meritorious proposals I have submitted to him is incalculable, yet my lord has never shown his teeth in a smile. Now, sir, how did you persuade my lord so as to cause him to be delighted like this?"

"I told him straightforwardly how I judge dogs and horses," said Ghostless Hsü.

"Just like that?" asked Nü Shang.

"Haven't you heard about the man who was exiled to Viet?" asked Ghostless Hsü. "After he'd been away from his country for several days, whenever he saw someone he knew it made him happy. After he'd been away from his country for a month or so, whenever he saw someone he'd seen before in his country it made him happy. By the time a full year had elapsed, whenever he saw someone who looked vaguely familiar, it made him happy. Isn't this because the longer you're away from someone, the more deeply you think of him? Suppose that someone flees into a deserted valley where weasel runs are choked with pigweed and goosefoot. After a protracted stay in its emptiness, should he hear the tramping sound of human footsteps, he will feel happy. How much more so if it were the mirthful murmurs of his brothers and relatives by his side! For too long there have been no mirthful murmurings of a true man by the side of my lord!"

2

Ghostless Hsü had an interview with Marquis Wu, and the marquis said to him, "For too long, sir, you have dwelt in the mountain forests eating chestnuts and acorns and sating yourself with onions and leeks, neglecting my humble self! Have you come now because you're old? Because you desire to try the taste of wine and meat? Or because you want to bring blessings to my humble altars to the gods of the land and grain?"

"I was born into poverty," said Ghostless Hsü, "and would never dare to eat and drink my lord's meat and wine. I have come, rather, to console my lord."

"What?" said the lord. "How can you console my humble self?"

"I shall console your spirit and your form."

"What do you mean?" asked Marquis Wu.

"The nurture of heaven and earth is integral," said Ghostless Hsü. "Someone who climbs high should not think that he is esteemed; someone who dwells low should not think that he is debased. You may be the sole sovereign with ten thousand chariots at your disposal, my lord, but you use your position to embitter the people of your country and to nourish the cravings of your eyes, ears, mouth, and nose. Your spirit, however, will not consent to this. Now, the spirit prefers harmony and abhors dissipation. Dissipation is a disease, therefore I console you because of it. Why are you, my lord, particularly prey to this disease?"

"I have long wished to see you, sir," said Marquis Wu. "I wish to love the people and through righteousness to halt war. Will that suffice?"

"No," said Ghostless Hsü. "Loving the people is the source of harming the people; halting war through righteousness is the root that produces war. If you act on these premises, my lord, you are unlikely to accomplish your aims. The intentional effort to accomplish something fine is a poor device for doing so. Though you may act through humanity and righteousness, my lord, it is tantamount to hypocrisy. For just as surely as form produces form, accomplishment yields vaingloriousness and deviation produces external combativeness. You must not amass forma-tions of troops amidst your elegant watchtowers, my lord, and you must not have infantry and cavalry in the sequestered sanctuaries of your palace. Do not harbor contrariness in your achievements; do not gain victory over others through cleverness; do not gain victory over others through scheming; do not gain victory over others through battle. If I kill another's nobles and people, if I incorporate his territory to nourish my self and my spirit, one does not know who the better person is in such a battle and wherein the victory lies. If you feel compelled to do something, cultivate the sincerity in your breast in order to respond to the circumstances of heaven and earth without con-flict. Thus the people will already have escaped death, so what need there be for my lord to halt war?"

3

The Yellow Emperor went to visit Great Clump at Mount Shady.

Square Bright acted as his charioteer,
Brilliant Canopy rode along as his assistant.
Vernal Eurus and Autumnal Zephyr went before his
      horses,
Dusky Gates and Gaudy Wag followed behind his
      carriage.

When they arrived at the wilderness of Hsiangch'eng,
The seven sages had all become lost,
      and there was nowhere for them to ask the way.

By chance they encountered a lad who was pasturing some horses, so they asked him the way.

"Do you know Mount Shady?" they asked.

"Yes."

"Do you know where Great Clump exists?"

"Yes."

"What a strange little boy you are!" said the Yellow Emperor. "You not only know about Mount Shady, you also know where Great Clump exists. Let me ask you about all under heaven."

"Taking care of all under heaven," said the little boy, "is also just like this—no big deal! When I was young, I wandered by myself within the six reaches of the universe. As I was just then afflicted with blurred vision, an elder taught me, saying, 'Ride in the chariot of the sun and wander in the wilderness of Hsiangch'eng.' Now my affliction has improved somewhat, and I am wandering, but this time outside the six reaches of the universe. Taking care of all under heaven is also just like this— no big deal to me!"

"Taking care of all under heaven," said the Yellow Emperor, "is indeed not your business, my son. Nonetheless, let me ask you about taking care of all under heaven."

The little boy declined to answer, but when the Yellow

Emperor asked him again, the little boy said, "How is taking care of all under heaven any different from pasturing horses? All that it takes is to get rid of whatever would harm the horses!"

The Yellow Emperor bowed twice and kowtowed, then, addressing the boy as "Heavenly Teacher," he withdrew.

4

Without the transformations of their thought, intellectuals have no joy; without the orderliness of their discussions, disputers have no joy; without the busyness of their investigations, examiners have no joy. All of them are confined by things.

Those who attract the attention of the age rise in court; those who hit it off with the people glory in officialdom; those who have muscular strength tackle difficulties; those who are brave and daring rouse themselves against troubles; those who are adept with weapons and shields joy in battle; those who are withered and wizened rest on their fame; those who are familiar with the law broaden the scope of government; those who are proficient in ceremonial doctrines respect appearances; those who emphasize humaneness and righteousness honor relationships. Without the busyness of their weeding, farmers are discomfited; without the business of their markets, merchants are discomfited. When ordinary people have employment from morning till evening they are encouraged; when the various types of artisans are skilled with their tools and machines they flourish. If their wealth and property do not accumulate, the greedy are worried; if their power and influence do not amass, the boastful are sad. Such adherents of influence and material things joy in transformation. If they encounter a moment when there is use for them, they cannot but act. They all follow along with the times and change along with things. They race their physical forms and their natures, sinking them under the myriad things, without ever turning back their whole life. How sad!

5

Master Chuang said, "If an archer hits the target without taking aim in advance and we declare that he is a skilled archer, then all under heaven would be Yis. Is that a permissible statement?"

"Yes," said Master Hui.

"Given that there is no publicly recognized conception of what is right for all under heaven," said Master Chuang, "and that each individual takes as right what she considers right, then all under heaven must be Yaos. Is that a permissible statement?"

"Yes," said Master Hui.

"Well, then," said Master Chuang, "there are the four schools of the Confucians, the Mohists, the Yangists, and the Pingists. Adding yours, master, it makes five. Which of you is actually right? Or may it be someone like Hasty Ninny? His disciple said to him, 'I have attained your way, master. In winter I can light a cooking fire under a three-legged vessel and in summer I can make ice.' 'That's merely to attract yang with yang and yin with yin,' said Hasty Ninny. 'It's not what I mean by the Way. I will show you my Way.' Thereupon he tuned two zithers. He placed one of them in the hall and the other in an inner chamber. When he plucked the note *do* on one, *do* resonated on the other, and when he plucked the note *mi* on one, *mi* resonated on the other. It's because their harmonies were the same. If he had retuned one of the strings so it didn't match any note in the pentatonic scale, and had then plucked it, all twenty-five strings on the other zither would have resonated, not because there was any fundamental difference in the sound, but because it was the note that dominated all the rest. May it be that you thinkers are all like this?"

"Just now," said Master Hui, "the Confucians, the Mohists, the Yangists, and the Pingists were disputing with me. We oppose each other with our words and overwhelm each other with our voices, yet they have never proven me wrong. How can you imply that I am like them?"

"A man of Ch'i," said Master Chuang, "sent his son on a sojourn to Sung. His instructions to the gatekeeper there did not include the use of a bolt, but when he acquired a chime or a bell he would wrap it up tightly. In seeking his missing son, he wouldn't even leave his own territory. There are such heedless types, you realize! Then there was the man of Ch'u who had an altercation with the gateman at the place he was staying and in the middle of the night when no one was around had a fight with his boatman, so that before he had even left the shore he had already done enough to provoke the boatman's enmity."

6

Master Chuang was accompanying a funeral when he passed by the grave of Master Hui. Turning around, he said to his attendants, "There was a man from Ying who sent for carpenter Shih to slice off a speck of plaster like a fly's wing that had splattered the tip of his nose. Carpenter Shih whirled his ax so fast that it produced a wind. Letting the ax fall instinctively, he sliced off every last bit of the plaster but left the nose unharmed, while the man from Ying stood there without flinching. When Lord Yüan of Sung heard about this, he summoned carpenter Shih and said, 'Try to do the same thing for me.' 'Your servant used to be able to slice off plaster like that,' said carpenter Shih, 'but my "chopping block" died long ago.' Since your death, Master Hui, I have had no one who can be my 'chopping block.' I have had no one with whom to talk."

7

Kuan Chung having fallen ill, Duke Huan went to inquire how he was, saying, "Your illness, Father Chung, is serious, but it's something that I cannot refrain from mentioning. Should it end up in the great illness, to whom could I entrust the state?"

"To whom does your honor wish to give it over?" said Kuan Chung.

"Pao Shuya," said the duke.

"He won't do. His behavior is that of a fine nobleman, unsullied and honest. But he will not associate with those who are not like him and when he hears of another person's faults, he never forgets them for the rest of his life. If you were to have him govern your state, above he would goad you and below he would counter the people. It would not be long before he offended you, my lord."

"Then to whom can I give it?" said the duke.

The reply was, "If I am compelled to speak, Hsi P'eng will do. His behavior is such that he would be oblivious of those above him and would not cause the disaffection of those below him. He is ashamed that he is not equal to the Yellow Emperor and pities those who are not equal to himself. Someone who shares his integrity with others is called a sage; someone who shares his wealth with others is called a worthy. Someone who overawes others with his worthiness will never succeed in gaining their affection; someone who subordinates himself to others with his worthiness will never fail to gain their affection. In matters of state, there are things such a man chooses not to hear and, in family affairs, there are things such a man overlooks. If I am compelled to speak, Hsi P'eng will do."

8

The King of Ngwa, floating on the Yangtze River, disembarked to climb a hill noted for its monkeys. When the host of monkeys saw him, they all ran off in terror, fleeing into the deep thickets. There was one monkey, however, that kept casually cavorting and saucily swinging through the branches, showing off its cleverness to the king. The king shot at it, but the monkey deftly grabbed the arrow. The king ordered his attendants to hurry up and shoot it, and thus the monkey died forthwith.

Turning to address his friend, Doubtless Countenance, the king said, "This monkey, by displaying its cleverness and relying on its agility, was arrogant to me, and so it ended up perishing like this. Take warning from it! Ah, do not be haughty to others with your looks!"

Doubtless Countenance returned home and became a student of Regulate Firm in order to hoe his looks. He put away joy and bid adieu to flamboyance. After three years, the people of the kingdom extolled him.

9

Sir Motley of Southunc sat leaning against his low table. He looked up to heaven and exhaled slowly. Master Countenance Complete entered and, upon seeing him, said, "Master, you are most excellent among all things! Can you really make your body become like a withered carcass and your mind like dead ashes?"

"I used to live in a mountain grotto. T'ien Ho once came to see me and the multitudes of the state of Ch'i thrice congratulated him. I must first have had a reputation, therefore he knew about me. I must have traded on my reputation, therefore he came to purchase it. If I had not had a reputation, how would he have been able to know about me? If I had not traded on my reputation, how would he have been able to purchase it? Alas! I pitied people who destroy themselves. I also pitied those who pity others, and I also pitied those who take pity on the pitifulness of others. Later on, however, I distanced myself from all that day by day."

10

When Confucius went to Ch'u, the King of Ch'u ordered that wine be poured for him. Sun Shu'ao stood by holding a chalice and Yiliao of Southmarket, having received some of the wine, poured a libation.

"Oh, man of the ancients!" said he. "Please speak to us on this occasion."

"I, Hillock, have heard of unspoken speech, but I have never tried to speak it. Shall I try to speak it on this occasion? Yiliao of Southmarket kept juggling his balls and the difficulties between the two houses were resolved; Sun Shu'ao, grasping his feather-fan, kept sleeping sweetly and the people of Ying threw down their weapons. Would that I had a beak three feet long!"

That refers to the Way that cannot be walked upon and *this* refers to the disputation that is without words. Therefore, integrity that is summarized in the unity of the Way and speech that rests in what is unknown through knowledge are the ultimate. Yet integrity is not identical with that which is the unity of the Way and disputation cannot instance that which is unknowable through knowledge. To give names to these things, like the Confucians and the Mohists, brings evil. Therefore, the nonrejection of the eastward-flowing streams by the sea is the ultimate of greatness. The sage embraces all of heaven and earth and his benefits reach to all under heaven, but we do not know who he is or to which clan he belongs. For this reason, he may have no titles when alive and no epithets when dead. He neither gathers riches nor establishes his fame. Him we may call a great man.

A dog is not considered to be good because it barks well; a man is not considered to be worthy because he speaks well—how much less is he considered great! He who acts great is not qualified to be considered great—how much less is he to be considered as having integrity! Now, there is nothing greater than heaven and earth, but do they strive for anything to make themselves so great and all-encompassing? He who knows how to be great and all-encompassing seeks nothing, loses nothing, and abandons nothing. He would not change himself for any-thing. Returning to himself, he is inexhaustible; complying with antiquity, he is ineffaceable. This is the sincerity of the great man.

11

Sir Motley had eight sons. Having lined them up before himself, he summoned Nonagon Impediment and asked, "Would you read the features of my sons for me so I may know which is the most auspicious?"

"K'un's the most auspicious," said Nonagon Impediment.

"How so?" asked Sir Motley with happy surprise.

"K'un will eat together with the ruler of a state his whole life."

"Why should my son arrive at such an extremity?" asked Sir Motley, his tears falling despondently.

Nonagon Impediment said, "The benefits of one who eats together with the ruler of a state will reach to the three clans of his relatives, how much more to his father and mother! Now, master, for you to weep upon hearing this is to ward off good fortune. The son is auspicious, but the father is inauspicious."

"Impediment," said Sir Motley, "how are you capable of recognizing whether K'un is auspicious? Granted that his mouth and nose may be completely stuffed with wine and meat, but how are you capable of knowing where they will come from? I have never been a shepherd, yet a ewe was born in the southwest corner of my house. I have never liked to hunt, yet a quail was born in the northwest corner of my house. If these are not considered prodigies, what would be? The place where my son and I wander is between heaven and earth. I pray with him for joy from heaven and I pray with him for food from earth. I do not get involved in affairs with him, do not undertake plans with him, do not effect prodigies with him. I mount with him on the sincerity of heaven and earth and thus do not come into conflict with things. I am entirely self-content with him and with him am unconcerned about the appropriateness of affairs. Now, however, there is this worldly compensation for him. Whenever there are prodigious proofs, there must be prodigious behaviors. Perilous!—but it's not through any fault of my son and me. Heaven must be visiting this upon us. That is why I wept."

Not long thereafter, K'un was sent on a mission to Yen and was waylaid by robbers along the way. It would have been difficult to sell him if he were unmutilated, so they thought it better to chop off one of his feet. They proceeded to do so and sold him in Ch'i. There he was put in charge of the private quarters of the palace of Duke K'ang and was able to eat meat till the end of his life.

12

Gnaw Gap chanced to meet Hsü Yu and asked him, "Where are you going?"

"I am fleeing from Yao."

"What do you mean?"

"Yao is so assiduously humane that I am afraid he'll be laughed at by all under heaven and that future generations of men will eat each other. It is not difficult to gather the people around oneself. Love them and they will be affectionate; profit them and they will come to you; praise them and they will be encouraged; bring upon them what they dislike and they will scatter. Love and profit derive from humaneness and righteousness, but those who confer humaneness and righteousness are few while those who profit from them are numerous. The practice of humaneness and righteousness is thus merely insincere and a pretext for predators. For this reason, should one man by his own determinations and decisions aim to benefit all under heaven, his vision may be compared to that of a fleeting glimpse. Yao knew how the worthy man could profit all under heaven, but didn't know how he could thieve from all under heaven. Only someone who has gotten beyond worthiness knows this."

13

There are the smugly satisfied, the complacently content, and the bent-waistedly busy.

The so-called "smugly satisfied" study the words of a single master, then—all smug and satisfied—they are secretly pleased with themselves and consider themselves to be quite sufficient, without realizing that they haven't begun to learn anything. Hence they are called "smugly satisfied."

The complacently content are like lice on a pig. They select a spot where the bristles are far apart, considering that they have found themselves a spacious palace or a large park. Within the slits of its hooves, inside the folds of its skin, between its nipples, betwixt its thighs—they consider these to be comfortable chambers and profitable places. But they do not realize that one morning the butcher, swinging his arms, will spread some grass and wield his torch, scorching both themselves and the pig. Thus do they prosper along with their environment and flounder along with their environment. They are the so-called "complacently content."

Shun is an example of the bent-waistedly busy. Mutton is not fond of ants, but ants are fond of mutton because it is rank. Shun must have had rank behavior, for the hundred clans were pleased with him. Therefore, when he thrice changed his residence, each of them became a capital, and when he arrived at the wastes of Teng, he had more than ten thousand families with him. Yao heard of Shun's worthiness and elevated him from these barren lands, saying, "I hope for the benefits of his coming." When Shun was elevated from these barren lands, he was already advanced in years, and his hearing and eyesight were failing, yet he was not able to rest or return home. He was one of the so-called "bent-waistedly busy."

For this reason, the spiritual man dislikes the arrival of the multitudes. Should the multitudes arrive, there will be discord;

should there be discord, it will be disadvantageous. Therefore, there are none with whom he is very intimate and there are none with whom he is very distant. He embraces integrity and nurtures harmony so as to be in accord with all under heaven. This is called the "true man. . . ."

He uses his eye to look at his eye, his ear to listen to his ear, his mind to respond to his mind. This being so, his levelness is straight as a ruler and his transformations are orderly. The true man of old attended the human with the heavenly instead of using the human to interfere with the heavenly. The true man of old looked upon success as life, upon failure as death; he looked upon success as death, upon failure as life.

Take medicines, for instance. There are crow's head, kikio root, fox nut, and the root of pig's dung. Each has a time when it is the sovereign prescription, but it is impossible to describe them all.

Kou Chien took refuge on Mount K'uaichi with three thousand troops wearing armor and bearing shields. Only Chung was capable of knowing how the defeated state of Yüeh could be preserved, yet only Chung did not know the sorrows that awaited himself. Therefore it is said, "The owl's eye has that for which it is suited; the crane's leg has that for which it is fitted—to cut them away would be tragic."

Therefore it is said, "When the wind passes over it, a river is diminished; when the sun passes over it, a river is likewise diminished. But let the wind and the sun together guard the river, and the river will feel that they have not even begun to come in conflict with it. Relying on its sources, it flows on." Therefore, water is affirmed when it is guarded by soil, shadows are affirmed when guarded by men, things are affirmed when guarded by things.

Therefore, the eye is imperiled by keen sight, the ear is imperiled by keen hearing, the mind is imperiled by ardent thought, and any capability is imperiled by its latency. When the peril becomes real, it cannot be averted, and misfortunes will be

prolonged in increasing amounts. Turning back is due to effort, a fruitful result requires persistence. Yet men consider such capabilities to be their personal treasures—is this not sad? Therefore, there is an endless forfeiture of states and massacre of the people because no one knows how to inquire into their causes.

Therefore, although the earth upon which our feet tread is restricted, by relying on those places where we have not stepped before, we later become good at going far; although human knowledge is small, by relying on what we do not know, we later come to know what is meant by heaven. To know the great unity, to know the great yin, to know the great eye, to know the great equality, to know the great method, to know the great verity, to know the great stability—that is the ultimate! The great unity comprehends it, the great yin explains it, the great eye sees it, the great equality rationalizes it, the great method embodies it, the great verity examines it, the great stability maintains it.

In the uttermost there is heaven; in order there is illumination; in darkness there is a pivot; in the beginning there was that. Thus, its explanation was as though there were no explanation, its knowledge was as though there were no knowledge. Only through unknowing can it be known. Inquiring after it, one cannot have limits, yet one cannot be without limits. In slippery vagueness there is a reality that has not been displaced from antiquity till today, nor can it be depleted. Thus, may we not call it "the great summation"? Why not make inquiries into this? Why act so confused about it? Explain what is confusing with what is not confusing so that you may return to unconfusion, and this will be the greatest unconfusion.

25

SUNNY

Another long chapter with diverse content, it begins by rehabilitating the concept of the sage as a wise man at rest with the world, at peace with himself, and capable (though not always willing) of advising the ruler. It concludes with the longest poetic passage in the book, a reverie by Grand Just Harmonizer on the futility of words (especially philosophical language) to describe the Way.

1

When Sunny was traveling in Ch'u, Even Constant spoke of him to the king, but before the king granted an interview, Even Constant returned home. Sunny went to see Princely Kernel and asked, "Master, why don't you mention me to the king?"

"I am not as good for that as Ducal Happyrest," said Princely Kernel.

"What does Ducal Happyrest do?" asked Sunny.

"In winter he spears turtles in the Yangtze River, and in summer he rests in the foothills of the mountains. When passersby ask him what he's doing there, he says, 'This is my house.' Since Even Constant was not able to make an introduction for you, how much less can I, who am not as good for that as him!

Now, as a person, Even Constant lacks integrity but has knowledge. He does not permit himself thereby to spiritualize his dealings with others. Instead, he gets firmly bogged down in situations that emphasize wealth and honor. He does not assist others with integrity but assists them negatively. A person who is freezing would borrow spring as his clothing; a person who is sweltering would have winter come back with its cold winds. Now, as a person, the King of Ch'u has a respectful bearing and is stern. Toward offenders, he is as unforgiving as a tiger. Unless one were eloquent and of upright integrity, who could make him bend?

"Therefore, when the sage is in straits, he causes the members of his family to forget their poverty; when he is successful, he causes kings and dukes to forget their titles and allowances, transforming them into humble men. Regarding things, he takes pleasure together with them. Regarding people, he enjoys communicating things with them, but protects himself while doing so. Therefore, while he may not speak, he enables men to imbibe harmony. He stands side by side with other men and causes them to be transformed, as would be suitable for a parent and child. When they have a place to return and reside, he dispenses his favors with utter impartiality. So distant is he in his bearing toward the minds of men. Therefore, I said, 'Wait for Ducal Happyrest.' "

2

The sage achieves intertwining so that he becomes a single body with all around him, yet he does not know how this is so—it is his nature. In the operation of fulfilling his destiny, he takes heaven as his teacher. Men thus follow him and style him a sage. If he were troubled by knowledge and what he practiced were always ephemeral, he would be stymied, and then what could he do about it?

Men serve as a mirror for one who is born with excellences.

If they did not tell him, he would not know that he is more excellent than others. Whether he knows it or does not know it, whether he hears it or does not hear it, his happiness, in the end, never ceases and men's admiration of him also never ceases—it is his nature. Because the sage loves other men, they give him a name. If they did not tell him, he would not know that he loves others. Whether he knows it or does not know it, whether he hears it or does not hear it, his love of others, in the end, never ceases and men's finding security in him also never ceases—it is his nature.

When one gazes upon her old country or her old city, she is exhilarated. Even if its hills and mounds are obscured by grasses and trees that have invaded nine-tenths of the land, one will still be exhilarated. How much more would she feel so having seen what she has seen and heard what she has heard! It would be like a terrace eighty feet high suspended amidst the crowd.

3

The clansman Jan Hsiang located himself in the center of the circle of things, thereby following them along to completion and accompanying them without beginning and without end, without periodicity and without time. He who daily transforms along with things has a unity that does not transform. How could he have ever given it up? If we strive to take heaven as our teacher but do not succeed in doing so, we will perish together with things. How would that do for managing our affairs? Now, the sage has never begun to have a heaven, has never begun to have men, has never begun to have a beginning, has never begun to have things. He goes along with the world but does not substitute himself for it; his goings are comprehensive but not excessive. How would it do for him to yoke himself in that fashion?

When T'ang acquired his palace guard and gateman, Teng Heng, he made him his tutor. Following him as teacher, he became unconstrained and was enabled to acquiesce in completion. He put him in charge of his name and his name became fully emulatable, having acquired a dual vision. Because Confucius exhausted his thoughts, he was made a tutor. The clansman Jungch'eng said, "If days are omitted, there will be no years; if there is nothing internal, there will be nothing external."

4

Ying, the King of Wei, made a treaty with Marquis T'ien Mou of Ch'i, but Marquis T'ien Mou violated it. Ying of Wei was angry and intended to send a man to assassinate him.

When the minister of war heard about this, he was ashamed of it and said to the king, "You are the ruler of ten thousand chariots, my lord, yet you would avenge yourself by means of an ordinary man. I request that I receive from you two hundred thousand troops in armor to attack him for you, my lord. I will capture his people, rope his cattle and horses, and cause the hot ire within him to be so great that it will erupt from his back, after which I will uproot him from his capital. His general, T'ien Chi, will flee from it, after which I will beat his back and snap his spine."

When Master Chi heard about this, he was ashamed of it and said to the king, "If we are constructing a city wall eighty feet high and destroy the wall when it is already nine-tenths finished, this would embitter the conscript laborers. Today it has been seven years since troops were raised; this is the foundation of your kingship. Yen [the minister of war] is a person who would bring disorder. He cannot be listened to."

When Master Hua heard about this, he was repelled by it and said, "He who is good at saying 'Attack Ch'i!' is a person who would bring disorder. He who is good at saying 'Don't attack!' is also a person who would bring disorder. He who declares that those who advocate attack and those who advocate not to attack are both persons who would bring disorder is himself a person who would bring disorder."

"So, then what am I to do?" said the ruler.

"You should just seek the Way and that is all."

When Master Hui heard about this, he introduced Tai Chinjen to the king and Tai Chinjen said to him, "There is a creature called the snail. Do you know about it, my lord?"

"Yes."

"On the left horn of the snail there is a person named Clansman Butt who has set up a kingdom and on the right horn there is a person named Clansman Barbarossa who has set up a kingdom. The two kingdoms often compete with each other for territory and go to war, strewing the ground with tens of thousands of corpses. The victors pursue the vanquished for fifteen days before returning to their base."

"Tush!" said the ruler. "That's just empty talk!"

"Please allow me to demonstrate the real significance of it for you, my lord. Do you conceive of space—the four directions plus up and down—as being finite?"

"It is infinite," said the ruler.

"Knowing how to let your mind wander in infinity, when you turn to contemplate kingdoms that can be apprehended, doesn't it seem as though they barely exist?"

"Yes," said the ruler.

"Among kingdoms that can be apprehended, there is Wei, and in Wei there is its capital Liang, and in Liang there is a king. Is there any distinction between that king and Clansman Barbarossa?"

"There is no distinction," said the ruler.

The guest went out, leaving the ruler absent-minded, as if he were lost. After the guest had gone out, Master Hui came in to see the king.

"That guest is a great man," said the ruler. "Even a sage could not match him."

"If you blow into a bamboo pipe," said Master Hui, "there will be a full-bodied whistling sound, but if you blow into the pommel of a sword, all you'll get is a faint hiss. Yao and Shun are praised by men, but to talk of them before Tai Chinjen would be like making a faint hiss."

5

When Confucius went to Ch'u, he lodged with a sauce-maker on Ant Hillock. At the neighboring house, the husband and wife, together with their male and female servants, had climbed up on the roof.

"What are those people doing up there milling about?" asked Tzulu.

"The man is a disciple of the sages," said Confucius. "He buries himself among the people and hides himself among the pathways that divide the fields. His reputation has dissipated, but his will is infinite. Although he speaks with his voice, his mind has never spoken. What's more, he runs counter to the world and his mind disdains to associate with it. He is someone who can submerge himself on dry land. Isn't he like Yiliao of Southmarket?"

Tzulu requested permission to go and summon the man.

"Leave him alone!" said Confucius. "He knows that I am stuck on myself and that my coming to Ch'u is to have the King of Ch'u summon me to his court, so he considers me a glib flatterer. Being such a person, he would be embarrassed to hear the words of a flatterer, and even more so to see a flatterer in person! And what makes you think he'll remain there?"

Tzulu went over to see the man, but his rooms were empty.

6

The border warden at Tall Tree inquired of Tzulao, saying, "A ruler should not be heedless in carrying out his administration nor haphazard in governing the people. In the past when I was planting, if I plowed heedlessly the grains paid me back heedlessly, and if I weeded haphazardly the grains paid me back haphazardly. In recent years I've changed my methods. I plow deeply and harrow thoroughly, so the plants flourish abundantly and I have plenty to eat all year long."

When Master Chuang heard about this he said, "Nowadays, in governing their physical forms and in ordering their minds, most people are like what the border warden described. In their multitudinous activities, they hide from heaven, negate their natures, erase their emotions, and stifle their spirits. Therefore, he who is heedless of his nature, whose likes and dislikes are seeds of retribution, will find his nature choked with reeds and rushes. At first their sprouts seem to support our physical forms, but gradually they eradicate our natures until we erupt in festering pus that breaks out everywhere from tumors and ulcers, internal fevers, and chylous urine. That's what will happen!"

7

Rap Rule, who was studying with Old Longears, said, "I request permission to wander through all under heaven."

"No need for that," said Old Longears. "All under heaven's the same as here."

Again he made the request, upon which Old Longears asked, "Where will you start?"

"I'll start from Ch'i."

When he arrived in Ch'i, Rap Rule saw the displayed corpse of an executed criminal. He pushed it so it lay stretched out full length, then took off his court robes and covered it with them. Calling out to heaven, he cried and said, "Sir! Oh, sir! There will be a great calamity for all under heaven. It's just that you were the first to encounter it. We are told, 'Do not be a robber! Do not be a murderer!' But when glory and disgrace are established, we subsequently witness the abuse that arises; when goods and property are accumulated, we subsequently witness the conflict that arises. Now, if we establish what men abuse and accumulate what men have conflicts over, we place them in such extreme distress that they have no time for rest. Even if we wished that they wouldn't end up like this, how could it be achieved?

"The superior man of ancient times attributed his success to the people and his failures to himself; he attributed what was correct to the people and what was erroneous to himself. Therefore, if a single physical form were lost, he would withdraw and blame himself. Now, however, it is not so. Rulers are excessive in the things they want done and rebuke those who are unaware of them. They create great difficulties and condemn those who dare not cope with them. They impose heavy duties and punish those who cannot bear them. They send people on distant errands and execute those who do not fulfill them. When the strength and the knowledge of the people are exhausted, they follow them up with falsity. When the ruler daily perpetrates much falsity, how can his nobles and his people not engage in falsity? Insufficiency of strength leads to falsity, insufficiency of knowledge leads to deceit, insufficiency of property leads to robbery. Whom should we blame for such acts of robbery and theft?"

8

When Ch'ü Poyü was in his sixtieth year, he had been through sixty transformations. There had never been a time when he began by considering something right that he didn't end up dismissing it as wrong. He didn't know whether what he now called right might not be what he had considered wrong for fifty-nine years. The myriad things all have that which gives them birth, but no one sees their root; they all have that which produces them, but no one sees their gate. Men all respect what their knowledge enables them to know, but no one knows how to rely on what their knowledge doesn't enable them to know so that later they could really know. May this not be called the great perplexity? Enough! Enough! There's no escaping from it. This ostensible "so it is!"—is it really so?

9

Confucius inquired of the Grand Scribes, Big Bow-case, Poch'ang Ch'ien, and Hsiwei, saying, "Duke Ling of Wey was so besotted with wine and immersed in pleasures that he paid no attention to the administration of his state. He was so addicted to hunting with nets and arrows that he did not respond to the meetings of the feudal lords. For what reason was he canonized as Duke Ling ('Numinous')?"

"It was for precisely these reasons," said Big Bow-case.

"Duke Ling had three wives," said Poch'ang Ch'ien, "with whom he would bathe in the same tub. But when Shih Ch'iu entered his presence bearing imperial presents, he would have someone carry the gifts for him and others support him under the arms. His crudeness could be as great as it was in the former instance, but when he saw a worthy, he could be as reverent as in the latter instance. It is for this reason that he was canonized as Duke Ling."

"When Duke Ling died," said Hsiwei, "the divination for burying him in the old family tomb was unfavorable, while the divination for burying him in Sandy Hillock was favorable. After we had dug several fathoms in the sand, we came upon a stone coffin. Having washed it off, we examined the coffin and found on it an inscription that said, 'Without relying on his descendants, Duke Ling may snatch this and settle himself in it!' Duke Ling has already been numinous for a long time. How would these two men be capable of recognizing it?"

10

Little Knowledge inquired of Grand Just Harmonizer, saying, "What is meant by 'village words'?"

"A village," said Grand Just Harmonizer, "determines its customs by the combination of ten surnames and a hundred names. When they combine their differences they are the same;

when they dissociate their similarities they are different. Now, if we point to the various parts of a horse, there is no longer a horse, but when the horse is tied up in front of us standing there with all of its various parts, we may refer to it as a horse. Hence hills and mountains may be thought of as the accumulation of what is minute so that it becomes high; the Yangtze and the Yellow rivers may be thought of as the confluence of small streams so that they become great; the great man may be thought of as combining all humanity so that he becomes just. For this reason, when something enters him from without, though he has a subjective stance he does not insist upon it; when something issues from within, though he may have the correct position he does not reject others. The vital breaths of the four seasons are dissimilar, but heaven is not partisan toward any of them, therefore the year is complete. The duties of the five offices are dissimilar, but the ruler is not partial to any of them, therefore the state is governed. The capabilities of the civil and the military realms are dissimilar, but the great man is not partisan toward either of them, therefore their integrity is realized. The principles of the myriad things are dissimilar, but the Way is not partial to any of them, therefore it has no name.

> Having no name, it does nothing;
> Doing nothing, there is nothing that it does not do.
> The seasons have their endings and beginnings;
> The ages have their transformations and evolutions.
> Misfortune and fortune fluctuate;
> Their arrival may bring that which is disagreeable,
>   and that which is agreeable.
> Each self ascribing to different orientations,
> There is that which is correct,
>   and that which is deviant.

> We may compare this to a great marsh
> In which all the varieties of vegetation are fitting;

We may observe this on a great mountain,
Where the trees and stones share the same fundament.
This is what is meant by 'village words.' "

"So," asked Little Knowledge, "then is it sufficient if we refer to them as the Way?"

"Not so," said Grand Just Harmonizer. "Now, if we calculate the number of things, it does not stop at ten thousand, but the reason we limit it by saying 'the myriad things' is because that is an expression for referring to a large number. Hence, heaven and earth are the greatest physical forms; yin and yang are the greatest vital breaths. But it is the Way that is all-encompassing. Because of its greatness, to refer to it by that expression is permissible, but does having such a term imply that it is comparable to anything else? To dispute about it in this fashion is like comparing horses and dogs. Is it not certain to be far off the mark?"

Little Knowledge asked,

"Within the four directions
    and inside the six reaches of the universe,
How did the birth of the myriad things arise?"

Grand Just Harmonizer said,

"The yin-moon and yang-sun shone upon each other,
Covering each other up and governing each other;
The four seasons replaced each other,
Giving birth to each other and destroying each other.
Desires and dislikes, renouncing and acceding,
As a result, conspicuously arose;
The separation and the union of male and female,
As a result, commonly occurred.

Security and danger alternated with each other,
Misfortune and fortune gave birth to each other,

Indolence and urgency rubbed against each other,
So that gathering and dispersal were thereby
        completed.

The realities of these names can all be noted,
Their essential subtleties can all be recorded.
The principles by which they follow in sequence upon
        one another,
The mutual causation through which they
        conspicuously revolve,
Their reversal after reaching an extreme,
Their beginning after coming to an end—
These are the qualities inherent in things.
Where words are exhausted,
Where knowledge terminates,
They are delimited by things and that is all.
Men who see things through the Way
Do not pursue them to where they disappear,
Do not trace them to where they arise;
This is where their deliberation ends."

Little Knowledge asked,

"Chi Chen's nonfacticity
And Master Chieh's contingent causation—
Between the deliberations of these two schools,
Which is correct with regard to attributes?
Which is prejudiced with regard to principles?"

Grand Just Harmonizer said,

"Chickens cackle and dogs bark—
This is what men know.
Although they may have great knowledge,

They cannot explain with words whence they have
     evolved,
Nor can they surmise with ideas what they will
     become.

If we analyze things in this fashion,

Their fineness would be beyond comparison,
Their largeness could not be encompassed.
Contingent causation and nonfacticity,
Not being free of things,
End up in error.

If we accept contingent causation, there is reality,
If we accept nonfacticity, there is vacuity.
When there is both name and reality,
We dwell in the realm of things;
When there is neither name nor reality,
We exist in a vacuity of things.
We can speak and can think,
But the more we speak, the further off we are.
What is not yet born cannot be forbidden,
What is already dead cannot be prevented.
Death and birth are not distant,
It's their principle that cannot be seen.
Contingent causation and nonfacticity
Are suppositions which are premised on doubt.

When I observe their roots,
They go back infinitely;
When I seek their culminations,
They go forward interminably.
Infinite and interminable,
They are beyond words,
Yet they share the same principle with words.

Contingent causation and nonfacticity
Are roots for words;
They end and begin together with things.

The Way cannot be held to exist, nor can it be held to be nonexistent. 'The Way' as a name operates as a supposition which is premised. Contingent causation and nonfacticity are but one corner of things. What have they to do with the great method? If words were satisfactory, we could speak the whole day and it would all be about the Way; but if words are unsatisfactory, we can speak the whole day and it will all be about things. The Way is the delimitation of things. Neither words nor silence are satisfactory for conveying it. Without words and without silence, our deliberations reach their utmost limits."

26

EXTERNAL THINGS

Containing some of the strangest and most vivid stories in the book, this chapter comments upon a wide range of Taoist topics, including distrust of petty knowledge, the usefulness of uselessness, wandering, and the fundamental insignificance of words. The ultimate man pays attention to what is essential, that is, what is within.

1

External things cannot be depended upon. Therefore, Lungp'ang was executed, Pikan was murdered, Master Chi went mad, Olai died, and Chieh and Chow perished. Sovereigns invariably desire the loyalty of their ministers, but that loyalty does not necessarily inspire their trust. Therefore, Wu Yüan was left to drift down the Yangtze River and Ch'ang Hung died in Shu, where his blood was preserved for three years till it turned into moss-green jade. Parents invariably desire the filialness of their sons, but that filialness does not necessarily inspire their love. Therefore, Filial Self was anxious and Tseng Shen was sad.

When wood is rubbed against wood, it will ignite; when metal is kept in close proximity with fire, it will flow. When yin and yang are out of kilter, heaven and earth will be greatly disturbed. Consequently, there will be a crash of thunder and there will be fire amidst the water that can incinerate big trees. Facing the twin pitfalls of pleasure and trouble, men have nowhere to escape. Like frantic insects, they cannot complete anything and their hearts are as though suspended between heaven and earth. Melancholy and gloom, benefit and harm rub against them, giving birth to many fires of anxiety within which incinerate the harmony of the mass of men. Indeed, their lunar intelligence cannot cope with these fires. Consequently, they collapse and are bereft of the Way.

2

Chuang Chou's family was poverty-stricken, so he went to borrow some grain from the marquis who was overseer of the Yellow River.

"All right," said the marquis who was overseer of the Yellow River, "I will be getting the tax money from my fief and will lend you three hundred pieces of gold. Is that all right?"

Chuang Chou flushed with anger and said, "Yesterday as I was coming here, there was a voice that called out from the middle of the road. When I turned around to look, I saw that there was a golden carp in the carriage rut. 'Well, golden carp,' I asked it, 'what are you doing here?' To which it replied, 'I am minister of the waves in the Eastern Sea. Do you have a gallon or a pint of water to keep me alive, sir?' 'Yes,' I said, 'I'm just wandering south to the lands of Ngwa and Viet and will channel water from the West River to meet you. Is that all right?'

"The golden carp flushed with anger and said, 'I've lost my normal environment and have no place to stay. If I get a gallon or a pint of water it will keep me alive. Rather than do what you propose, sir, you might as well go looking for me in a dried-fish shop pretty soon!'"

3

The scion of the Duke of Jen, having readied a great hook with a gigantic black rope and fifty steers as bait, hunkered on Mount K'uaichi and threw his line into the Eastern Sea. Dawn after dawn he fished, but a whole year passed and he didn't catch anything. At last, a great fish swallowed the bait and dove down, dragging the gigantic hook with him. Then it raced upward and, flailing its fins, raised mountainous white waves. The sea waters seethed with a ghostly sound, spreading terror for a thousand tricents.

Having caught such a fish, the scion of the Duke of Jen sliced and salted it. From the Chih River east and from Mount Ts'angwu north, there was no one who was not sated by that fish. In later generations, satirists of minor ability would all tell it to each other with alarm. Yet if the scion had snatched up his pole and line and scurried off to a ditch or drain to watch for salamanders and carp, surely it would have been hard for him to catch a great fish. Those who embellish their petty persuasions to curry favor with district magistrates are surely far from great perceptivity. For this reason, those who have not heard about the customs of clansman Jen are surely far from being able to participate in the government of the world.

4

Some literati were breaking open a grave mound in accordance with the *Odes* and the *Ritual.* The chief literatus shouted down to the others,

> "The sun is rising in the east!
> How is the affair getting on?"

The lesser literati said,

"We haven't taken off his skirt and jacket yet,
But there's a pearl in his mouth."

"Indeed, it is said in the *Odes:*

'The green, green wheat
Grows on the slopes of the tumulus.
While alive, he made no donations,
In death, why let him hold a pearl in his mouth?'

Grab hold of the hair on his temples and pull down on his beard.
By tapping on his chin with a metal mallet, you should be able to
open his jaws slowly, but don't damage the pearl in his mouth."

5

A disciple of Old Master Chenopod who had gone out to collect
firewood encountered Confucius. Upon his return, he told his
master about it, saying, "There's a man there whose upper body
is long and whose lower body is short. He's slightly hunchbacked
and his ears hang back. When he looks about, it's as though he
were managing all within the four seas. I wonder who he might
be?"

"It's Hillock," said Old Master Chenopod. "Call him here."
And after Confucius arrived, he said, "Hillock! Get rid of your
pompous attitude and your knowing look, then you'll really be a
superior man." Confucius bowed and was withdrawing when he
abruptly changed countenance and asked, "Will my enterprise
thereby be advanced?"

"You cannot bear the sufferings of a single age," said Old
Master Chenopod, "but you are oblivious to the troubles of
myriad ages. Is it because you were originally a simpleton, or
because your strategy is just not up to it? Your obliviousness
stems from your joy in dispensing favors, but it is your lifelong
shame. Only the behavior of a mediocre man would advance in

this fashion. You lead others on with fame, you bind yourself to others with subterfuge. Rather than praising Yao and condemning Chieh, it would be better for you to forget both of them and bring a close to your condemnation and praise. Contrariness is inevitably injurious, officiousness is inevitably depraved. The sage is hesitant in initiating affairs, so he always achieves success. And what may be said of your doings? Haughty to the very end!"

6

At midnight, Lord Yüan of Sung dreamed that a man with disheveled hair peeped in at him from a side door and said, "I'm from the Gulf of Tsailu. I was commissioned by the clear Yangtze River to go to the place of the Earl of the River, but was caught by the fisherman, Feeish."

When Lord Yüan awoke, he had someone divine the matter. The man said, "This is a sacred tortoise."

The lord said, "Is there a Feeish among the fishermen?"

"There is," said his attendants.

The lord said, "Order Feeish for a meeting at court."

The next day, Feeish appeared in court.

The lord said, "What fish have you caught?"

"I caught a white tortoise in my net," was the reply. "It's five feet in circumference."

The lord said, "Present your tortoise."

When the tortoise arrived, the lord both wanted to kill it and to keep it alive. His mind filled with doubt, the lord consulted a pyromantic oracle on the matter who said, "To kill the tortoise for purposes of pyromancy would be auspicious." Whereupon they cut the tortoise open. They drilled seventy-two holes, not one of which failed to give an accurate response.

"The sacred tortoise could appear in a dream to Lord Yüan," said Confucius, "but it couldn't escape Feeish's net. Its knowledge enabled the tortoise to respond accurately without fail when seventy-two holes were drilled in it, but not to escape from

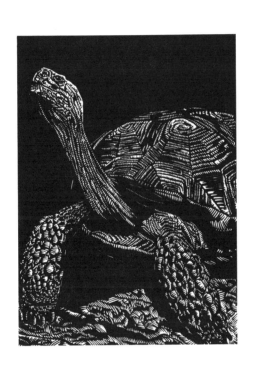

the calamity of having its intestines cut open. Such being the case, there are instances in which knowledge is encumbered and in which sacredness is ineffectual. Although someone may have ultimate knowledge, myriad men may scheme against him. Fish do not fear nets but they do fear pelicans. Get rid of small knowledge and your great knowledge will be illuminated; get rid of goodness and you will naturally be good. An infant when it is born can learn to speak without an eminent teacher because it dwells together with those who can speak."

7

Master Hui said to Master Chuang, "Sir, your words are useless."

"You can only begin to speak of what is useful with someone who knows what is useless," said Master Chuang. "Now, the earth is definitely broad and great, but what a man uses of it need only accommodate his feet. However, if one were to dig away the earth from around his feet all the way down to the Yellow Springs, would it still be of any use to the man?"

"It would be useless," said Master Hui.

"Then the usefulness of the useless is quite clear," said Master Chuang.

8

Master Chuang said, "If a man is capable of wandering, what's to keep him from wandering? If a man is incapable of wandering, will he ever get to wander? An escapist will and effacing behavior, alas! are not the business of one who has ultimate knowledge and substantial integrity. Some capitulate altogether and never turn around; some rush about furiously and never look back. Although they may be in the relationship of ruler and subject, it's only a matter of time before the age will change and there will be no reason for the one to despise the other.

Therefore, it is said, 'The ultimate man is not intransigent about his behavior.'

"To respect antiquity and belittle modernity is the habit of scholars. However, if we observe the modern world through the habit of the clansman Hsiwei, who would not be awash? Only the ultimate man can wander through the world without deviation, accommodating others without losing himself. Though he doesn't study their doctrines, he can accept ideas without being dismissive."

9

Acute eyes make for keen vision; acute ears make for keen hearing; an acute nose makes for keen smell; an acute mouth makes for keen taste; an acute mind makes for keen knowledge; acute knowledge makes for integrity. Whatever is the Way does not like to be obstructed. If it is obstructed, then it becomes choked. If it is unceasingly choked, then it becomes stagnant. If there is stagnation, a host of injurious effects are born.

That things may have knowledge depends on their breathing. If it is not plentiful, that is not to be blamed on heaven. Heaven penetrates them with it day and night without intermission, but man contrarily blocks up the openings. The abdominal cavity is spacious; the mind has its heavenly wanderings. If their chambers are not roomy, wife and mother-in-law will quarrel; if the mind has not its heavenly wanderings, the six senses will interfere with each other. The excellence of great forests, hills, and mountains for men is because their spirits cannot vanquish them.

10

Integrity overspills into fame, fame overspills into violence. Scheming is due to urgency; knowledge derives from competition; stoppage is born from conservatism; bureaucratic affairs result from acceding to the masses. When spring rains are timely, plants grow exuberantly. Thereupon, people start to weed them out with spade and hoe. Yet the plants that sprout back up to life are more than half, and nobody knows why.

11

Quietness can serve as a tonic for illness; massage can stave off old age; stillness can halt agitation. Although it is like this, these are what those who are vexed pay attention to; those who are at ease have never had to ask about them. Nor has the spiritual person ever had to ask how the sage admonishes all under heaven. Nor has the sage ever had to ask how the worthy man admonishes the world. Nor has the worthy man ever had to ask how the superior man admonishes his state. Nor has the superior man ever had to ask how the petty man accords with the times.

12

There was a man from the vicinity of the Yen Gate who, upon the death of his parents, was so skillful in emaciating himself that he was rewarded with the title of Official Teacher. As a result, half of the people in his village who emaciated themselves in emulation of him died. When Yao gave the rulership of all under heaven to Hsü Yu, the latter fled. When T'ang gave his to Wu Kuang, the latter was angry. When Chi T'o heard about it, he led his disciples to settle by the River K'uan, causing the feudal lords to mourn him for three years. Consequently, Shent'u Ti threw himself into the Yellow River.

13

A fish-trap is for catching fish; once you've caught the fish, you can forget about the trap. A rabbit-snare is for catching rabbits;

once you've caught the rabbit, you can forget about the snare. Words are for catching ideas; once you've caught the idea, you can forget about the words. Where can I find a person who knows how to forget about words so that I can have a few words with him?

27

METAPHORS

Perhaps the most difficult chapter in the book, "Metaphors" probes the question of language itself. The problem is how to convey ideas, sentiments, and meanings effectively through an inadequate medium. A sense of wonder at all the phenomena of the universe, big and small, pervades. Sensitive individuals are capable of transforming gracefully along with other creatures through life and death.

1

Metaphors are effective nine times out of ten and quotations seven times out of ten, but impromptu words come forth every day and harmonize within the framework of nature.

Metaphors are effective nine times out of ten because they borrow externals to discuss something. A father does not act as a matchmaker for his son. It's better for someone who is not the father to praise the son than for the father himself to do so. Then it won't be his own fault, but somebody else's fault. If someone agrees with oneself, one responds favorably, but if someone does not agree with oneself, one opposes them. One considers to be right those who agree with oneself and considers to be wrong those who disagree with oneself.

Quotations are effective seven times out of ten because their purpose is to stop speech. They are from our elders, those who precede us in years. But those who fill up the years of their old age without grasping what is significant and what is rudimentary are not really our predecessors. If a man has not that whereby he precedes others, he lacks the way of humanity. If a man lacks the way of humanity, he may be called a stale person.

Impromptu words pour forth every day and harmonize within the framework of nature. Consequently, there is effusive elaboration so that they may live out their years. Without speech, there is equality. Equality plus speech yields inequality; speech plus equality yields inequality. Therefore, it is said, "Speak nonspeech." If you speak nonspeech, you may speak till the end of your life without ever having spoken. If till the end of your life you do not speak, you will never have failed to speak. There are grounds for affirmation and there are grounds for denial. There are grounds for saying that something is so and there are grounds for saying that something is not so. Why are things so? They are so because we declare them to be so. Why are things not so? They are not so because we declare them to be not so. Wherein lies affirmation? Affirmation lies in our affirming. Wherein lies denial? Denial lies in our denying. All things are possessed of that which we may say is so; all things are possessed of that which we may affirm. There is no thing that is not so; there is no thing that is not affirmable. If it were not for the impromptu words that pour forth every day and harmonize within the framework of nature, who could last long?

The myriad things are all from seeds, and they succeed each other because of their different forms. From start to finish it is like a circle whose seam is not to be found. This is called the celestial potter's wheel, and the celestial potter's wheel is the framework of nature.

2

Master Chuang said to Master Hui, "When Confucius was in his sixtieth year, he had been through sixty transformations. What in the beginning he had considered right, he ended up considering wrong. He didn't know that what he now called right wasn't what he had considered wrong for fifty-nine years."

"Confucius applied himself to knowledge with diligent determination," said Master Hui.

"Confucius rejected that," said Master Chuang, "and never spoke about it. Confucius said, 'We receive our ability from the great root and restore our numinosity through living. When we sing it should match the pitch-pipes; when we speak it ought to match the laws. With profit and righteousness arrayed before us, likes and dislikes, right and wrong merely cause men to submit verbally. If, however, we are to have men submit in their hearts and not stand up against us, we must stabilize that which stabilizes all under heaven.' Enough! Enough! I cannot keep up with him."

3

When Master Tseng took office for a second time, his mind having undergone a second transformation, he said, "When I took office while my parents were still alive, although my grain allotment was only three pecks, my heart was happy. When I took office later, although my grain allotment was three thousand bushels, I couldn't share it with my parents, so my heart was sad."

The other disciples asked of Confucius, "May we say that such a one as Shen is free of the offense of entanglement?"

"But he *was* entangled. If he had had no entanglements, could he have had such sadness? He would have looked upon three pecks and three thousand bushels as though he were observing sparrows or mosquitoes passing before him."

4

Sir Wanderer of Countenance Complete declared to Sir Motley of Easturb, "From the time when I began to hear your words, the first year I was still in the wilderness, the second year I just followed along, the third year I understood, the fourth year I identified with things, the fifth year things came to me, the sixth year I was inspirited, the seventh year my heavenly nature was complete, the eighth year I was no longer aware of death or life, the ninth year I comprehended the great wonder."

5

Life has its actions, and that is death. Let the public be exhorted that there is a cause for their deaths. But the yang quality of their lives is without a cause. Is it really so? Where is it all headed? Where is it all not headed? Heaven has its astronomical enumerations; earth has its human occupations. Where shall I seek them? No one knows where they'll end, but how can they be without destiny? No one knows where they started, so how can they have a destiny? Where there are mutual correspondences, how can there be no spirits? Where there are no mutual correspondences, how can there be spirits?

6

Penumbra inquired of Shadow, saying, "A moment ago you were looking downward, but now you are looking upward; a moment ago you had your hair tied up, but now it is disheveled; a moment ago you were sitting down, but now you're standing up; a moment ago you were walking, but now you've stopped. Why is this?"

Shadow said, "I just flit about. Why ask about something so trivial? I have movement but don't know why. I seem like cicada shells or snake sloughs but am not. I coalesce when there's fire or sun; I dissolve when there's yin or night. Are these what I must depend upon? How much more so is it like this when there's nothing upon which to depend! When they come, I come with them; when they go, I go with them. When they are powerful, then I am powerful along with them. Since they are so powerful, why ask about them either?"

7

Sir Sunny Dweller went south to P'ei while Old Longears was wandering westward in Ch'in. Sir Sunny Dweller invited Old Longears to meet in the borderlands and then traveled to Liang where he encountered the Old Master. In the middle of the road, the Old Master looked up to heaven and sighed, saying, "At first I thought you could be taught, but now I realize that you cannot be."

Sir Sunny Dweller made no reply. When they reached their lodgings, Sir Sunny Dweller brought in water for the Old Master to wash his hands and to rinse his face, as well as a towel and a comb. Then he took his shoes off outside the door and, walking forward on his knees, said, "Just now your disciple wanted to request instruction from you, Master, but as you were walking you had no leisure and for that reason I dared not ask. Now that you are at leisure, I beg to ask about my faults."

The Old Master said,

"You have a supercilious
And haughty look;
Who would dwell with you?

'The greatest whiteness seems grimy,
The fullest integrity seems insufficient.'"

Sir Sunny Dweller abruptly changed countenance and said, "Respectfully I hear your commands."

When he first arrived at the lodge, the people there came out to welcome him. The master of the house brought him a mat and the wife brought him a towel and comb. The people in the lodge left their places at the mat and those who were warming themselves by the fire left their places at the stove. When he returned from his interview with the Old Master, the people in the lodge competed with him for places at the mat.

28

ABDICATING KINGSHIP

The best ruler is he who does not covet rulership—the people will follow him anywhere. The truly wise man, on the other hand, would not accept rulership or wealth and honor under any circumstances—poverty is a natural state of affairs for him.

1

Yao wished to abdicate his rulership of all under heaven to Hsü Yu, but Hsü Yu would not accept it. He then tried to abdicate to Sir Township Branch Father, but Sir Township Branch Father said, "It would be possible to make me the son of heaven. However, it so happens that I am suffering the illness of melancholia. While I am trying to cure it, I have no spare time to govern all under heaven." Now, the rulership of all under heaven is of ultimate importance, but he would not accept it for fear that it would harm his life. How much less would he let other things harm him! Only one who does not wish to take on the rulership of all under heaven may be entrusted with the rulership of all under heaven.

Shun wished to abdicate the rulership of all under heaven to

Sir Township Branch Uncle, but Sir Township Branch Uncle said, "It so happens that I am suffering from the illness of melancholia. While I am trying to cure it, I have no spare time to govern all under heaven." Therefore, although the rulership of all under heaven is a great instrument, he would not exchange his life for it. This shows wherein one who possesses the Way differs from common men.

Shun wished to abdicate the rulership of all under heaven to Goodroll, but Goodroll said, "I stand in the middle of universal space and time. In winter I wear skins and furs; in summer I wear clothes made from the fibers of arrowroot hemp. In spring I plow and plant, my physical form ready for the laborious toil; in autumn I gather in the harvest, my body ready for the rest and sustenance. When the sun comes up I work; when the sun sets I cease. I roam through heaven and earth and satisfy myself with the thoughts in my mind. Why would I want to take on the rulership of all under heaven? How sad, sir, that you do not understand me!" Thereupon, he refused to accept the offer. So he left and entered into the deep mountains, no one knew where.

Shun wished to abdicate the rulership of all under heaven to his friend, the farmer of Stone Door, but the farmer of Stone Door said, "As a person, your excellency, you're all contorted from your striving. You're someone who trusts his strength." Believing that Shun's integrity had not reached the ultimate, he loaded his belongings on his back and on his wife's head and, leading his son by the hand, went off to sea, never to return for the rest of his life.

2

When the Great King Pater Tan was dwelling in Pin, the Dik people attacked him. He presented them with skins and silks, but they would not accept them. He presented them with dogs and horses, but they would not accept them. He presented them with pearls and jade, but they would not accept them. What the Dik people sought was his territory.

The Great King Pater Tan said, "To dwell with people's older brothers and cause their younger brothers to be killed, to dwell with people's fathers and cause their sons to be killed—this I cannot bear. I urge all of you, my children, to remain where you are. What difference is there in being my subjects or in being subjects of the Dik people? And I have heard that a ruler should not employ what he uses for nourishment to harm those whom he nourishes." Thus taking his staff and riding-whip, he went away. But the people followed him in an unbroken line, whereupon he reestablished his state at the base of Mount Ch'i.

We may say that the Great King Pater Tan was able to respect life. A person who is able to respect life, though he be honored and wealthy, would not injure his person on account of what nourishes him, and though he be poor and lowly, would not burden his physical being on account of what profits him. The people of the present age who occupy high offices and who hold honorable titles all look seriously upon the prospect of losing them, but when they see a possibility of profit, they make light of the risk to their persons. Are they not deluded indeed?

3

In three successive generations, the people of Viet assassinated their ruler. Troubled by this, Prince Sou fled to the Cinnabar Caves, leaving the state of Viet without a ruler. The people searched for Prince Sou but could not find him, till finally they tracked him to the Cinnabar Caves. Prince Sou was unwilling to come out, but they smoked him out with mugwort and made him ride in the royal chariot. As Prince Sou held on to the straps to mount the chariot, he looked up to heaven and cried out, "A ruler! Oh, to be a ruler! Couldn't I alone have been spared from this?" Prince Sou did not dislike being ruler; he disliked the troubles inherent in being ruler. We may say that such a person as Prince Sou would not injure life on account of the state, and this was precisely why the people of Viet wanted to get him to be their ruler.

4

Han and Wei were competing with each other over some land that had been invaded. Sir Master Hua went to see Marquis Chaohsi who had a mournful look.

Sir Master Hua said, "Supposing, my lord, that all under heaven were to sign an agreement before you stating that 'Should the left hand seize it, the right hand will be disabled; should the right hand seize it, the left hand will be disabled. Yet he who seizes it will certainly gain all under heaven.' Would you seize it?"

"I would not seize it," said Marquis Chaohsi.

"Very good!" said Sir Master Hua. "Judging from this, your two arms are more important than all under heaven, but your person is even more important than your two arms. Han is far less significant than all under heaven, but what you are competing over now is far less significant than Han. Why, my lord, must you worry your person and injure your life by fretting over something you can't get?"

"Excellent!" said Marquis Hsi. "Many are those who have instructed me, but I have never heard this sort of advice."

Sir Master Hua may be said to have known what was insignificant and what was important.

5

The Lord of Lu, hearing that Yen Ho was a person who had attained the Way, dispatched a man to go before him with gifts. Yen Ho was waiting by a rustic village gate, wearing hempen clothing and feeding a cow by himself. When the messenger of the Lord of Lu arrived, Yen Ho himself received the man.

"Is this Yen Ho's house?" asked the messenger.

"It is Ho's house," answered Yen Ho.

As the messenger was presenting the gifts, Yen Ho responded by saying, "I'm afraid that you heard incorrectly and that the one who sent you with the presents will blame you. You had better check."

The messenger returned and, having checked over the matter, came back again to seek Yen Ho but could not find him. Thus does someone like Yen Ho truly dislike wealth and honor.

Therefore it is said,

"The truth of the Way
Is for governing the person.

Its remnants
Are for managing the state and family.
Its scraps
Are for governing all under heaven."

Judging from this, the achievements of emperors and kings are the leftover affairs of the sages, not that which fulfills the person or nourishes life. Most of the worldly gentlemen of today endanger their persons and abandon life in their greed for things. Is this not sad?

Whenever the sage makes a movement, he is certain to examine what his purpose is and what he is doing. If now, however, we suppose that there were a man who shot at a sparrow a thousand yards away with the pearl of the Marquis of Sui, the world would certainly laugh at him. Why is this? It is because what he uses is important and what he wants is insignificant. And is not life much more important than the pearl of the Marquis of Sui?

6

Sir Master Lieh was poverty stricken and his countenance had a starved look. A visitor spoke of this to Tzuyang, prime minister of Cheng, saying, "I believe that Lieh Yük'ou is a gentleman who possesses the Way, yet he dwells poverty stricken in your honor's state. Could it be that your honor does not like such gentlemen?" Tzuyang of Cheng immediately ordered an official to send him some grain. When Sir Master Lieh saw the messenger, he bowed twice but declined the grain.

After the messenger left, Sir Master Lieh went inside. Beating her breast, his wife said to him with resentment, "I have heard that the wife and children of one who possesses the Way all enjoy peaceful pleasure, but now we have a starved look. His honor recognized his error and sent you some food, but you, sir, would not accept it. Could we be so ill-fated?"

"His honor himself does not know me," Sir Master Lieh said to her with a laugh. "He sent me the grain because of what someone told him. Ultimately, he may also hold me a criminal because of what someone tells him. That's why I did not accept it."

In the end, the people actually did riot and killed Tzuyang.

7

When King Chao of Ch'u lost his kingdom, the sheep butcher Happy followed the king in his flight. When King Chao returned to his kingdom and was going to reward those who had followed him, he came to sheep butcher Happy, who, "When our great king lost his kingdom, I lost my sheep butchery. When he returned to his kingdom, I likewise returned to my sheep butchery. His subject's titles and emoluments have already been restored, so why should he reward me any further?"

"Force it upon him!" said the king.

"The great king's loss of his kingdom was not due to any crime of mine," said sheep butcher Happy, "therefore I would not presume to submit to punishment for that. The great king's return to his kingdom was not due to any achievement of mine, therefore I would not presume to receive a reward for that."

"Admit him to my presence!" said the king.

"The laws of the kingdom of Ch'u," said sheep butcher Happy, "require that one be admitted to the presence of the king only upon the receipt of a heavy reward for great achievement. Now, my knowledge was insufficient to preserve the kingdom and my courage was insufficient to kill the invaders. When the armies of Ngwa entered Ying, fearing the difficulties, I ran away from the invaders. I did not follow our great king on purpose. Now, our great king wishes to abrogate the law and rescind the regulations by admitting me into his presence. This is not what I would want to have heard about me everywhere under heaven."

"Sheep butcher Happy occupies a lowly position," said the king to his minister of war, Tzuchi, "but his display of righteousness is very high. You may extend to him on my behalf the position of one of the three banners."

"I know that the position of 'three banners' is more honorable than a sheep butcher's stall," said sheep butcher Happy, "and that an emolument of ten thousand bushels would make me wealthier than the profits from my sheep butchery. Yet, out of greed for titles and emoluments, how could I give my ruler a name for reckless bestowal? I would not presume to receive them but would rather return to the stall of my sheep butchery." Accordingly, he refused to accept the king's rewards.

8

When Yüan Hsien was dwelling in Lu, the walls of his house were only a few yards around. It was thatched with live grass; had a thornwood door that was incomplete, a mulberry branch for a door-pivot, and bottomless earthen jars for windows; the two rooms were separated by a serge cloth. It leaked above and was damp below, but there he sat squarely, strumming and singing.

Tzukung, wearing a purple inner garment and a white robe, went to see Yüan Hsien riding in a carriage drawn by large horses, the top of which was so high that it would not fit into the alley. Yüan Hsien, wearing a cap of mulberry bark and slippers tied together with string, and supporting himself on a chenopod cane, went to answer the door.

"Gracious!" said Tzukung. "What distress are you suffering from, sir?"

"I have heard," responded Yüan Hsien, "that to be without property is called poverty and that inability to put one's learning into practice is called distress. Now, I may be poor, but I'm not in distress."

Tzukung shrank back with an embarrassed look.

"To strive for worldly approbation in one's practice," said Yüan Hsien with a laugh, "to form cliquish friendships, to pursue learning for the sake of impressing others, to teach for the sake of one's own aggrandizement, to cloak oneself in humaneness and righteousness, and to flaunt one's chariots and horses—these are not what I, Hsien, can bear to do!"

9

When Master Tseng was dwelling in Wey, he wore a robe quilted with hemp whose outer layer was missing. His face was swollen and inflamed, his hands and feet were callused. He would go three days without lighting a fire and ten years without having any clothes made. If he tried to put his cap on straight, the throatband would break; when he tugged at his lapels, his elbows would be revealed; and when he put on his shoes, the heels would split. His shoes tied on with string, he would shuffle along singing the "Lauds of Shang." The sound of his voice filled heaven and earth, as though it came from a bronze bell or a stone chime. The son of heaven could not get him to be a minister, the feudal lords could not get him to be their friend. Thus, he who nourishes his determination forgets about his physical form, he who nourishes his physical form forgets about profit, and he who applies himself to the Way forgets about mind.

10

"Come here, Hui," said Confucius to Yen Hui. "Your family is poor and your dwelling is lowly. Why don't you take office?"

"I'm unwilling to take office," replied Yen Hui. "I have fifty sixth-acres of fields beyond the outer walls of the city, which are sufficient to provide me with biscuits and gruel. I have ten sixth-acres within the outer walls of the city, which are sufficient to supply me with silk and hemp. Strumming my lute is sufficient for entertaining myself and your doctrines which I study are sufficient for enjoying myself. I'm unwilling to take office."

Abashed, Confucius changed countenance and said, "Your thoughts are excellent, Hui! I have heard 'One who knows what is sufficient would not burden himself for profit. One who understands self-contentment will not be frightened by loss. One who practices cultivation within will not be chagrined at having no position.' Long have I, Hillock, been preaching this, but today I have at last seen it in Hui. This is my gain."

11

Prince Mou of Chungshan said to Master Chan, "My person is situated by the rivers and the sea, but my heart dwells at the court of Wei. What's to be done?"

"Emphasize life," said Master Chan. "If you emphasize life, then you will look upon profit as insignificant."

"Although I know this," said Prince Mou of Chungshan, "I have not been able to conquer myself."

"If you cannot conquer yourself, then follow your inclinations."

"Wouldn't that be an offense against the spirit?"

"If you cannot conquer yourself and force yourself not to follow your inclinations, this is called 'double injury.' A person who is doubly injured will not be classed among the long-lived."

Mou of Wei was the prince of a state with ten thousand chariots. For him to seek reclusion amid crags and caves was more difficult than it would have been for a common scholar. Although he had not attained the Way, we may say that he had an idea of it.

12

When Confucius was isolated between Ch'en and Ts'ai, he had no cooked food to eat for seven days, but only some chenopod soup without any rice mixed in. His face looked very exhausted, but he still kept strumming and singing in his room. Yen Hui was outside picking vegetables, while Tzulu and Tzukung, who were talking together, said to him, "Our master was twice driven out of Lu, had his traces obliterated in Wey, had a tree he was resting under chopped down in Sung, was impoverished in the capitals of the old Shang duchy and the Chou kingdom, and is besieged in the area between Ch'en and Ts'ai. If someone were to kill our master, he would be guiltless, and there is no prohibition against holding him prisoner. And yet he keeps strumming his lute and singing without a break in the sound. Can a superior man be so shameless as this?"

Having nothing with which to respond to them, Yen Hui went in and reported to Confucius what they had said. Confucius pushed his lute aside and said with a deep sigh, "Tzulu and Tzukung are petty men. Summon them to come here and I'll speak to them."

Tzulu and Tzukung entered. "It may be said that, in this sort of situation, you are really isolated!" said Tzulu.

"What are you talking about?" said Confucius. "When the superior man communicates with the Way, it is called 'communication.' When he is isolated from the Way, it is called 'isolation.' Now, I embrace the way of humaneness and righteousness to encounter the troubles of a disordered age. How can you say that I am isolated? Therefore, through introspection, I am not isolated from the Way. Though I confront difficulties, I do not lose my virtue. When great cold has arrived and frost and snow have descended, we may know thereby the vegetal vigor of the arborvitae. The perils of Ch'en and Ts'ai are a blessing for me!"

Confucius returned to playing his lute and singing ardently to its accompaniment, while Tzulu picked up a shield and danced energetically.

Tzukung said, "I did not know heaven's height nor earth's depth!"

The ancients who attained the Way were joyful both in isolation and in communication, but what made them joyful was not the isolation nor the communication. When the Way is attained in this fashion, isolation and communication are as the sequence of winter cold and summer heat, of wind and rain. Therefore, Hsü Yu found pleasure north of the Ying River and the Earl of Kung attained his ambition on the top of Mount Kung.

13

Shun wished to abdicate the rulership of all under heaven to his friend, Northerner Nonprefer, who said, "What a strange man the ruler is! When he was dwelling among his channeled fields, he aspired to wander at the gate of Yao. But it's not only this. Now he wants to sully me with his disgraceful conduct. I would be ashamed to see him." Whereupon he threw himself into the watery depths of Ch'ingling.

14

When T'ang was about to attack Chieh, he consulted with Follow Transform, who said, "It's none of my business."

"Whom may I consult?" asked T'ang.

"I don't know."

T'ang then consulted with Oblivious to Glory, who said, "It's none of my business."

"Whom may I consult?" asked T'ang.

"I don't know."

"How about Yi Yin?" asked T'ang.

"He has a powerful ability to endure infamy. I don't know anything else about him."

Thereupon T'ang consulted with Yi Yin, attacked Chieh, and subdued him, after which he wished to abdicate to Follow Transform, who declined the offer, saying, "When your majesty was about to attack Chieh and consulted with me, you must have thought I was a brigand. Having conquered Chieh and wishing to abdicate to me, you must think that I am greedy. I was born into a disordered age, and a man who is without the Way comes to me twice and sullies me with his disgraceful conduct. I cannot endure listening to the repetition of these things." Whereupon he threw himself into the Chou River and died.

T'ang then wished to abdicate in favor of Oblivious to Glory, saying, "He who is wise planned it; he who is valiant carried it out; he who is humane should occupy it—that was the way of antiquity. Why, sir, do you not take the position?"

Oblivious to Glory declined, saying, "To depose one's sovereign is to be unrighteous; to kill the people is to be inhumane. If another person risks difficulty and I reap the benefits therefrom, I would be dishonest. I have heard it said, 'If it is not righteous, one does not accept the salary; in an age that lacks the Way, one does not tread upon the soil.' How much less should I accept this position of honor! I cannot endure seeing this any longer." Whereupon, carrying a stone on his back, he drowned himself in the Lu River.

15

Long ago, at the rise of the Chou dynasty, there were two noblemen named Poyi and Shuch'i who lived in Kuchu. The two men spoke together, saying, "We have heard that in the west there is a man who, it would seem, possesses the Way. Let us go and observe him."

When they had arrived south of Mount Ch'i, King Wu heard about them and sent Uncle Tan to see them and make a covenant with them, saying, "Bestow wealth of the second rank on them and appoint them as officials of the first grade." The covenant was to be smeared with the blood of a sacrificial animal and buried.

The two men looked at each other and laughed, saying, "Ha! How strange! This is not what we would call the Way. Of old, when the Divine Farmer possessed all under heaven, he sacrificed at the proper seasons and with the utmost reverence, but did not pray for blessings from the gods. Toward men, he was loyal and sincere, doing his utmost to govern them, but without seeking anything from them. He enjoyed administering for the sake of administering; he enjoyed governing for the sake of governing. He did not fulfill himself through the ruin of others; he did not exalt himself by debasing others; he did not profit himself by taking advantage of the times. Now the Chou, seeing the disorder of the Yin, have seized the administration. They conspire with those on high and circulate bribes to those below. They presume upon their troops to preserve their majesty. They slaughter sacrificial animals and make covenants to demonstrate their faith. They flaunt their deeds to please the masses. They kill and attack in their desire for gain. This is to displace disorder by exchanging it for tyranny. We have heard that the noblemen of antiquity did not shirk their duties when they encountered an age of good government and did not dishonorably cling to survival in an age of disorder. Now all under heaven is in darkness; the integrity of the Chou has declined. Rather than ally with the Chou and thereby besmirch our persons, it would be better to shun them and thereby preserve the purity of our conduct."

The two princes went north to Shouyang Mountain where they died of starvation. Men such as Poyi and Shuch'i, when it comes to wealth and honor, even if they could obtain them, would certainly not depend upon them. Their lofty moral principles and zealous conduct, their solitary joy in their own will, their not serving in their age—such were the ideals of these two noblemen.

29

ROBBER FOOTPAD

The most sustained and integral narrative in the Chuang Tzu *occupies the first half of this chapter. An elaboration of a theme from Chapter 10, it is an incredibly powerful denunciation of Confucius by a brigand. The remainder of the chapter consists of censures against wealth and power. The wise man eschews fame and gain, tending instead to his spiritual equanimity.*

1

Confucius was a friend of Underwillow Chi, who had a younger brother named Robber Footpad. Robber Footpad had nine thousand troops who followed him and who marched at will everywhere under heaven, encroaching violently upon the feudal lords. They bore through walls and wrenched off doors, drove off people's cattle and horses, and carried away people's wives and daughters. In their greed for gain, they forgot their kin, disregarded their parents and brethren, and did not sacrifice to their ancestors. Wherever they passed through a region, the people in the bigger states guarded their city walls, while those in the smaller states entered their fortifications. Myriads of people suffered because of them.

"Those who are fathers," said Confucius to Underwillow Chi, "should certainly be able to appeal to their sons, and those who are older brothers should certainly be able to instruct their younger brothers. If fathers cannot appeal to their sons and older brothers cannot instruct their younger brothers, there is no honor in the relationship between father and son, between older brother and younger brother. Now, sir, you are a nobleman of ability in this age and your younger brother is Robber Footpad. He harms all under heaven, yet you cannot instruct him. I must admit, sir, that I am embarrassed for you. Let me go speak to him for you."

"Sir," said Underwillow Chi, "you say that those who are fathers should certainly be able to appeal to their sons, and those who are older brothers should certainly be able to instruct their younger brothers. But if sons will not listen to the appeals of their fathers and younger brothers will not accept the instructions of their older brothers, even though one may have your powers of disputation, sir, what can be done about it? What's more, Footpad is a person whose mind is like a bubbling spring and whose thoughts are like a whirlwind. He is strong enough to repel his enemies and his powers of disputation are sufficient to gloss over his wrongs. If you go along with his mind he's happy, but if you go against his mind he'll get angry. He readily abuses others when he speaks. You must not go to him, sir."

Confucius did not heed his advice. With Yen Hui as his charioteer and Tzukung on his right, he went to see Robber Footpad, who was just then resting his troops to the south of Mount T'ai and eating a dinner of hashed human liver. Confucius got down from his carriage and went forward. Upon seeing the officer in charge of receiving visitors, he said, "I, Hillock K'ung of Lu, have heard of the general's lofty righteousness." Respectfully, he bowed twice to the officer.

The officer entered to announce the visitor. When Robber Footpad heard that Confucius had come, he was greatly angered. His eyes blazing like stars and his hair rising till it touched his cap, he asked, "Is not this fellow Hillock K'ung, the clever hypocrite from the state of Lu? Tell him for me, 'You make speeches and compose phrases, recklessly citing kings Wen and Wu. You wear a cap decorated with twigs and branches and a cummerbund of dead ox hide. You are wordy and prone to exaggerate. You eat without plowing, dress without weaving. You flap your lips and wag your tongue, presumptuously fabricating right and wrong, thereby confusing the rulers of all under heaven and causing the scholars of all under heaven not to return to what is fundamental. You recklessly propound filial devotion and fraternal duty, yet try your luck with the feudal lords, the wealthy, and the honored. Your crimes are great, your offenses enormous. Go back where you came from quickly! Otherwise, I'll supplement my lunch with your liver!' "

Confucius sent in another communication, saying, "I have received the favor of your brother Chi and hope that I shall be permitted to step beneath your curtain."

After the officer in charge of receiving visitors had communicated this message, Robber Footpad said, "Have him come before me!"

Confucius hurried forward but, declining to be seated on a mat, hastily turned back and then bowed twice to Robber Footpad. This greatly angered Robber Footpad who stretched out both his legs, placed his hand on his sword, and said with glaring eyes and a growl like a nursing tigress, "Come before me, Hillock! If what you say goes along with my thoughts you will live, but if it goes against what's in my mind you will die."

"I have heard," said Confucius, "that all under heaven have three virtues. To grow up tall and big, to be peerlessly handsome and good, to please everyone who sees him, be they young or old, honored or lowly—this is to have superior virtue. To have knowledge that ties together heaven and earth, to be able to dispute on all manner of things—this is to have middling virtue. To be brave and bold, decisive and daring, to gather in multitudes and lead on troops—this is to have inferior virtue. Whoever has one of these virtues is capable of facing south and styling himself 'solitary.' Now you, general, are someone who combines all three. Your person is eight feet two inches tall, your face is radiant, your lips are like shining cinnabar, your teeth are like even cowry shells, your voice is tuned to the Yellow Bell, and yet you are named Robber Footpad. I must admit, general, that I am ashamed for you and cannot approve of this.

"If you are of a mind to listen to me, general, permit me to go south to Ngwa and Viet as your ambassador, to go north to Ch'i and Lu as your ambassador, to go east to Sung and Wey as your ambassador, to go west to Chin and Ch'u as your ambassador. I will have them build a great city of several hundred tricents for you, general, will have them establish an appanage of several hundred thousand households for you, and will have them respect you, general, as a feudal lord. You will begin anew with all under heaven, will disband your troops and demobilize your soldiers, will collect and nourish your brothers, and will reverently sacrifice to your ancestors. This would be the conduct of a sage and a nobleman of ability and what all under heaven wish for."

Greatly angered, Robber Footpad said, "Come before me, Hillock! Those who reprimand with gain and remonstrate with words may all be said to be stupid and crude commoners. To be tall and big, to be handsome and good, and to please those who see me—these are virtues inherited from my parents. Even if you had not praised me for them, do you think that I wouldn't have known about them myself?

"Moreover, I have heard that those who are fond of praising others to their face are also fond of slandering them behind their back. Now, your telling me about a great city and multitudes of people is because you want to reprimand me with gain and treat me as a commoner. How could that last long? The greatest city cannot be greater than all under heaven. Yao and Shun possessed all under heaven, but their sons and grandsons did not even have land enough in which to stick an awl. T'ang and Wu were established as sons of heaven, but their later generations were severed. Wasn't this because their gains had been great?

"Moreover, I have heard that in ancient times birds and beasts were many and men were few, so the people lived in nests in order to avoid them. By day they would gather acorns and chestnuts, and at evening they would roost in their trees. Therefore, they were called the people of the clansman of the freehold at Nest. In ancient times the people did not know the use of clothes. In summer they would accumulate much firewood and in winter they would warm themselves with it. Therefore, they were called people who knew how to take care of their lives. In the age of the Divine Farmer, when the people lay down they were content and when they got up they were peaceable. The people knew their mothers but not their fathers. They lived together with elk and deer. They plowed so they would have food; they wove so they would have clothes. They had no mind to harm one another. This is the fullness of ultimate virtue. The Yellow Emperor, however, could not maximize his virtue. He fought with Ch'ihyu in the wilds of Cholu and the blood flowed for a hundred tricents. When Yao and Shun arose, they established their crowd of ministers. T'ang banished his sovereign and King Wu killed Chow. Ever after this, the strong oppressed the weak and the many tyrannized the few. Ever since T'ang and Wu, they have all been a bunch who bring disorder to the people.

"Now you, sir, cultivate the way of Wen and Wu; you manipulate the disputations of all under heaven to instruct later ages. With your ample robe and broad belt, your dissembling words and fraudulent conduct, you confuse and delude the sovereigns of all under heaven, wishing thereby to seek wealth and honor. There are no greater robbers than you, sir. Why don't all under heaven call you Robber Hillock instead of calling me Robber Footpad? With your sweet phrases, you persuaded Tzulu to become a follower of yours. You had him get rid of his peaked cap and remove his long sword, so as to receive your instructions. All under heaven say that Confucius can stop tyranny and prevent wrongs. In the end, however, when Tzulu wished to kill the Lord of Wey, the affair miscarried and they displayed his pickled corpse on the east gate of Wey. This shows the imperfection of your teaching, sir.

"Do you call yourself a nobleman of ability and a sage? But you were twice driven out of Lu, had your traces obliterated in Wey, were isolated in Ch'i, and were besieged in the area of Ch'en and Ts'ai, leaving no place under heaven where your person might be accommodated. It was your instructions that brought upon Tzulu this calamity of being pickled. You, as superior, can do nothing for your own person, and your subordinates can do nothing for others. Is your way worth honoring, sir?

"There is no one whom the world esteems as much as the Yellow Emperor, but even the Yellow Emperor was unable to perfect his virtue and fought in the wilds of Cholu, causing blood to flow for a hundred tricents. Yao was unkind, Shun was unfilial, Yü was partially withered, T'ang banished his sovereign, and King Wu attacked Chow. . . . These are the six men whom the world esteems, but if we discuss them thoroughly, they were all deluded by gain and forcefully opposed their own emotions and natures. Their conduct is thus quite shameful.

"Those whom the world considers worthy noblemen include Poyi and Shuch'i. Poyi and Shuch'i took leave of the Lord of Kuchu and starved to death at Shouyang Mountain, their bones and flesh remaining unburied. Pao Chiao glamorized his conduct and criticized the world, but he died with his arms wrapped around a tree. When Shent'u Ti's criticisms went unheeded, he threw himself into the river carrying a stone on his back and was eaten by fishes and turtles. Chieh Tzut'ui, being of utmost loyalty, cut flesh from his own thigh to feed Duke Wen. When Duke Wen later turned his back on him, Tzut'ui became angry and went away, wrapping his arms around a tree and being burnt to death. Tailborn had an appointment with a girl beneath a bridge, but the girl did not come. The water rose, but he would not leave, and he died with his arms wrapped around a pillar of the bridge. These six men were no different from a dog whose carcass is hung outside the door to ward off evil spirits, a pig that is sacrificed to the god of the river, or a starved beggar who has frozen to death in a ditch but still holds his alms gourd. They all put a premium on fame and despised death, paying no regard to the fundamental nourishment of their allotted life span.

"There are none whom the world considers such loyal ministers as Prince Pikan and Wu Tzuhsü. Yet Tzuhsü's body was cast into the Yangtze River and Pikan's heart was cut open. The world considered these two men loyal ministers, but in the end they were laughed at by all under heaven. Judging from the above cases, down to Tzuhsü and Pikan, none are worth honoring.

"As for what you're trying to persuade me with, if you tell me about the affairs of ghosts, that's something I can't know anything about; if you tell me about the affairs of men, it's no more than this—what I've already heard about and know.

"Now, sir, I shall tell you about the human condition. The eyes desire to see colors; the ears desire to hear sounds; the mouth desires to taste flavors; the will and vital breath desire fulfillment. Man's highest longevity is a hundred years, medium longevity is eighty, and lowest longevity is sixty. If we exclude illness, death, and dread, the days that remain on which we can open our mouths to laugh amount to no more than four or five in a month. Heaven and earth are timeless, but the death of man is fixed in time. If we take an entity that is fixed in time and entrust it to timelessness, its brevity will be no different from that of Piebald Thoroughbred passing a crack in a wall. None who are unable to gratify their volition and to nourish their allotted life span are in communication with the Way.

"Everything you have spoken, Hillock, is what I have rejected. Go back immediately. Speak no more! Your way is a frenzied and frantic affair that is deceitful, clever, vain, and hypocritical—not what can be used to fulfill the truth. It's not worth discussing!"

Confucius bowed twice and hurried away. He went out the door and mounted his carriage. Three times the reins fell from his grasp. His eyes were so blurred that he couldn't see anything and his complexion was like dead ashes. Leaning against the crossbar with head bowed, he could scarcely catch his breath. When he returned to Lu, he happened to meet Underwillow Chi outside the east gate. "Regrettably," said Underwillow Chi, "I haven't seen you for the last few days and your carriage and horses look as though you've been traveling. Could it be that you went off to see Footpad?"

Confucius looked up to heaven and said with a sigh, "Yes."

"Might it be that Footpad went against your ideas as I predicted he would?" asked Underwillow Chi.

"Yes," said Confucius. "I may be said to be one who cauterizes himself when he's not even sick. I ran off hastily to grab the tiger by his head and tweak his whiskers, and I narrowly escaped his mouth."

2

Tzuchang asked Fully Ill-Gotten, "Why don't you behave virtuously? If you don't behave virtuously, you won't be trusted; if you're not trusted, you won't be appointed to office; and if you're not appointed to office, you will not realize any gain. Therefore, if you judge the matter on the basis of fame or estimate it on the basis of gain, righteousness is truly the right course. But if you reject fame and gain and reflect on the matter in your mind, you will find that the gentleman's virtuous behavior cannot for a day fail to be without righteousness."

"Those who are without shame become wealthy," said Fully Ill-Gotten, "and those who are much trusted become prominent. The greatest fame and gain would seem to lie in shamelessness and trust. Therefore, if you judge the matter on the basis of fame or estimate it on the basis of gain, trust is truly the right course.

But if you reject fame and gain and reflect on the matter in your mind, you will find that the gentleman's virtuous behavior is to embrace heaven."

"Long ago," said Tzuchang, "Chieh and Chow were honored as sons of heaven, and they possessed the wealth of all under heaven. Now, if we were to say to a pilferer, 'Your conduct is like that of Chieh and Chow,' he would blush and, in his heart, would not submit to such an accusation. Thus they are despised even by petty men. Confucius and Mo Ti were poverty-stricken commoners, but if we were now to say to a prime minister, 'Your conduct is like that of Confucius and Mo Ti,' he would change countenance in embarrassment, declaring that he is not worthy of such a comparison. Thus they are sincerely honored by noblemen. Therefore, though one may be powerful as the son of heaven, he will not necessarily be honored; though one may be poverty stricken as a commoner, he will not necessarily be despised. The distinction between honor and contempt lies in the quality of one's conduct."

"Small robbers are arrested," said Fully Ill-Gotten, "and great robbers become feudal lords. It is within the gates of the feudal lords that the righteous nobleman is preserved. Of old, Hsiaopo, who was Duke Huan, killed his older brother and took in his sister-in-law as a wife, yet Kuan Chung served as his minister; Viscount Fieldborn, Ch'ang, murdered his ruler and usurped the state, yet Confucius accepted presents from him. In their discussions Kuan Chung and Confucius despised them, but in their conduct they were subservient to them. Thus the emotions stemming from their words and their conduct were in a fractious war within their breasts. Is this not perverse? Therefore, it is said in a book, 'Who is good? Who is bad? He who is successful takes the headmost; he who is unsuccessful takes the hindmost.'"

"If you do not behave virtuously," said Tzuchang, "there will be no distinction between distant and close relatives, there will be no usages for the honored and the despised, there will be no order for the old and the young. Then how will you distinguish among the five relationships and the six positions?"

"Yao killed his eldest son," said Fully Ill-Gotten, "and Shun exiled his half-brother—did they maintain a distinction between distant and close relatives? T'ang banished Chieh and King Wu killed Chow—did they maintain the usages for the honored and the despised? Prince Junior assumed the legal succession and the Duke of Chou killed his elder brothers—did they maintain the order between young and old? Given the specious phraseology of the Confucian literati and the universal love of the Mohists, would there be a distinction among the five relationships and the six positions?

"Moreover, sir, your goal is fame and my goal is gain. The actualities of fame and gain are not in accord with principle and are not illuminated by the Way. The other day, I put our argument before Bondless, who said, 'The petty man sacrifices himself for property; the superior man sacrifices himself for fame. While the distortion of their attributes and the change of their nature may be different, they are identical in that they end up by rejecting what they should be doing and sacrificing themselves for what they should not be doing. Therefore, it is said,

"Do not be a petty man,
Turn and sacrifice yourself for heaven;
Do not be a superior man,
Follow the principles of heaven.

Whether a thing be crooked or straight,
View it in the pinnacle of heaven;
Facing the four directions, observe—
Ebb and flow with the times.

Whether a thing be right or wrong,
Hold fast to the circular mechanism;

Alone, complete your ideas,
And roam with the way.

Do not be exclusive in your conduct,
Do not complete your righteousness,
Or you will fail in what you are doing.

Do not hasten toward wealth,
Do not sacrifice yourself for completion,
Or you will lose the heaven in you."

" 'Pikan had his heart cut out; Tzuhsü had his eyes plucked out—such are the misfortunes brought about by loyalty. Straightup witnessed against his father; Tailborn drowned—such are the calamities brought about by trustworthiness. Master Pao dried out standing up; Master Shen did not defend himself—such are the harms brought about by honesty. Confucius would not see his mother; Master K'uang would not see his father—such are the failings brought about by righteousness. These are cases transmitted from former ages that are talked about in later ages. They demonstrate that noblemen, by rectifying their speech and regularizing their conduct, submit to tragedy and meet with calamity.' "

3

Insufficient inquired of Know Harmony, saying, "Among the masses of men, there are none who do not aspire to fame and go after gain. People turn to those who are wealthy. Having turned to them, they are subservient and, being subservient, they honor them. To be honored by the subservient is the way to long life, rest for the body, and a joyous intent. Now, sir, do you alone not aspire to this because your knowledge is insufficient? Or may it be that you know about it but that you don't have the strength to be able to carry it out? Do you purposely push for rectitude and never forget it?"

"Now, let us suppose," said Know Harmony, "that there is this sort of man who believes that, in comparison with his own contemporaries and his own compatriots, he is a nobleman who has broken with vulgarity and transcended the world. But in his examination of the ancient and the contemporary, in his distinguishing between right and wrong, he is totally without a controlling rectitude and evolves along with the vulgarity of his age. He gets rid of what is most important and he rejects what is most respected in order to do what he does. Is this not far from 'the way to long life, rest for the body, and a joyous intent' which has been discussed? Upon grievous anxiety and tranquil repose, he reflects not in his body; upon timorous fear and gleeful happiness, he reflects not in his mind. He knows that he does what he does but does not know why he does it. For this reason, though he may be honored as the son of heaven and have the wealth of all under heaven, he will not be free from calamities."

"Wealth," said Insufficient, "is in every respect beneficial to man. The exhaustive appreciation of beauty and the thorough exercise of power are not what the ultimate man can grasp nor what the worthy can reach. By commandeering the brave strength of others, one may assume majestic might; by employing the wise counsels of others, one may assume intelligent discrimination; by borrowing the virtues of others, one may assume worthy goodness. Then, even though he does not possess the state, a man will be as awe-inspiring as the ruler-father. Furthermore, the effect of sound, color, flavors, authority, and power upon man is such that the mind enjoys them without having to learn from others and the body takes pleasure in them without having to emulate others. Desires, dislikes, aversions, and predilections, indeed, do not require a teacher—this is the nature of man. Even though all under heaven may contradict me, who can dismiss these traits?"

"The action of the wise man," said Know Harmony, "is intentionally initiated on behalf of the hundred clans. He does not violate the statutes and, for this reason, feeling that what he has is sufficient, he does not compete for more. Having no reason for acting he does not seek anything. If what he has is insufficient, he seeks what he needs, competing in all quarters without considering himself greedy. If he has an excess, he will decline any more, rejecting all under heaven without considering himself incorrupt. For him, the reality of incorruption and greed is not compelled by externals, but by turning inward to reflect on his own measure. He may wield the power of the son of heaven, but he would not be arrogant to others on account of his honor; he may have the wealth of all under heaven, but he would not be contemptuous of others on account of his property. He estimates risks and contemplates contrarieties. If he believes that something may be harmful to his nature, declining, he will refuse to accept it, but not because he wants fame or praise. Concord prevailed when Yao and Shun were emperors; not because they were humane to all under heaven, but because they did not harm life with what was deemed attractive. Goodroll and Hsü Yu were offered the emperorship but refused to accept it, not because they declined with vain phrases, but because they did not harm themselves with affairs. These men all acceded to what was beneficial and declined what was harmful, and all under heaven declare them worthy for that. Thus, they may have such renown, but not because they attempted to enhance their fame and praise."

"By necessarily maintaining their fame," said Insufficient, "they embitter their bodies and deprive themselves of all sweetness. By maintaining their life with restricted sustenance, they are merely staving off death through prolonged illness and lengthy crisis."

"Equanimity," said Know Harmony, "is blessedness, and having an excess is harmful. It is so with all things, but particularly with property. Now, the ears of the wealthy man are entranced by the sounds of bells, drums, pipes, and flutes, and his mouth is sated with the flavors of domesticated animal flesh, thick wines, and liqueurs. Consequently, his thoughts are stimulated so he ignores his true enterprise—we may say that he is disordered. He is immersed in plenitude, as though he were walking up a slope bearing a heavy burden—we may say that he is embittered. He tries to derive solace from his greed for property; he tries to derive fulfillment from his greed for authority. If he dwells quietly, he becomes depressed; if his body is sleek, he becomes manic—we may say that he is diseased. In his desire for wealth and penchant for gain, the walls of his home are stuffed full but he doesn't know how to escape, relying on his possessions and not being able to give them up—we may say that he is disgraced. He amasses property that is of no use to him, clings to it fervently and won't give it up. His mind thoroughly vexed, he seeks ever more and doesn't know when to stop—we may say that he is troubled. Within, he suspects filching, begging thieves; without, he fears harm from bandits and robbers. At home, he builds crenelated towers all around; abroad, he dares not walk alone—we may say that he is frightened. These six conditions are the ultimate harm for all under heaven, but everyone is ignorant of them and no one knows how to examine himself for them. When calamity arrives, he seeks with the utmost of his nature and by exhausting his property to bring back just one undisturbed day but he cannot. Therefore, he searches for fame but it cannot be seen; he seeks for gain but it cannot be found. His thoughts are enmeshed and his body is broken in competition for these things—is he not deluded?"

30

DISCOURSING ON
SWORDS

This short chapter consists of a single tale in which Master Chuang takes the role of an accomplished swordsman. Speaking metaphorically, he defeats all of his formidable opponents with his razor-sharp tongue. In the process, he jolts a king who is addicted to swordfighting back to his senses.

1

Long ago, King Wen of Chao was fond of swords. More than three thousand swordsmen clustered around his gate as guests. Day and night they dueled before him. There were more than a hundred casualties a year, but he was so enamored of their bouts that he never grew weary of them. It was like this for three years, but the kingdom declined, so the other feudal lords began to plot against Chao.

Troubled by this, the heir apparent K'uei summoned his attendants and said, "Whoever can persuade the king to put a stop to these swordsmen, I will reward with a thousand pieces of gold."

"Master Chuang surely can," said the attendants.

Thereupon the heir apparent sent men with a thousand pieces of gold to offer to Master Chuang. Master Chuang would not accept them, but went back together with the messengers. When he saw the heir apparent he said, "What instructions do you have for me, heir apparent, that you should present me with a thousand pieces of gold?"

"I have heard, sir," said the heir apparent, "that you are a brilliant sage, so I am respectfully offering you a thousand pieces of gold as gifts for your followers. But if, sir, you do not accept them, I wouldn't dare to say anything further."

"I have heard," said Master Chuang, "that the reason you wish to employ me is to free the king from his passion. Suppose that, in trying to persuade his majesty, I should go against his wishes on the one hand and fail to satisfy you on the other, I would be punished with death. Of what use would the gold be to me then? Or suppose that I should succeed in persuading his majesty on the one hand and satisfying you on the other, what might I seek in the kingdom of Chao that I would not get?"

"However," said the heir apparent, "the only people whom my father, the king, will see are swordsmen."

"Yes," said Master Chuang, "but I am skilled in wielding swords."

"However," said the heir apparent, "all the swordsmen whom my father, the king, sees have disheveled hair, locks that bulge out from their temples, drooping caps with plain throatbands, coats that are short in back, glaring eyes, and combative speech, all of which delight the king. Now, sir, you will certainly go to see the king wearing literati garb, and this is something that will certainly run greatly against his liking."

"Allow me to make ready a swordsman's garb," said Master Chuang. After three days, his swordsman's garb made ready, Master Chuang went to see the heir apparent, who went together with him to see the king. The king unsheathed the naked blade of his sword and waited for him. When Master Chuang entered the doorway to the hall, he did not rush forward, and he did not bow when he saw the king.

"With what do you wish to instruct me," asked the king, "that you would have the heir apparent introduce you?"

"I have heard that your majesty likes swords, and therefore I have come to see you with my sword."

"How can your sword suppress the enemy?" said the king.

"My sword cuts down one man every ten paces, and for a thousand tricents it doesn't pause in its march forward."

Greatly pleased, the king said, "There's no match for it under heaven!"

"One who wields a sword," said Master Chuang,

"Reveals his emptiness to his opponent,
Gives him an advantageous opening,
Makes his move after him,
Arrives before he does.

I'd like a chance to try out my skill for you."

"Go to your lodgings to rest, sir," said the king, "and await my orders. I will arrange for the contest and then invite you." Thereupon the king tested his swordsmen for seven days, during which there were more than sixty casualties. He selected five or six men and made them come to the lower part of his hall bearing their swords, whereupon he called Master Chuang. "Today I shall have my men try out their swordsmanship against you," said the king.

"I have been looking forward to this for a long time," said Master Chuang.

"How long is the weapon that you'll be using?" asked the king.

"Whichever sword your subject is made to bear will be all right. However, I have three swords that I may employ for you, oh King. Allow me to describe them first and then try them out."

"I would like to hear about the three swords," said the king.

"There is the sword of the son of heaven, the sword of the feudal lord, and the sword of the common man."

"What is the sword of the son of heaven like?" asked the king.

"The sword of the son of heaven has a point made of Swallow Gorge and Stone Wall, a blade edge made of Mount Tai in Ch'i, a spine made of Chin and Wey, a haft made of Chou and Sung, and a pommel made of Han and Wei. It is embraced by the four uncivilized tribes, encircled by the four seasons, and wrapped around by the Sea of Po. It is guided by the enduring hills, regulated by the five elements, assessed with punishment and virtue, initiated with yin and yang, maintained with spring and summer, activated with autumn and winter. When this sword goes straight, nothing stands before it; when raised, nothing lies above it; when pressed down, nothing lies below it; when whirled around, nothing lies beyond it. Above, it pierces the floating clouds; below, it penetrates the fundament of earth. Once this sword is put to use, it rectifies the feudal lords and causes all under heaven to submit. This is the sword of the son of heaven."

Lost in stupefaction, King Wen asked, "What is the sword of the feudal lord like?"

"The sword of the feudal lord has a point made of wise and brave noblemen, a blade edge made of pure and incorrupt noblemen, a spine made of worthy and good noblemen, a haft made of loyal and sage noblemen, and a pommel made of valiant and heroic noblemen. When this sword goes straight, nothing stands before it either; when raised, nothing lies above it either; when pressed down, nothing lies below it either; when whirled around, nothing lies beyond it either. Above, it models itself on round heaven so as to accord with the three luminaries; below, it models itself on square earth so as to accord with the four seasons; in the middle, it harmonizes with the thoughts of the people so as to pacify the habitations in the four directions. Once this sword is put to use, it is like a crash of thunder. There are none within the four borders who will refuse to submit and to acquiesce in the ruler's commands. This is the sword of the feudal lord."

"What is the sword of the common man like?" asked the king.

"The sword of the common man has disheveled hair, locks that bulge out from the temples, a drooping cap with a plain throatband, a coat that is short in back, glaring eyes, and combative speech. It duels before you; above, it chops through neck and throat; below it perforates liver and lungs. This is the sword of the common man. It is no different from a fighting cock. One morning its life is cut off and it is of no use in the affairs of state. Now, your majesty occupies the position of the son of heaven, yet has a preference for the sword of the common man. I venture to deplore it on your behalf."

The king thereupon led Master Chuang to the top of the hall. The cook served a meal around which the king circled three times.

"Sit down calmly and settle your spirits," said Master Chuang. "I have already finished my presentation on the business of swords."

Thenceforth, King Wen did not leave his palace for three months, and the swordsmen all committed suicide in their rooms.

31

AN OLD FISHERMAN

A very wise old fisherman mercilessly satirizes Confucius for his officiousness and hypocrisy. The Taoist venerable, by contrast, concentrates on cultivating his true nature. Confucius is stunned by his meeting with a real sage.

1

Confucius was wandering in the forest of Black Curtains and sat down to rest at Apricot Altar. His disciples were reading their books and Confucius himself was singing a song while strumming on his lute. He had not finished half of his canto when an old fisherman got out of his boat and came toward them. With a gleaming white beard and eyebrows, disheveled hair, and flapping sleeves, he walked up from the bank and stopped when he reached the elevated land. His left hand resting on his knee and his right hand holding his chin, he listened. When the canto was ended, he beckoned to Tzukung and Tzulu, both of whom responded.

"What does he do?" asked the stranger, pointing at Confucius.

"He's the superior man of Lu," replied Tzulu.

The stranger asked about his clan, to which Tzulu replied, "He belongs to the K'ung clan."

"And how does clansman K'ung occupy himself?" asked the guest.

Before Tzulu responded, Tzukung replied, "Clansman K'ung by nature is devoted to loyalty and trust and in his person practices humaneness and righteousness. He embellishes rites and music and codifies human relationships. Above, he applies loyalty to the reigning sovereign; below, he applies education to the ordinary people. His aim is to benefit all under heaven. This is how clansman K'ung occupies himself."

"Is he a ruler who has territory?" the guest went on to ask.

"No," said Tzukung.

"Is he the assistant to a marquis or a king?"

"No," said Tzukung.

Whereupon the stranger laughed and turned to leave, saying as he walked, "He may well be humane, but I am afraid he won't be able to escape harm to his person. He taxes his mind and toils his body, thereby endangering his true nature. Alas! How far he has diverged from the Way!"

Tzukung returned and reported this to Confucius. Pushing aside his lute, Confucius got up and said, "He must be a sage!" whereupon he went down in search of the stranger. When he reached the edge of the marsh, the stranger was just about to pole his boat away with an oar. Glancing back, he saw Confucius, then turned around and stood facing him. Confucius retreated, bowed twice, and went forward.

"What do you seek from me, sir?" asked the stranger.

"A while ago, master, you made some enigmatic remarks and then left," said Confucius. "I am unworthy and do not understand what you said, so I venture to wait here deferentially in hopes that I shall be so fortunate as to hear a few fine phrases from you that, in the end, will be of help to me."

"Hai!" said the stranger, "great, indeed, is your love of learning!"

Confucius bowed twice, then rose and said, "I have cultivated learning from my youth up till today when I am sixty-nine years old, but I never had the opportunity to hear the ultimate teaching. Dare I not seek instruction from you in all humility?"

The guest said, "Similar categories follow each other and similar sounds respond to each other. Indeed, this is the principle of heaven. Allow me to explain what I have so as to analyze what you are engaged in, sir. What you are engaged in, sir, are human affairs. When the son of heaven, the feudal lords, the grand masters, and the common people, these four classes, correct themselves, we have the beauty of order. But when these four classes leave their proper positions, there is no greater disorder. When the officials take care of their duties and the common people attend to their affairs, there is no room for encroachment. Therefore, barren fields, leaking rooms, insufficient food and clothing, unpaid taxes, disharmony among wives and concubines, disarray among old and young—these are the worries of the common people. Inability to fulfill their responsibilities, official business left uncared for, conduct lacking probity, subordinates who are slipshod and lazy, absence of merit and excellence, failure to maintain titles and allowances—these are the worries of the grand masters. Absence of loyal ministers, state and family in chaos, inept workers and craftsmen, lack of excellence in tribute items, falling behind in spring and autumn audiences with the emperor, disaccord with the son of heaven—these are the worries of the feudal lords. Disharmony of yin and yang, untimeliness of winter cold and summer heat that injure all things, feudal lords who are rebellious and who usurpingly attack each other to the detriment of the people, rites and music unrestrained, property and resources exhausted, human relationships out of kilter, the hundred clans licentiously disordered—these are the worries of the son of heaven. Now you, sir, do not have the superior power of rulers and lords who have control of governments, nor do you have the subordinate office of a great minister who is in charge of affairs, yet you usurp for yourself the embellishment of rights and music and the codification of human relationships so as to educate the ordinary people. Are you not being overly officious?

"Moreover, there are eight defects in men and four infirmities in their handling of affairs that must be examined. To involve oneself in an affair that is not one's business is called presumptuousness. To go forward when no one pays attention to oneself is called insinuation. To guide one's words by catering to the ideas of others is called sycophancy. To speak without regard for right or wrong is called flattery. To be fond of speaking about men's failings is called defamation. To divide friends and separate relatives is called malevolence. To extol and deceive in order to bring about the ruin of others is called wickedness. Without choosing between good and bad, to accommodate both ambivalently so as to extract stealthily what one desires is called treachery. Without, these eight defects bring disorder to others and, within, injury to oneself. A superior man will not befriend one who has them; an enlightened ruler will not use him as a minister. Then there are the four so-called infirmities. To be fond of managing great affairs, transforming and changing what has been constant, in order to scheme for merit and fame, is called ambitiousness. To monopolize knowledge and arrogate affairs, encroaching upon what belongs to others and appropriating it for one's own use, is called greediness. To see one's errors without altering them and to hear criticisms but be all the more inured to them is called perverseness. To approve of another when he agrees with oneself, but when he disagrees with oneself to say that he is not good, even though he may be good, is called conceitedness. These are the four infirmities. Only if one can get rid of the eight defects and not exercise the four infirmities can one be taught."

Abashed, Confucius sighed. He bowed twice, then rose and said, "I was twice driven out of Lu, had my traces obliterated in Wey, had a tree I was resting under chopped down in Sung, and was besieged in the area of Ch'u and Ts'ai. I don't know what mistakes I made that I should have suffered these four vilifications."

Grieved, the stranger changed countenance and said, "How very difficult it is, sir, for you to comprehend! There was a man who, afraid of his shadow and disliking his footprints, tried to run away from them, but the more frequently he raised his feet the more numerous were his footprints, and the faster he ran the closer his shadow stayed to his person. He thought he was still going too slow, so he kept going faster and faster without stopping until his strength was exhausted and he died. He didn't realize that, by staying in the shade, he could eliminate his shadow and that, by staying still, he could extinguish his footprints. How very stupid he was! You, sir, inquire into the sphere of humaneness and righteousness, examine the boundary between sameness and difference, observe the transformations of movement and stillness, comply with measures for giving and receiving, adjust the emotions of liking and disliking, harmonize the moments of happiness and anger—and yet you have barely been able to escape all these troubles. Diligently cultivate your person; attentively guard your true nature; let things return to the keeping of others—then there will be nothing in which you will be implicated. But now, instead of cultivating your own person, you seek to cultivate others. Is this not paying attention to externals?"

"Allow me to ask what you mean by 'true nature,'" said Confucius, abashed.

"One's true nature," said the stranger, "is the ultimate expression of pure sincerity. If one is neither pure nor sincere, one cannot move others. Therefore, he who forces himself to cry, though he may seem sad, is not really sorrowful; he who forces himself to be angry, though he may seem stern, is not really awe-inspiring; he who forces himself to be affectionate, though he may smile, is not really sympathetic. True sadness, even without any sounds, is sorrowful; true anger, even without any temper, is awe-inspiring; true affection, even without a smile, is sympathetic. She who has truth within will be spiritually animated without; for this reason, we honor the truth. As for its application to human relations, in serving parents, it elicits kindness and filialness; in serving one's lord, it elicits loyalty and honesty; in winedrinking, it elicits pleasure and joy; in situations of mourning, it elicits sadness and sorrow. In loyalty and honesty, merit is primary; in winedrinking, joy is primary; in situations of mourning, sorrow is primary; in serving parents, compliance is primary. The beauty of merit accomplished does not always leave identical traces; in serving parents with compliance, one does not discuss the means; in winedrinking for joy, one is not choosy about the utensils; in situations of mourning with sorrow, one is not inquisitive about the rites. The rites were devised by the vulgar people of the world; one's true nature is that which was received from heaven, so naturally it cannot be changed. Therefore, the sage models himself on heaven and honors the truth; he does not cling to the vulgar. The stupid do the opposite of this. They cannot model themselves on heaven but are distressed by man. They do not know to honor the truth but dully undergo the transformations of the vulgar. Therefore they are inadequate. 'Tis pity, sir, that you were so early immersed in human hypocrisy and heard of the great Way so late."

Again, Confucius bowed twice, then rose and said, "My meeting you today is as though it were a stroke of heavenly fortune. If, master, you would not be ashamed to include me among the ranks of those who render service to you and to teach me personally, I venture to see where your dwelling is so that I may be permitted to receive instructions from you and finish my learning of the great Way."

"I have heard," said the stranger, "that, if it is someone with whom you can walk along, go with him even to the wondrous Way. But, if it is someone with whom you cannot walk along, someone who knows not the Way, take care not to go with him, and then your person will be blameless. Exert yourself, sir, for I must leave you! I must leave you!" Whereupon he left, poling his boat through the green reeds.

Yen Yüan turned the carriage around and Tzulu handed Confucius the strap for mounting, but he paid no attention to it.

He waited until the ripples had subsided and was willing to mount the carriage only after the sound of poling could no longer be heard.

Following beside the carriage, Tzulu questioned him, saying, "Long have I had the opportunity to be your servant, but I have never seen you so awe-inspired by any other person you've met, master. I have seen you with rulers of ten thousand chariots and lords of a thousand chariots; they have always shared their halls with you and treated you as an equal, while you, master, wore a look of haughtiness. Now this old fisherman stood across from you leaning on his oar, and you bent at the waist like a stone chime. When he spoke, you bowed before responding. Isn't this a bit much? Your disciples all think it strange of you, master. How could the fisherman affect you like this?"

Confucius leaned against the crossbar and said with a sigh, "It's very difficult to transform you, Yu! You've been immersed in rites and righteousness for quite a while, but till this day you have not gotten rid of your crude, mean heart. Come nearer and I will tell you. If you meet an elder and are not respectful to him, that is impolite; if you see a worthy and do not honor him, that is inhumane. If he were not an ultimate man, he would not be able to make others humble themselves and if those who humble themselves are insincere, they will not obtain the truth. Therefore, they would cause lasting injury to their persons. Alas! There is no greater misfortune for man than to be inhumane, but you alone, Yu, would arrogate that to yourself. Moreover, the Way is that whence the myriad things derive. When things of all sorts lose it they die; when they attain it they live. In handling an affair, if you go against it you will fail, if you accord with it you will succeed. Therefore, wherever the Way exists, the sage honors it. Now, we may say that the old fisherman possesses the Way. Dare I not respect him?"

32

LIEH YÜK'OU

The nominal hero of this chapter is Master Lieh, the third most famous Taoist master after the Old Master(s) and Master Chuang, but he is sharply upstaged by Uncle Obscure Dimbody. The chapter also censures sycophancy, literati learning, ostentatious skills, punishments, and egocentrism. It closes with two charming sketches of the simplicity and humility of Master Chuang.

1

Lieh Yük'ou was going to Ch'i but he turned back when he was halfway there. He met Uncle Obscure Dimbody who asked, "What prompted you to turn back?"

"I was startled."

"What startled you?"

"I had eaten in ten soup-shops and in five of them they attentively served me first."

"But if that's how they treated you," asked Uncle Obscure Dimbody, "why were you startled?"

"If one's inner sincerity is not released, the physical form will divulge a realized light. When one subdues others' minds with one's external appearance, causing them to belittle the honored and the elderly, various troubles will ensue. The soup-shop owner's particular business is to sell soup and he doesn't have a lot of excess earnings. The profit he makes is slight and the authority he wields is little. If even they were like this, how much more so would a ruler of ten thousand chariots be! His person wearied by the state and his knowledge exhausted by affairs, he would employ me in his affairs and have me devote myself to achievement. That's why I was startled."

"Excellent observation!" said Uncle Obscure Dimbody. "But if you stay by yourself, people will still flock to you."

Not much later, he went to visit Lieh Yük'ou and saw that the space outside the door was filled with shoes. Uncle Obscure Dimbody stood facing north with his chin propped on his upright staff. He stood there for a while then left without saying a word.

When the servant who received guests told Master Lieh what had happened, the latter picked up his shoes and ran barefoot after the visitor. Catching up with him at the outer gate, he said, "Since you have come, sir, won't you issue me a prescription?"

"There's no point. I surely told you that people would flock to you and, indeed, they have done so. It's not that you can cause people to come to you, but rather that you cannot cause them not to come. What use is there in stirring up the pleasures of others by showing how different you are? For you will certainly stir up and agitate your own ability, and then nothing may be said for it.

> What's more, those who wander with you
> Do not warn you of this.
> Those petty words of theirs
> Are all so much poison for a man.
> Unawakened, unenlightened—
> How can they be familiar with each other?
> The clever are wearied and the wise are worried,

But he who is incapable seeks nothing.
He eats his fill and goes a-rambling,
Drifting like an unmoored boat—
An empty rambler 'tis he."

2

There was a man from Cheng named Deliberate who intoned his lessons at the place of clansman Furrobe. In only three years, Deliberate had become a literatus. As the waters of the Yellow River moisten the land for nine tricents, so did his benefits reach to the three clans of his relatives. He had his younger brother study Mohism. When he, the Confucian literatus, and his brother, the Mohist, would have disputes, their father would take the side of the Mohist. After ten years, Deliberate committed suicide. He appeared to his father in a dream, saying, "It was I who had your son become a Mohist. Why have you not viewed my grave, since I have become the fruits of the catalpa and the arborvitae?"

In endowing human beings, the creator of things does not endow the human in them, but rather the heavenly that is within the human in them. Because they are like that, she causes them to be that. This man, thinking that he was different from others, despised his own parent, as when the people of Ch'i who were drinking out of a well grappled with each other. Therefore it is said, "All the people of this age are Deliberates." They think themselves to be right, but a person of integrity considers this to be ignorance. How much more so would a person of the Way! The ancients called what happened to people like Deliberate "the punishment of fleeing from the heavenly."

The sage seeks security in what is secure; he does not seek security in what is insecure. The masses seek security in what is insecure; they do not seek security in what is secure.

Master Chuang said, "To know the Way is easy; not to speak of it is difficult. To know but not to speak of it is that which pertains to heaven; to know and to speak of it is that which pertains to man. The men of antiquity pertained to heaven and not to man."

3

Dwarfy Diffuse learned how to butcher dragons from Scattered Plus. Having depleted the family fortune of a thousand pieces of gold, he perfected his techniques within three years, but there was nowhere for him to use his skill.

4

The sage considers what is necessary to be unnecessary, therefore he has no hostility. The masses consider what is unnecessary to be necessary, therefore they have much hostility. Therefore, the behavior of those who go along with hostility will be demanding. Whoever relies on hostility will perish.

The wisdom of the small man never gets beyond gift wrap and calling cards. He wears out his spirit with trivialities, yet wishes without distinction to assist and guide things to the emptiness of form of the grand unity. A man like this becomes confused by space and time, burdening his form but not knowing the grand beginning. The spirit of the ultimate man, however, reverts to beginninglessness and sleeps sweetly in Never-never Land. He is like water flowing through formlessness and gushing forth from grand purity.

How sad! You direct your knowledge toward hairlike trifles but know nothing of great peacefulness!

5

There was a man of Sung named Ts'ao Shang who was sent by the King of Sung on a mission to Ch'in. For his journey there, he received several carriages from the King of Sung and the King of

Ch'in, who was pleased with him, added a hundred more carriages. Upon his return to Sung, he saw Master Chuang, to whom he said, "To live in a narrow lane of a poor village, to be so poverty stricken that I have to weave my own sandals, to have a scrawny neck and a sallow complexion—these are what I'm bad at. But immediately to enlighten the ruler of ten thousand carriages and to be granted a retinue of a hundred carriages, that's what I'm good at."

"When the King of Ch'in is ill," said Master Chuang, "he summons a physician. One who lances an abscess or drains a boil will receive one carriage. One who licks his hemorrhoids will receive five carriages. The lower the treatment, the greater the number of carriages received. Did you treat his hemorrhoids, sir? How did you get so many carriages? Begone!"

6

Duke Ai of Lu asked Yen Ho, "If I make Confucius the pillar of my government, will the ills of the state be cured?"

"Perilous! Precarious! Confucius would even decorate a feather with paint and, in carrying out affairs, he uses flowery diction. He takes offshoots as his main theme and is headstrong in what he shows the people, but is neither wise nor trustworthy. He accepts all this in his mind and is controlled by it in spirit, so how is he fit to be set above the people? Is he suitable for you? Shall you give over the rearing of the people to him? You might do so by mistake, but now if you were to cause the people to depart from reality and learn artifice, this is not what to show the people. Thinking for later generations, it would be better to dismiss the idea."

7

It is difficult to govern. To bestow favors on others but to be ever mindful of them is not heaven's manner of conferring. That is why merchants are disregarded by others. But even if, on account of some business, regard is paid to them, the spirit will disregard them.

8

External punishments are inflicted by metal and wood; internal punishments are inflicted by agitation and excess. When small men encounter external punishment, it is metal and wood that interrogate them; when they encounter internal punishment, it is yin and yang that eat at them. Only the true man can avoid internal and external punishment.

9

Confucius said, "In general, the mind of man is more dangerous than mountains and rivers, more difficult to know than heaven. Heaven, at least, has its periods of spring and autumn, summer and winter, morning and evening, but man has an impenetrable appearance and deep emotions. Therefore, he may have an honest appearance but be overbearing, may seem superior yet be unworthy, may seem circumspect but be straightforward, may seem stiff but be lax, may seem deliberate but be impetuous. Therefore, he may hasten to righteousness as though he were thirsty, but then may run away from it as though from a fire.

Therefore, the superior man will send a person on a distant mission to observe his loyalty, send him on a nearby mission to observe his respect, send him on an irksome mission to observe his ability, question him suddenly to observe his wisdom, set an urgent appointment for him to observe his trustworthiness, entrust him with property to observe his humaneness, warn him of danger to observe his steadfastness, make him drunk on wine to observe his standards, place him in mixed company to observe his sexuality. Through the application of these nine tests, the unworthy man may be discovered."

When Longlived Father, the Correct,

Received his first honorary appointment,
  his head drooped;
When he received his second honorary appointment,
  his back stooped;
When he received his third honorary appointment,
  his waist swooped,
And he went scurrying along the wall.
Who would dare not follow his example?

But if it's one of those ordinary fellows,

When he receives his first honorary appointment,
  he struts and he prances;
When he receives his second honorary appointment,
  in his carriage he dances;
When he receives his third honorary appointment,
  the names of his uncles he advances.
Who can compare with T'ang and Hsü Yu?

10

There is no greater affliction than for integrity to be possessed by the mind and for the mind to be possessed by its eye. Once ruled by the mind's eye, a person looks inward, and when she looks inward she is defeated. There are five types of malevolent integrity and the chief among them is egocentric integrity. What is meant by "egocentric integrity"? She who has egocentric integrity is possessed by self-love and ridicules whatever she does not do herself.

11

There are eight extremities leading to failure, three necessities leading to success, six repositories leading to punishment. Beauty, beard, height, size, stoutness, elegance, bravery, and daring—when one surpasses others in all of these eight respects, he will fail as a result of them. Being compliant, supine, and constrained, as though one were not equal to others—when one is adept in all three of these respects, he will succeed. Knowledgeable wisdom, external communication, brave movement, many complaints, humane righteousness, and many rebukes—it is these six which bring on punishment.

She who comprehends the attributes of life is gigantic; she who comprehends knowledge is petty; she who comprehends a great fate conforms with it; she who comprehends a small fate meets it.

12

There was a man who, having had an audience with the King of Sung and having been presented ten carriages by him, proudly showed them off to Master Chuang.

"Near the Yellow River," said Master Chuang, "there was a poor man who supported his family by weaving artemisia. His son dove into a deep pool and found a pearl worth a thousand pieces of gold. 'Bring a rock and smash it to bits,' said the father to his son. 'A pearl worth a thousand pieces of gold must have been nestled under the chin of a black dragon at the bottom of the ninefold depths. That you were able to get the pearl must have been because you came upon him when he was asleep. If the black dragon had awakened, you wouldn't have had the slightest chance!' Now, the kingdom of Sung is deeper than the ninefold depths of that pool and the King of Sung is fiercer than that black dragon. That you were able to get the carriages must have been because you came upon him when he was asleep. If the King of Sung had awakened, you would have been ground to a pulp!"

13

Some ruler sent gifts to Master Chuang with an invitation to accept office under him. Master Chuang responded to the messenger, "Have you seen a sacrificial ox, sir? It is garbed in patterned embroidery and fed with chopped grass and legumes, but when the time comes for it to be led into the great temple, though it wishes that it could once again be a solitary calf, how could that be?"

14

When Master Chuang was on the verge of death, his disciples indicated that they wished to give him a sumptuous burial. Master Chuang said, "I shall have heaven and earth for my inner and outer coffins, the sun and moon for my paired jades, the stars and constellations for my round and irregular pearls, and the myriad things for my mortuary gifts. Won't the preparations for my burial be quite adequate? What could be added to them?"

"We are afraid that the crows and the kites will eat you, master," said the disciples.

Master Chuang said, "Above, I'd be eaten by the crows and the kites; below, I'd be eaten by mole crickets and ants. Why show your partiality by snatching me away from those and giving me to these?"

If you even things out with what is uneven, the evenness that results will be uneven; if you verify things with what is unverified, the verification that results will be unverified. The keen-sighted person is merely employed by others, whereas the person of spirit verifies them. Long has it been that keen sight does not win out against spirit, yet those who are stupid rely on what they see and attribute it to other men. Their achievement being external, is it not sad?

33

ALL UNDER HEAVEN

Just as the entire Chuang Tzu *functions as an exposition and critique of the intellectual debates that were going on during the Warring States period, so does its last chapter serve as a survey and summation of all the major (and a few minor) thinkers of that period. "All Under Heaven" is by far the best and most authentic contemporary review of early Chinese thought. The wide variety of schools active at the time is remarkable and merits close comparison with parallel trends in Western and Indian philosophy.*

This chapter is surprisingly evenhanded in its treatment of the diverse philosophers it assesses. Among its more captivating portraits is that of Master Chuang himself, with his "absurd expressions, extravagant words, and unbounded phrases." The first place in the chapter is given to Master Mo, the most earnest and "right" thinker of the time. The final place is reserved for Master Chuang's favorite mental sparring partner, Master Hui. Confucius is beyond the pale—hardly worth mentioning after being devastated in the rest of the book.

1

Many are those under heaven who attend to their theories and techniques, and they all believe that nothing can be added to the ones that they possess. But where is the so-called "technique of the Way" of antiquity?

"It is everywhere."

"Whence does the spirit descend? Whence does intelligence emerge?"

"Sagehood has that from which it is born, kingship has that from which it is formed, but both find their source in Unity."

He who is not separated from the ancestral may be called a heavenly man; he who is not separated from the essential may be called a spiritual man; and he who is not separated from the true may be called an ultimate man. He who takes heaven as his ancestor, he who takes integrity as his root, he who takes the Way as his gate, and he who is foreshadowed by transformation and evolution may be called a sage. He who takes humaneness as kindness, he who takes righteousness as principle, he who takes ritual as conduct, he who takes music as harmony, and he who is suffused by compassion and humaneness may be called a superior man. To take the law as their lot; to take names as their representation; to take participation as validation; to take investigation as determination; and to consider counting off one, two, three, four as deciding what is right—this is how the hundred offices of government intermesh. To take administrative affairs as their constant occupation; to take the provision of food and clothing as their main task; to propagate, rear, and store; to think of the young and the old, the orphaned and the widowed, so that they will all have that whereby they may be nourished—this is the principle of caring for the people.

How well prepared were the men of antiquity! They complemented spiritual intelligence, imitated heaven and earth, fostered the myriad things, and harmonized with all under heaven. Their benefits reached to the hundred clans; they were enlightened with regard to rudimentary regulations; they were familiar with regard to particular rules; and they comprehended the six directions of the universe and the four regions. Big and little, coarse and fine—their operation was everywhere. Of their intelligence as it existed in regulations and rules, much was still transmitted in the old laws for generations by the historians. Of what existed in the *Odes, Documents, Ritual,* and *Music,* many of the masters who were noblemen of Tsou and Lu or members of the official class could understand it. . . . Of their regulations that were scattered under heaven and established in the Middle Kingdom, some of the hundred schools of learning occasionally stated and declared them.

Then there was great disorder under heaven and the worthies and the sages no longer illuminated it. The Way and virtue were no longer unified and, for the most part, all under heaven narcissistically held to one aspect of them. This may be compared to the ears, eyes, nose, and mouth. They all have that which they illumine, but they are not interchangeable. Likewise, the various experts of the hundred schools all have their strong points and those moments when they are useful. Nevertheless, they are neither comprehensive nor inclusive but scholars whose views are partial. When they judge the beauty of heaven and earth, analyze the principles of the myriad things, examine the wholeness of the ancients, few can encompass the beauty of heaven and earth or declare the features of spiritual intelligence. For this reason, the Way of internal sagehood and external kingship has become obscure and unillumined, constrained and unexpressed. But all men under heaven, because of their individual desires in these matters, devise their own theories. How sad that the hundred schools go along their own ways without turning back so that they will of necessity never join together! The students of later generations have unfortunately not seen the simplicity of heaven and earth. The techniques of the Way as they were so greatly embodied by the men of antiquity are being sundered by all under heaven.

2

Not to instill extravagance in later generations, not to be wasteful of the myriad things, not to be ostentatious with regulations and rules, to restrain oneself with codes of conduct, and to be prepared for the crises of the age—a portion of the ancient techniques of the Way lay in these practices. Mo Ti and Ch'in Kuli heard of such usages and delighted in them, but they were too overwrought in their doings and too insistent in their abstinence. They formulated an "antimusic" policy and put it under the rubric of "economy of expenditure." In life they were against singing and in death they were against graveclothes. Master Mo advocated love overflowing to all, the sharing of profits, and the rejection of fighting. His way was against anger. Moreover, he was fond of learning and was erudite. Though he did not strive to be different, he was not the same as the former kings and criticized the rituals and music of the ancients.

The Yellow Emperor had his "The Pond of Totality," Yao had his "Great Stanzas," Shun had his "Great Splendors," Yü had his "Great Hsia," T'ang had his "Great Diffusion," King Wen had his "Royal Concord," and King Wu and the Duke of Chou composed "The Martial."

In the funeral rites of the ancients, there were different ceremonies for the honored and the despised, there were different degrees for those above and those below. The coffin of the son of heaven had seven layers, that of a feudal lord had five, that of a great officer three, and that of a retainer two. But now Master Mo alone was against singing in life and against graveclothes in death. His legal guidelines called for a coffin made of paulownia wood three inches thick and no outer shell. I am afraid that, by instructing others with these doctrines, he did not love others and, by practicing them himself, he certainly did not love himself. This is not to overthrow the way of Master Mo altogether. Nevertheless, people will sing, yet he rejected singing; people will wail, yet he rejected wailing; people will make music, yet he rejected music. Does this really seem human? For him, life was toilsome and death was contemptible—his way was greatly deficient. Because it caused men to worry and to be sad, it was difficult to put into practice. I am afraid that it cannot be taken as the Way of the sages. Whatever is contrary to the mind of all under heaven, all under heaven will not bear it. Although Master Mo alone might have been able to endure it, how could all under heaven? Having left all under heaven behind, its distance from kingship was also far.

Master Mo declared, "Long ago, when Yü was trying to stem the flood waters, he cut channels from the Yangtze and the Yellow rivers and opened communications with the four uncivilized tribes and the nine regions. There were three hundred famous rivers, three thousand branch rivers, and countless smaller ones. Yü personally handled the basket and the shovel, interconnecting the rivers of all under heaven, till there was no down on his calves and no hair on his shins. He was bathed by the pouring rains and combed by the gusting winds as he laid out the myriad states. Yü was a great sage, and he wearied his physical form on behalf of all under heaven like this." He caused Mohists of later ages, for the most part, to wear furs and clothes made of arrowroot hemp and to put on wooden clogs and grass sandals. Day and night, they never rested, considering self-misery to be perfection. They said, "If one cannot be like this, he is not following the way of Yü and is unworthy of being called a Mohist."

The disciples of Hsiangli Ch'in, the adherents of Wu Hou, the southern Mohists such as Bitter Harvest, Bite Self, and Master Tengling all recited the Mohist canon, but their divergent distortions were so different that they called each other "aberrant Mohists." They reviled each other with their disputations over "hard" and "white" and over "sameness" and "difference," as well as with their rejoinders to each other over the disparity between "odd" and "even." They considered their giants to be sages and all were willing to accept them as their leaders, hoping that they would be accepted by later generations, but to this day the controversy has not been resolved.

The ideas of Mo Ti and Ch'in Kuli were right, but their practice was wrong. They were to cause the Mohists of later generations to weary themselves till there was no down on their calves and no hair on their shins, urging each other forward to the very end. The results were superior to disorder but inferior to order. Nonetheless, Master Mo was truly one of the best men under heaven, and it would be hard to find another like him. Though he became withered and wasted, he never gave up. He was indeed a scholar of ability!

3

Not to be entangled in vulgarity, not to ornament oneself with things, not to be caustic toward others, not to be hostile toward the masses, to desire peaceful repose for all under heaven so as to preserve the lives of the people, to stop when nourishment for others and for oneself is quite sufficient and thereby to make plain one's mind—a portion of the ancient techniques of the Way lay in these practices. Sung Chien and Yin Wen heard of such usages and delighted in them. They made Mount Hua caps to distinguish themselves and their first premise in their contact with the myriad things was to dispense with enclosures. In describing the capacity of the mind, they named it "the action of the mind." Through pliability they joined happily in blending all within the seas and they wished to establish this as their chief doctrine. By not feeling disgraced when insulted, their aim was to save the people from fighting; by prohibiting aggression and halting troops, their aim was to save the world from war. With these tenets, they walked all around under heaven trying to persuade those above and instructing those below. Although all under heaven did not adopt their tenets, they kept up a forceful clamor and never gave up. Therefore, it is said, "Those above and below are tired of seeing them, but they force themselves to be seen."

Nonetheless, they were too much concerned with others and too little concerned with themselves. They said, "We merely wish to have five pints of rice set before us and that will be enough." I am afraid that the masters never got their fill and the disciples, although hungry, never forgot all under heaven. Day and night, they never rested, saying, "We will certainly be able to go on living!" How proud were the plans of these noblemen who would save the world! They said, "The superior man does not make exacting examinations, nor does he permit his person to be subjugated by things." They believed that, rather than elucidate what was of no value to all under heaven, it would be better to desist. They took the prohibition of aggression and the halting of troops as their external policy, the diminution of desires as their internal policy. This was the big and the little, the coarse and the subtle of their theories. In their practice, they reached just to this and then stopped.

4

Public-minded and nonpartisan, easygoing and impartial, decidedly without subjectivity, not to be duplicitous in one's approach to things, not to be preoccupied by one's thoughts, not to scheme for knowledge, to make no choices among things, going along with everything—a portion of the ancient techniques of the Way lay in these practices. P'eng Meng, T'ien P'ien, and Shen Tao heard of such usages and delighted in them. They made equality of the myriad things their primary doctrine, saying, "Heaven can cover but it cannot support; earth can support but it cannot cover; the great Way can embrace but it cannot discriminate." They knew that the myriad things all have that wherein they are affirmable and that wherein they are not affirmable. Therefore, they said: "Any selection is biased; any instruction is imperfect; it is only the Way that omits nothing."

For this reason, Shen Tao abandoned knowledge and rejected self, acquiescing in inevitability. He was indifferent toward things and took this as his principle of the Way, saying, "When you know that you do not know, you will be one who disparages knowledge and tramples upon it." He went along with things and set himself no particular task, and he laughed at all under heaven for paying esteem to worthies; he was unrestrained and uncultivated, and he criticized all under heaven for giving prominence to sages. Hammering, slapping, lathing, cutting—he went round and round with things. He renounced right and wrong so that he might carelessly avoid involvement. He mastered nothing from knowledge and thought; he knew nothing of precedence and sequence—he merely remained sublimely disengaged. He would only go forward if he were pushed and he would only follow along if he were dragged. His movement was like the turning of a whirlwind, the circling of a falling feather, the revolving of a millstone. He was whole and without fault, his deportment was without error, and he was always without guilt. What was the reason for this? Things that are without knowledge are without the troubles that result from self-assertiveness and are without the entanglements that result from the application of knowledge. In their deportment, they never depart from principle, so consequently they are without praise till the end of their life. Therefore, he said, "May I merely arrive at the state of being like a thing without knowledge. There's no use for worthies and sages—it's the clod that doesn't lose the Way!" The valiant and the heroic laughed at him to each other and said, "The way of Shen Tao is not based on the conduct of the living; instead, he has arrived at the principle of the dead. There's really something strange about it!"

It was the same with T'ien P'ien. He studied with P'eng Meng, but what he got from him was noninstruction. P'eng Meng's teacher said, "The ancient men of the Way arrived at a state where there was nothing right and nothing wrong, that's all. His usages were so vague that they cannot be described in words. He often opposed others so no one heeded him, yet he could not avoid being rounded and cut off. What he called the way was not the Way, and what he said was right could not avoid being wrong.

P'eng Meng, T'ien P'ien, and Shen Tao did not know the Way. Nonetheless, it would appear that they had all heard about it.

5

To take the root as essential and to take things as extraneous, to take accumulation as insufficiency, to dwell alone tranquilly with spiritual intelligence—a portion of the ancient techniques of the Way lay in these practices. Yin, the Director of the Pass, and Old Longears heard of such usages and delighted in them. They set up the concept of eternal nonbeing and being and made grand unity their chief doctrine. They took soft weakness and humility as their distinguishing features and took vacuity and nondamage to the myriad things as their inner substance.

Director Yin said,

"To one who does not dwell in himself,
The forms of things will manifest themselves.

His movement is like water,
His stillness is like a mirror.

His response is like an echo,
Indistinct as though it were absent,
Quiet as though it were pure.

In sameness there is harmony,
In getting there is loss."

He never went before others but always followed after them.

Old Longears said,

> "Know masculinity,
> Maintain femininity,
>   and be a ravine for all under heaven.

> Know whiteness,
> Maintain insult,
>   and be a valley for all under heaven."

"Men all take the first place; he alone takes the last, saying, 'I will accept the filth of all under heaven.' Men all take substantiality; he alone takes emptiness. He does not store up, therefore he has a surplus. . . . In the conduct of his person, he is slow but not wasteful. He acts not and laughs at cleverness. Men all seek blessings; he alone is preserved whole through bending, saying, 'If only I can avoid affliction.' He takes depth as rudimentary and thrift as regulatory, saying, 'If it is hard it will be damaged; if it is sharp it will be blunted.' " He was always magnanimous toward things and not trenchant toward men. He may be said to have arrived at the apex.

Ah, Director Yin and Old Longears! They were indeed ample true men of antiquity!

6

Obscure and formless, ever transforming and inconstant. Are we alive? Are we dead? Do we coexist with heaven and earth? Do we go along with spiritual intelligence? How nebulous! where are we going? How blurred! where are we aiming? The myriad things being arrayed all around, there is none fit for us to return to—a portion of the ancient techniques of the Way lay in these practices. Chuang Chou heard of such usages and delighted in them. With absurd expressions, extravagant words, and unbounded phrases, he often gave rein to his whims but was not presumptuous and did not look at things from one angle only. Believing that all under heaven were sunk in stupidity and could not be talked to seriously, he used impromptu words for his effusive elaboration, quotations for the truth, and metaphors for breadth. Alone, he came and went with the essential spirits of heaven and earth but was not arrogant toward the myriad things. He did not scold others for being right or wrong, but abode with the mundane and the vulgar. Although his writings are exotic and convoluted, there is no harm in them; although his phraseology is irregular and bizarre, it merits reading. His fecundity is inexhaustible. Above he wanders with the creator of things, and below he is friends with those who are beyond life and death and without beginning or end. Regarding the root, he is expansive and open, profound and unrestrained; regarding the ancestor, he may be said to be attuned and ascendant. Nonetheless, in his response to evolution and in his emancipation from things, his principles are not exhaustive and his approach is not metamorphosing. How nebulous! How cryptic!—someone who has never been fully fathomed.

7

Hui Shih had many theories. His books filled five carts, but his way was contradictory and his words were off the mark. In his successive estimation of things, he said:

"That which is so great that there is nothing outside it may be called 'the great one'; that which is so small that there is nothing inside it may be called 'the small one.' "

"That which has no thickness and cannot be accumulated is a thousand tricents in size."

"Heaven is as low as the earth; a mountain is as level as a marsh."

"As soon as the sun is at noon it declines; as soon as a thing is born it dies."

"Given that there is a difference between great similarity and small similarity, this is called a small difference of similarity; given that the myriad things are ultimately similar yet ultimately different, this is called a great difference of similarity."

"The southern direction is limitless yet it has a limit."

"One sets out for Viet today but came there yesterday."

"Linked rings can be separated."

"I know the center of all under heaven: it is north of Yen and south of Viet."

"If there is general love of the myriad things, heaven and earth are one body."

Considering that these statements were great, Hui Shih revealed them to all under heaven and explained them to the sophists. All the sophists under heaven enjoyed adding their own to his:

"An egg has feathers."

"A chicken has three legs."

"Ying possesses all under heaven."

"A dog can be taken as a sheep."

"A horse has eggs."

"A frog has a tail."

"Fire is not hot."

"Mountains produce mouths."

"A wheel does not roll on the ground."

"An eye does not see."

"To indicate is not to arrive at; arrival is not absolute."

"A turtle is longer than a snake."

"An L-square is not square and a compass cannot make a circle."

"A chisel does not surround its helve."

"The shadow of a flying bird has never moved."

"Swift as the barbed arrow may be, there is a time when it neither moves nor is at rest."

"A puppy is not a dog."

"A sorrel horse and a black ox are three."

"A white puppy is black."

"An orphan colt never had a mother."

"If you take away half of a foot-long stick every day, it will not be exhausted in a myriad ages."

The sophists responded to Hui Shih with these statements endlessly throughout their lives.

Huan T'uan and Kungsun Lung were adherents of the sophists. They embellished the minds of men and changed the ideas of men. They could overcome others in debate but they could not subdue their minds—such were the limitations of the sophists. Hui Shih used his knowledge to dispute with others every day and he particularly devised strange propositions with all the sophists under heaven. This was the basis of his school.

However, in his colloquies, Hui Shih believed that he himself was the most worthy, saying, "Under heaven and on earth, is there another so magnificent?" He maintained his masculinity but was without technique. In the south there was an odd man named Huang Liao who asked him why heaven did not collapse and earth did not sink and the reason for wind, rain, and the crash of thunder. Not declining to respond, Shih replied thoughtlessly, volubly talking about the myriad things. He kept talking without a pause, voluminously and unceasingly, but still thinking that he was laconic and adding all sorts of strange remarks. He took contradicting others as his substance and wished to become famous by overcoming them, hence he did not get along with the masses. He was weak in virtue but strong in things. Arcane was his path!

If we observe Hui Shih's ability from the Way of heaven and earth, it was like the toiling of a mosquito or a gadfly. Of what use was he to things? It is acceptable to claim that he filled a certain role, but I say that, had he gone on to honor the Way, he would have been very close indeed. Hui Shih could not find any self-satisfaction in this, so he scattered himself insatiably among the myriad things, ending up being famed as a skillful debater. What a pity! With all of his abilities, he was like a runaway horse that could not be restrained. He went in pursuit of the myriad things and never came back. This is like trying to stifle an echo by shouting at it or pitting the body in a race against its shadow. How sad!

Glossary

The Glossary is divided into three parts: Names, Places, and Terms. In the interest of conciseness, not all possible entries are given. Items whose significance may be gained from the context are generally omitted, as are those for which nothing is known other than what the *Chuang Tzu* itself tells us and those explained in the Introduction. Many place names mentioned in the text can be located directly on the map on page lv and hence there is no need to provide a separate reference here. The page number after the entry in bold type usually refers to the first occurrence of the name or term.

Names

Ch'ang Chi (p. 42). Supposedly a disciple of Confucius, his name may be interpreted as "Constant Season."

Ch'ang Hung (p. 85). A worthy official of King Ching of the Chou dynasty who was executed by the sovereign over a difference of opinion concerning strategy.

Chao [Wen] (p. 17). The most famous lutanist of antiquity.

Chi Ch'e, Chianglü Mien (p. 110). The identity of these two men is not known.

Ch'ichi, Hualiu (p. 156). Fabulous horses; the Chinese counterparts of Bucephalus and Pegasus.

Chich'ü (p. 33). A mythical culture-hero.

Chieh (p. 31). A tyrant of high antiquity.

Chien Wu (p. 6). A fictitious practitioner of the Way.

Ch'ihyu (p. 302). Name of a mythical tribal chieftain who resisted the civilizing influences of the Yellow Emperor.

Ch'in Kuli (p. 336). One of Master Mo's closest disciples who had formerly studied under Tzuhsia, a high-ranking disciple of Confucius.

Chou and Shao (p. 142). Two dukes who assisted King Wu in establishing the Chou dynasty. The former is the famous Duke of Chou who was held up as a paragon by Confucius.

Chow (p. 31). A notorious tyrant of high antiquity; the last ruler of the Shang dynasty.

Chuang Chou (p. 24). Master Chuang (Chuang Tzu). The surname Chuang means "solemn" and Chou, his personal name, signifies "[all] round" or "whole."

Ch'ü Poyü (p. 36). A wise minister of the state of Wey.

Ch'ui (p. 87). A famous artisan who supposedly lived during the time of Yao and was said to be the deviser of the compass and L-square.

Chung (p. 251). Minister of the state of Viet who successfully advised Kou Chien in taking revenge against Ngwa in 473 B.C.E. Chung, however, was later forced by Kou Chien to commit suicide after having been slandered by others for disloyalty.

clansman . . . T'ai (p. 66). Supposedly the mythical first man, Fuhsi.

clansman . . . Yen (p. 135). This is supposedly the name of the Divine Farmer.

clansman . . . Yü (p. 66). The mythical emperor Shun. On page 204, there is a hidden allusion to the legend that Shun's own father and stepmother repeatedly tried to kill him when he was a child, but that his extreme filial piety finally won them over.

Deus (p. 146). Ti, the supreme deity; a deified royal ancestor. This word is sometimes translated as "God" or "gods." In later usage, it also came to mean "emperor."

Dik (p. 285). The so-called "Northern Barbarians." Some authorities have identified them as proto-Turkic and have even gone so far as to equate their name with the word "Turk."

Divine Farmer (p. 149). The mythical emperor, Shennung, who was the supposed inventor of agriculture.

Ducal Happyrest (p. 254). A fictitious personage.

Duke Chuang (p. 183). Of the state of Lu.

Duke Huan (p. 180). Of the state of Ch'i, the first of the five hegemons of the Warring States period who imposed their will on the other feudal states.

Duke Ling (p. 262). It is ironic that many dissolute rulers in Chinese history were awarded the posthumous epithet "Ling" ("Numinous," "Efficacious," "Ingenious," etc.).

Duke of Po (p. 156). T'ang and Wu were the founding kings of the Shang and Chou dynasties respectively. The Duke of Po was the grandson of King P'ing of Ch'u. His father, the crown prince, was demoted when the king became infatuated with a woman from the state of Ch'in. The prince fled to Cheng where he married a woman who gave birth to the Duke of Po. When the latter grew up, he returned to Ch'u and raised an armed insurrection in 479 B.C.E. to take revenge for his father, but was defeated and eventually committed suicide.

Duke Wei (p. 177). The son of Duke Huan and the younger brother of King K'ao (reigned 440–426 B.C.E.).

Earl of the River (p. 152). The god of the Yellow River.

Excalibur (p. 59). The text has "Moyeh," name of a famous ancient Chinese sword.

Fancypants Scholar (p. 126). Shih Ch'engch'i (literally, "Scholar [also a surname] Complete[ly]—Variegated Silk/Elegant Clothes"). With a name like this, it is not likely that we can expect to learn more about him from other, more historically reliable sources.

Filial Self (p. 268). Son of the famous Shang king, Wu Ting, he was driven out by his stepmother.

Follow Transform (p. 294). Pien Sui, presumably a wise recluse.

Four Masters (p. 7). Saintly hermits who lived on distant Mount Kuyeh.

Fuhsi (p. 33). A mythical culture-hero; the First Man.

Furrobe (p. 326). The surname signifies a Confucian in two ways: I. Confucian literati wore fur robes; 2. the word for "fur robe" in Old Sinitic sounds like Confucius's given name, Ch'iu ("Hillock").

Hillock (p. 22). Ch'iu, Confucius's personal name, possibly referring to the philosopher's high, knobby forehead or to his presumably illegitimate birth in the countryside.

Hohsü (p. 82). A mythical ruler.

Hsi Shih (p. I6). A fabled beauty of old.

Hsü Yu (p. 6). A legendary hermit. His name might be interpreted as "Promise Allow."

Hu Puhsieh, etc. (p. 394). All of these individuals were unbending moralists who were executed, ended up committing suicide, or went mad.

Huan Tou, etc. (p. 93). Although all three of these individuals are mentioned in the *Classic of Documents* (supposedly China's earliest book of history but of mixed date and reliability), they are mythological in nature. Several of the personal names and place names mentioned here have transparent meanings, e.g., Sanwei ("Triply Dangerous"), Kungkung ("Superintendent of Works"), Yutu ("Secluded Capital"), Mount Ch'ung ("Mount Lofty").

Huang Liao (p. 345). Apparently a singular sophist from Ch'u who asked Master Hui some tough questions when the latter was sent on a mission to that southern kingdom by the King of Wei.

Hui Shih. See **Master Hui.**

Idle Intruder (p. 28). Ch'in Yi, probably a fictional character, the meaning of whose name is not entirely clear.

Jan Ch'iu (p. 221). An introspective yet capable disciple of Confucius.

Jan Hsiang (p. 256). Supposedly a sagely king of highest antiquity, but nothing reliable is known of him.

Jungch'eng, etc. (p. 88). All twelve of these individuals were mythical emperors and kings or legendary founders of Chinese civilization. Only a few of them are even mentioned in the early histories. It is likely that over half of them were invented by the author of this chapter. Most of their names have a fairly transparent meaning that reflects their supposed role in the invention of civilization, such as "appearance completed," "great hall," "elder/earl/uncle resplendent," "center," "grain ripe," "black / pair of domestic animals," "carriage," "awe-inspiring crab," "venerable stove," "invoke fusing," "the first man," and "the divine farmer."

Kengsang Ch'u (p. 225). His name might well be explicated as Sharp[-witted] Long-lived Mulberry.

King Wen (p. 141). The King of Chou before it defeated the Shang and took over the empire. The King Wen of Chapter 30 who is so enamored of swordfighting was the king of a small state during the Warring States period.

King Wu (p. 114). Successor of King Wen and the first ruler of the Chou dynasty after it controlled the whole empire.

Kou Chien (p. 251). Ruler of the state of Viet (Yüeh) which had been defeated by the state of Ngwa (Wu) in 496 B.C.E.

Kuan Chung (p. 180). Prime minister of Duke Huan (q.v.) and the ostensible author of the book entitled *Master Kuan (Kuan Tzu)*. Kuan Chung died in 645 B.C.E., but the book that bears his name was manifestly compiled centuries later. It is highly eclectic, including even a few proto-Taoist and Yogic chapters. The roots of Legalism in China can be traced back to Master Kuan and he may also be viewed as the first economist in China, for it is he who began there the discussion of matters of finance and production.

Kuan Lungp'ang (p. 31). A worthy minister.

K'un (p. 3). An enormous fish that has often been likened to Leviathan.

Lieh Yük'ou. See **Master Lieh.**

Lien Shu (p. 6). A fictitious practitioner of the Way.

Longlived Father, the Correct (p. 329). Cheng K'aofu, supposedly a member of the ducal family of the state of Sung and Confucius's ancestor ten generations back.

Lord Yüan (p. 204). Duke Yüan, who ruled from 531 to 517 B.C.E.

Lotbridge Learner (p. 56). Puliang Yi or Pu Liangyi. His name might also be interpreted as "Lotmeasure Extraordinary."

Lungp'ang (p. 268). Kuan Lungfang (another reading of his name), a worthy minister of the Hsia-dynasty tyrant Chieh, who had him executed.

Maestro Chin (p. 136). Apparently a music teacher from the state of Lu.

Maestro K'uang (p. 17). A famous music teacher of old.

Mao Ch'iang (p. 21). A fabled beauty of old.

Marquis Chaohsi (p. 287). Marquis Hsi (as he is called near the end of the passage) of the state of Han.

Marquis Wu (p. 237). The founder of the state of Wei when it split off from the state of Chin. His son was the famous King Hui with whom Mencius had so many memorable discussions.

Master Chan (p. 292). This is Chan Ho, a Taoistic worthy of Wei.

Master Chi (p. 268). A relative of the Shang-dynasty tyrant Chow who was a worthy minister and who feigned madness rather than continue to stay at court and attempt to advise the king.

Master Hu (p. 69). Hu Tzu (or Master Pot) was Master Lieh's teacher.

Master Hui (p. 7). A friend and favorite philosophical sparring partner of Chuang Tzu, Hui Tzu was an important figure in the School of Names or Logicians. It is curious that his name and surname, perhaps only by accident, mean "kind bestowal." It is also curious that the author of the final chapter of the *Chuang Tzu* gives him such prominence, not only by placing him in the culminating position, but by devoting so much space to this otherwise largely neglected philosopher. There is, in fact, some evidence that this section of Chapter 33 may originally have been part of a separate chapter devoted to Hui Shih. Like Master Mo, he truly deserves to be called a philosopher, in contrast to the vast majority of other early Chinese thinkers who dealt with social problems rather than logic, ontology, epistemology, and so forth. Master Mo (see Introduction), interestingly enough, is similarly highlighted in this survey by being placed first and by being awarded extensive coverage.

Master K'uang (p. 308). A man of Ch'i who was driven away by his father for having criticized him. Once he left, he never saw his father again for the rest of his life.

Master Lieh (p. 5). Lieh Tzu, the best-known philosopher of early Taoism after Lao Tzu ("Old Master") and Chuang Tzu ("Master Chuang"). See Chapter 32.

Master Min (p. 48). A disciple of Confucius.

Master Tseng. See **Tseng Shen.**

Mengsun Ts'ai (p. 61). A wise man of the state of Lu.

Olai (p. 268). A deceitful minister of the tyrant Chow who was put to death together with his ruler by King Wu of the Chou dynasty.

Old Longears (p. 28). Intended as a reference to Lao Tzu (Old Master), the reputed author of the *Tao Te Ching.* For a discussion of his big ears, see Bibliography, Mair, "**File,**" p. 42, note I.

Old Master Chenopod (p. 271). Or "Old Master Goosefoot." This is Lao Lai Tzu, a shadowy Taoistic figure who is sometimes identified with Lao Tzu, the Old Master. There is no historical justification whatsoever for this identification.

Overlord of the Northern Sea (p. 153). His name was Jo.

Pao Chiao (p. 303). A recluse who committed suicide after being criticized by Tzukung, a disciple of Confucius.

Pao Shuya (p. 245). An old and close friend of Kuan Chung (q.v.) who was also an early supporter of Duke Huan.

Pater Tan (p. 285). T'ai Wang Tan Fu. He was also called Old Duke Pater Tan (Ku Kung Tan Fu). The word for father (Fu) in these names has a special tonal reading to indicate respect. The personal name Tan means "sincere, true." Pater Tan was the grandfather of King Wen, founder of the Chou dynasty.

P'eng (p. 3). A huge bird that has been compared to the roc of Western mythology and the *garuḍa* of Indian mythology.

P'eng Meng, T'ien P'ien, and Shen Tao (p. 339). Little is known of these three men except that the latter two, like Sung Chien and Yin Wen, were said to have been associated with the so-called Chihsia "academy" of the kings of Ch'i. Scattered fragments of Shen Tao's writings have survived, but nothing remains from the other two thinkers.

Pikan (p. 268). A relative of the Shang-dynasty tyrant Chow, who had his heart torn out after he made repeated admonitions.

Poleh (p. 80). According to legend, he was the finest judge of horses in antiquity.

Poli Hsi (p. 204). A famous statesman of the seventh century B.C.E. who rose from a lowly station to be the chief minister of

Duke Mu of the state of Ch'in. He is featured in the *Mencius* and other early Chinese texts.

Poyi and Shuch'i (p. 295). Celebrated hermit-martyrs of high antiquity who died for the sake of righteousness.

Prince Ch'ingchi (p. 190). The son of King Liao of the state of Wu, he fled to the state of Wey when his father was assassinated.

Prince Junior (p. 307). Wang Chi or Chili, son of a concubine, who displaced his two older brothers by the legal wife of his father. Wang Chi was the father of King Wen, founder of the Chou dynasty.

Progenitor P'eng (p. 4). P'engtsu, the Chinese Methuselah who lived in prehistoric times.

Shent'u Chia (p. 44). Presumably a wise man of the state of Cheng, his given name means "excellent." The surname Shent'u sounds suspiciously like the ancient Chinese transcriptions of the old name for India. It was the custom in China to name foreigners according to their place of origin.

Shent'u Ti (p. 303). A righteous personage of the Shang period. See the previous entry.

Shih Ch'iu (p. 76). A wise minister of the state of Wey who was an exemplar of Confucian rectitude.

Shu'erh (p. 78). A legendary gastronomical authority of ancient China.

Shun (p. 7). A sage-king of high antiquity. Shun is normally held up by Confucians as the epitome of filial devotion. There is, however, a late and somewhat untrustworthy account of his banishment of his blind father who had horribly abused him as a child, which might be operative in Chapter 29, section I. See also under **clansman . . . Yü.**

Sir High (p. 33). She Kung Tzukao, a minister of the southern kingdom of Ch'u.

Sir Motley of Southunc (p. 38). Perhaps the same imaginary person as Sir Motley of Southurb who appears at the beginning of the second chapter and Sir Sunflower of Southunc, who is featured in the sixth chapter.

Sir Motley of Southurb (p. 10). Probably a wholly fictional personage. His name may alternatively indicate that he had a sternly disciplined personality.

Sir Square Field (p. 198). T'ien Tzufang. Mentioned in many ancient texts, he was supposedly a close adviser of Marquis Wen, an enlightened ruler who occupied the throne of Wei from 446 to 397 B.C.E.

Sir Sunny Dweller (p. 68). Yang Tzuchü. This is probably Chuang Tzu's caricature of the hedonist philosopher, Yang Chu, whose pseudonym was Yang Tzuchü. This sounds exactly like the Modern Standard Mandarin pronunciation of the three sinographs for Sir Sunny Dweller, although the first one is written slightly differently from the surname of the famous philosopher. We may think of Sir Sunny Dweller as a sort of anti-Yang Chu, just as Chuang Tzu's Confucius often acts more like an anti-Confucius or, as we have styled him, a pseudo-Confucius.

Spidersight (p. 76). Lichu, a legendary figure of phenomenal eyesight who supposedly could see the tip of a feather or of a needle at a hundred paces.

Sun Shu'ao (p. 208). A famous statesman who engineered King Chuang (reigned 613–591 B.C.E.) of Ch'u's rise to the position of hegemon.

Sung Jung (p. 5). The same philosopher as Sung Chien who is discussed in the final chapter of this book.

Sunny (p. 254). Rendering of Tseyang, who is probably an imaginary character. In its only other occurrences, his name appears as P'eng Yang, which may be rendered as "Abundantly Sunny."

Tai Chinjen (p. 258). An imaginary personage whose name may be interpreted as "Truthbearer."

T'ang (p. 141). The founder of the Shang dynasty, the first Chinese dynasty that has been both historically and archeologically verified. The dynasty was established in roughly 1766 B.C.E., although details from the first part of the dynasty are still lacking.

T'ang and Yü (p. 149). The mythical rulers, Yao and Shun, here named after the principalities they inherited.

T'ien Ho (p. 246). The founding duke of the usurping T'ien lineage in the state of Ch'i.

T'ien Mou (p. 257). Ruled as King Wei of Ch'i from 357–320 B.C.E.

Tiger Yang (p. 161). A notorious marauder.

Torchman (p. 149). A mythical inventor of fire.

Tseng Shen (p. 76). A beloved disciple of Confucius who was a paragon of filial devotion. Nonetheless, he was despised by his own father who, according to one account, nearly beat him to death for having damaged the roots of some plants when he was weeding a melon patch.

Ts'ui Chü (p. 92). A fictional character.

Tzuchang (p. 305). An earnest, yet pragmatic, disciple of Confucius. His name may be interpreted as "Sir Open."

Tzuhsü (p. 85). A loyal adviser to kings of the state of Ngwa (Wu) who was forced to commit suicide because of a difference of opinion concerning relationships with the state of Viet (Yüeh). His body was sewn inside a sack of horse leather and thrown into the Yangtze River.

Tzukung (p. 60). One of Confucius's disciples. His cognomen may be interpreted as "Sir Tribute."

Tzulu (p. 125). A disciple of Confucius. His name may be rendered as "Sir Road."

Unadorned, Bridge Support, Yellow Emperor (p. 63). Three figures (the first two imaginary, the third mythical) who gave up their distinguishing abilities after hearing about the Way.

Uncle Tan (p. 296). Shutan, the Duke of Chou, younger brother of King Wu.

Underwillow Chi (p. 298). A worthy of the state of Lu.

Viscount Fieldborn (p. 85). A grandee of Ch'i, his real name was Ch'en Heng.

Wearcoat (p. 105). This is undoubtedly the same imaginary figure as Master Rushcoat who appears at the beginning of Chapter 7.

Wu Yüan (p. 268). Tzuhsü (see entry under that name).

Yao (p. 6). A sage-king of high antiquity. The usual Confucian image of Yao is that of great kindness. The reference on page 303, however, is to his setting aside his unworthy eldest son from the succession to the throne in favor of Shun.

Yellow Emperor (p. 56). This is Huang Ti, whose title might also be rendered as "Yellow / Blond Deus." According to legend, he is said to have subdued the warring tribes at the dawn of Chinese civilization and to have taught them medicine, mathematics, musical scales, and other vital aspects of culture.

Yen (p. 10). A disciple of Sir Motley. Yen was apparently his real name, Sir Wanderer his nickname.

Yen Ho (p. 36). A worthy scholar of the state of Lu in the employ of the state of Wey.

Yen Hui (p. 29). Confucius's favorite pupil.

Yen Yüan (p. 136). Yen Hui.

Yi, P'engmeng (p. 194). A famous bowman and his disciple.

Yin (p. 175). According to Taoist legend, this is the individual for whom Lao Tzu was said to have written down the *Tao Te Ching* before he went out through the pass guarding the central heartland of China and ultimately traveled to India.

Yin (p. 296). Another name for the Shang dynasty.

Yin Wen (p. 338). His dates are roughly 350–285 B.C.E., but few details are known of his life other than that he was associated with the kings of Ch'i.

Ying (p. 257). This is his personal name. His name as king was Hui.

Yu (p. 323). Tzulu's personal name.

Yü (p. 14). After Yao and Shun, the third sage-king of high antiquity. Yü is usually depicted as a man of great dynamism. On page 303, however, there is reference to his partial paralysis.

Yüan Hsien (p. 290). An eminent disciple of Confucius.

PLACES

Ch'en and Ts'ai (p. 137). Two small states, on the border of which Confucius once nearly lost his life. This famous incident is recorded in many ancient works (*Records of the Scribe, Analects, Mencius, Mo Tzu,* and *Hsün Tzu*) and occurs in the *Chuang Tzu* in the context of a whole series of disasters that plagued Confucius as he traveled from one state to another seeking a ruler who would put his doctrines into practice.

The first story tells of Confucius going on a tour of the state of Sung. He and his disciples stopped to rest under a large tree. The master instructed his disciples to practice their ritual and etiquette. Just at that moment, Huan T'ai, the minister of war for Sung, commanded that the tree be cut down and was about to have Confucius murdered when the latter fled. Huan T'ai's enmity for Confucius is said to have stemmed from the master's criticism of his cruelty and excess in the construction of his own tomb.

In the next story, the Duke of Wey permitted Confucius and his followers to enter his state, but he kept such a close watch on them that they decided to leave. As they were departing, the people of a border town, mistaking them for a band of robbers who had raided the area not long before, surrounded Confucius and his disciples. Only after five days did the local strongman release them, warning Confucius never to come back to the state of Wey.

The specific allusions to the Shang duchy and the Chou kingdom in this passage are not known, except to say that neither of these states heeded Confucius's counsel. They were also probably unwilling to foot the considerable bill for the master and his entourage.

The rulers of Ch'en and Ts'ai, afraid that Confucius would travel to help their powerful southern neighbor, the state of Ch'u, surrounded him when he passed through their states. He is said to have been released only through the intervention of Ch'u. It is reported that, while he was being detained, Confucius survived on chenopod soup for a week. "Chenopod" is the Latinate equivalent of "goosefoot." The Chenopodiaceae family includes pigweed, lamb's quarters, beets, spinach, the broom plant, and many common weeds. In old China, chenopods were associated with famine and poverty.

On page 303 there is reference to the story of Confucius having fled to Ch'i when there was chaos in Lu. Duke Ch'ing of Ch'i was impressed by Confucius's political advice and wanted to enfeoff him, but was prevented from doing so by the prime minister of Ch'i, Yen Ying.

Ch'i (p. 33). A powerful northern kingdom.

Chia (p. 193). The sinograph for Chia is probably a miswriting of the graphically similar character for Yin (i.e., the Shang dynasty), by which is intended its successor dukedom, Sung. The latter state was permitted to survive under the Chou dynasty as a haven for the remnants of the Yin aristocracy.

Chih River (p. 270). In Chekiang province.

Ch'in (p. 282). The modern province of Shensi.

Ch'ingling (p. 294). Said to be west of Nanyang district in Honan province.

Chungshan (p. 292). The fiefdom of Prince Mou of Wei. It was located in the modern Ting district of Hopeh province.

Dark Mountain (p. 132). An imaginary place of mystic associations in the distant north.

Han and Wei (p. 287). Two of the three new states into which the state of Chin was divided around the middle of the fourth century B.C.E. The third was Chao.

Hantan (p. 86). The capital of the state of Chao. The people there were said to have a stylishly distinctive strut.

Hao (p. 165). In Anhwei.

Hsiangch'eng (p. 241). There is still a district by this name in Honan province. The name of the place might be interpreted as "Raised City," that is, a walled town that lies above the surrounding area.

Hua (p. 106). This may refer to the area around Mount Taihua in the province of Shensi.

K'unlun (p. 105). These mountains are the seat of the Queen Mother of the West and the axis of the world in Chinese cosmology and mythology.

Liang (p. 282). Present-day K'aifeng in Honan province.

Lu (p. 192). Confucius's home state. It is supremely ironic that he was "twice driven out of Lu." He had held several posts in the administration of Lu, the highest being Minister of Justice, but he could not keep them for long because his puritanical activism and grandiloquent plans for good government often brought him into conflict with the ruler. Once, for example, during the reign of Duke Ting, the state of Ch'i purposely sowed seeds of discord between Confucius and his ruler by presenting the latter with 80 beautiful women and 124 fine horses. Confucius was unhappy about this, of course, because it diverted the ruler's attention from the all-important (to Confucius) business of governing the state well, so he felt that he had no choice but to leave Lu and attempt to persuade some other ruler to adopt his policies.

Middle Kingdom (p. 153). Still China's name for itself to this day. It originally signified a monarchical political entity located within a group of fortified passes in the present-day province of Shensi at the confluence of the Wei and Yellow rivers around modern Sian, i.e., "kingdom of the central plains." Later, however, the concept took on a more cultural coloring with China seeing itself as a uniquely civilized country surrounded by hordes of "barbarians." Places outside of the "central," or "middle" kingdom were considered to be cultural backwaters. During Chuang Tzu's time, that included everything south of the Yangtze River.

Mount Ch'i (p. 296). In Shensi, where King Wen established the Chou dynasty.

Mount Ch'ung (p. 93). See under the name "Huan Tou."

Mount K'uaichi (p. 251). Southeast of Shaohsing district in Chekiang province.

Mount Kung (p. 294). Near present-day Hui district in Honan. The Earl of Kung, named Kung Ho, was offered the throne of the Chou dynasty, but preferred to stay at his own fief near this mountain.

Mount K'unlun (p. 54). The axis of the world, located far to the west of China.

Mount Ts'angwu (p. 270). In the far southern province of Kwangsi.

Namviet (p. 188). South (*nam*) of the state of Yüeh (*viet*). This being unfamiliar territory to the Chinese during Chuang Tzu's time, its use here is to indicate a place that is remote.

Ngwa (p. 8). In the south of China. During Chuang Tzu's time, the people living here were far from being fully sinicized. In Modern Standard Mandarin, this name would be pronounced *Wu*.

P'ei (p. 138). In the modern district of the same name in Kiangsu province.

Pin (p. 285). In modern-day Hsünyi district of Shensi province.

P'u River (p. 164). In Shantung province.

Sea of Po (p. 315). The Gulf of Chihli in the northeast.

Shang (p. 131). This signifies the state of Sung where the descendants of the Shang dynasty were settled during the successor Chou dynasty.

Shang (Hillock) (p. 38). A place in Honan.

Shouling (p. 163). A place in the state of Yen.

Shouyang (p. 78). The name of a mountain in Shansi.

Shu (p. 268). Szechwan.

Sui (p. 288). Located near the P'u River (in the province of Hupeh) which produced fine pearls. A local legend tells how the

Marquis of Sui once healed a wounded snake and was rewarded by it with a particularly fine specimen that became known as the pearl of Sui.

Sung (p. 7). A kingdom in the central part of north China.

Teng (p. 250). In modern Honan province, near Nanyang.

Tsang (p. 205). Said to be on the Wei River in the vicinity of modern Sian, but the place is most likely imaginary.

Tsung, K'uai, and Hsü'ao (p. 20). Three small states (probably imaginary).

Ts'ungchih, Hsü'ao, Hu (p. 31). Small countries.

Tungling (p. 78). "The Eastern Mound," that is, the famous and sacred Mount T'ai in Shantung.

Viet (p. 7). In the south of China. During Chuang Tzu's time, the people living here were not yet sinicized. In Modern Standard Mandarin, this name would be pronounced *Yüeh*.

Wei (p. 198). One of the kingdoms during the Warring States period.

Wey (p. 29). An ancient state within the Chou dynasty.

Yellow Springs (p. 163). The Chinese equivalent of Hades.

Yen Gate (p. 276). One of the gates in the wall of the capital of the state of Sung.

Ying (p. 132). The capital of the state of Ch'u, which constituted the southernmost reach of the Chinese orbit in Chuang Chou's time.

Ying River (p. 294). North of Loyang in Honan. Hsü Yu rejected the offer of the throne from Yao and became a hermit there.

TERMS AND ALLUSIONS

all under heaven (p. 6). A traditional expression for the Chinese empire (literally, "heaven / sky-below") that occurs hundreds of times in the *Chuang Tzu*. In this translation, when considered collectively as "the world" or "the empire," it is grammatically treated as a singular noun phrase (as though it might be written "all-under-heaven"). When considered as the constituent elements, things, or men and women that go to make up the world or the empire, it is grammatically treated as a plural noun phrase.

animus, anima (p. 121). In ancient Chinese psychocosmology, each individual is thought to be possessed of both a male and a female soul.

artery, conduit (p. 25). Technical terms from traditional Chinese medicine. They are channels through which one's vital force (*ch'i*) flows, but in the *Chuang Tzu* they are used in a partially metaphorical sense.

bamboo seeds (p. 165). Since bamboo flowers (and hence produces seeds) only rarely, some species as seldom as once a century, the fact that the Yellow Phoenix (which itself only appears at great intervals) will eat only its seeds means that it is very particular about its food.

bear strides and bird stretches (p. 145). Readers familiar with Yoga will immediately recognize the regimen described in this sentence as a close Chinese adaptation of that ancient Indian discipline. See Mair, *Tao Te Ching*, pp. 159–60 and Mair, "**File**," pp. 35–37.

body, physical form. These terms are used throughout the *Chuang Tzu* in close conjunction. The former refers more to the individual being or to his / her personhood, the latter more to his / her corporeal existence.

breathing . . . from the heels (p. 480). A reminder of the close affinities between the Taoist sages and the ancient Indian holy men. Yogic breath control and *āsanas* (postures) were common to both traditions (see the previous note on "bear strides and bird stretches"). Even today, introductory Yoga instructors tell us to breathe from our heels, although this is a gross simplification of what really goes on in *prāṇāyāma* (yogic breath control).

cangue (p. 94). A heavy wooden yoke that is carried on the shoulders and through which the neck and arms pass. It was used as a form of punishment for minor criminals in China.

chop off . . . feet (p. 249). It was common in ancient China partially to immobilize individuals who were in servile positions. Female footbinding, though it developed erotic overtones, also functioned as a deterrent to free mobility.

clouds . . . rain (p. 131). A favorite Chinese metaphor for sexual activity.

coffers (p. 84). Boxes or covered baskets for storing treasure.

Confucians and Mohists (p. 15). Two schools of thought from the Warring States period. They are meant to stand for the whole gamut of contesting schools at that time.

contingent causation, nonfacticity (p. 265). The former expression implies that perhaps something causes things to exist /

happen, the latter implies that nothing does. Together, they are strongly reminiscent of the split between ancient Hindu realist philosophies such as *Saṁkhyā* and *Vaiśeṣika*, on the one hand, and idealist philosophies such as Yoga on the other. They also call to mind such central, and early, Buddhist concepts as dependent origination (Sanskrit *pratītya samutpāda*) and *anātmaka* (no individual, independent existence of conscious or unconscious beings), *māyā* (illusion), and *śunyatā* (emptiness).

culture (p. 149). In a narrower and more specific sense, the same sinograph (*wen*) signified "writing." In a broader and more basic sense, it signified "elegant pattern."

cure (p. 30). It should be noted that the word for "cure" is the same as that for "govern." The concept of governing in ancient China was premised upon the notion that the sage ruler, with the assistance of his worthy advisers, brought order where disorder would otherwise prevail. In other words, he healed the body politic.

customs . . . rules (p. 197). The sentiments are exactly the same as those expressed by St. Ambrose in his advice to St. Augustine: "When in Rome do as the Romans do."

dark (p. 23). In Taoist thought, darkness signifies many things, including mystery (cf. *Tao Te Ching*, chapter I), concentrated yin, origin, etc., and is associated with the north and water. This is the region where the Way (Tao) is most immanent.

disputation (p. 19). Philosophical argument, the favorite pursuit of the Sophists or Logicians.

divine (p. 205). The specific type of divination employed would have been to read the cracks on a scorched tortoise shell or an ox scapula. The shell or bone was prepared by drilling a small hole in it and then applying a heated poker to the hole. A ritual specialist was then called upon to interpret the pattern of the cracks that resulted. This was considered to be a particularly effective method for consulting one's deceased ancestors.

dorsal inductories (p. 39). A technical term in traditional Chinese medicine.

eight feet, two inches (p. 301). Roughly equivalent to six feet by modern standards.

emaciation (p. 276). A type of privation required of sons in mourning according to a strict application of the Confucian doctrine of filial piety.

essence (p. 146). The word for "essence" in Old Sinitic also meant "semen." Because of this identification, the Taoist adept was always very careful not to spill his semen thoughtlessly since that constituted a loss of spiritual essence. This helps to account for the elaborate regimes of sexual hygiene that were practiced in several branches of Taoism.

exuviae (p. 172). The dead skins sloughed off by various animals, especially snakes and certain insects.

fame (p. 30). The word for "fame" is the same as that for "name" in ancient Chinese (both are *ming*). It should further be noted that an important problem in classical Chinese philosophy was the relationship between name and reality. Hence, "the rectification of names" was a burning concern for several schools of ancient Chinese thought.

fifty-first year (p. 138). An allusion to Confucius's celebrated statement to the effect that, at age fifty, he understood the mandate of heaven. Like all early Chinese thinkers, Confucius accepted the importance of the Tao (Way). He and his followers, however, gave greater emphasis to T'ien (heaven), while the Taoists, as their name implies, put Tao in the highest position.

filialness (p. 132). *Hsiao* (also translated as "filiality," "filial piety," "filial duty," or "filial devotion") is a cornerstone of Confucian ideology.

five colors (p. 75). Cyan, yellow, red, white, and black—the primary colors plus black and white. Note that in Chinese the word for "color" may also mean "sex."

five constants (p. 131). This probably refers to the five phasal elements (see the next entry).

five elements (p. 315). Also called the five phases, these are metal, wood, water, fire, and earth.

five flavors (p. 78). Acrid, sour, sweet, bitter, salty.

five odors (p. 117). Rank, fragrant, aromatic, fishy, rotten.

five sounds (p. 76). The five notes of the ancient Chinese pentatonic scale.

five viscera (p. 75). Heart, liver, spleen, lungs, and kidneys. These were not, of course, considered to be mere physical organs but were also considered to be the seats of the emotions and of thought.

five ... weapons (p. 122). There are various enumerations (e.g., spear, lance, halberd, shield, and bow). The expression "five [categories of] weapons" signifies all types of weapons.

flexions (p. 145). Like channeling, a type of Yoga-inspired Taoist exercise designed to increase one's longevity.

forget (p. 52). An important word in the *Chuang Tzu* that became a technical term in later Taoism, especially for those schools that emphasized meditation. It signifies the emptying of the mind that brings utter calm and peace.

four seas (p. 93). The waters surrounding the continent inhabited by the ancient Chinese.

gibbon (p. 20). An arboreal ape with long arms and a slender body.

Great Clod (p. 12). A metaphor for the earth, the universe, or—in most cases—the Way (Tao).

Great Clump (p. 240). Probably an alternative reference to the Great Clod (see previous entry).

guards . . . vital breath (p. 175). Also the primary concern of the Yogin who preserves his *prāṇa* ("vital breath").

hegemon (p. 56). A ruler who is able to exert control over a number of competing states. The term is applied particularly to the leaders of Ch'i, Sung, Chin, Ch'in, and Ch'u during the Warring States period.

hemiculters (p. 398). Small fish found in rivers and lakes, loosely rendered on page 165 as "minnows." They are only a few inches long with thin, flat bodies that, according to old Chinese texts, are "shaped like a willow leaf."

hundred clans (p. 94). Literally, "the hundred surnames." This is generally understood to mean "the people," but the lowest classes in ancient China did not have surnames.

hungry tiger (p. 179). This recalls one of the best-known stories from the *Jātakas* (tales of the Buddha in former incarnations).

immortals (p. 107). A technically more precise translation of *hsien* would be "transcendents." They are immune to heat and cold, untouched by the elements, and can fly, mounting upward with a fluttering motion. They dwell apart from the chaotic world of man, subsist on air and dew, are not anxious like ordinary people, and have the smooth skin and innocent faces of children. The transcendents live an effortless existence that is best described as spontaneous. They recall the ancient Indian ascetics and holy men known as *ṛṣi* who possessed similar traits. In Master Chuang's time, the transcendents practiced meditation and forgetting (see above), but later generations of Taoists tried to acquire these remarkable traits by various alchemical, sexual, and hygienic regimes.

impersonator of the dead (p. 6). Also rendered as "representative of the dead" or "sacrificial officiant"; the two graphs literally mean "corpse invoker."

impromptu words (p. 278). There is an enormous variety of speculative opinion about the meaning of this expression (literally, "goblet words") and indeed about the sentence and even the section as a whole. I understand "goblet words" to be language that pours forth unconsciously and unpremeditatedly.

jugs (p. 116). Primitive earthenware musical instruments (like the ocarina or the jugs in a jugband). They can also punningly indicate alcohol.

just (p. 262). It should be noted that the ancient Sinitic word for "just" (*kung*)—as here and in the name of the speaker in this long monologue—also means "public." The same sinograph that is used to write "just, public" is used as well to write the homophonous title of nobility for "duke." It is not uncommon in ancient Chinese texts to pun on these various meanings of the graph in question (e.g., *Tao Te Ching*, Chapter 16).

knowledge (p. 275). As used in the *Chuang Tzu*, this word has many meanings. It ranges all the way from having positive implications of wisdom to expressing pejorative notions of cunning. For the more authentic parts of the text, it generally signifies the discursive, discriminating, rational consciousness of the human mind in contrast to the intuitive understanding of the "ultimate" or "true" person.

"Lauds of Shang" (p. 291). The earliest Confucians were specialists in the rituals of the old Shang dynasty.

loach (p. 20). A small eel, only three to four inches long, that lives in the mud of ponds and lakes.

lunar intelligence (p. 269). There is an old tradition in China of using the moon (yin) as a symbol of the human mind. Naturally, since passive yin and active yang are opposed, it will be easily consumed by the solar (yang) fires of anxiety.

magus (p. 131). A type of ancient Iranian ritual specialist who also became active in West Asia, Europe, and China during the first millennium B.C.E. The word is cognate with the English "magician."

measurements (p. 205). The standardization of measures was a serious problem in feudal society, one not effectively solved for China until the time of the first emperor of the Ch'in dynasty (late third century B.C.E.).

mind (p. 10). The word *hsin* means both "heart" and "mind." We may think of it as the heart-mind or heart /mind.

Mount Hua caps (p. 338). The people of the Warring States period had the curious custom of wearing distinctive caps (sometimes quite elaborate and even outlandish) to express some feature of their character that they especially prized. Mount Hua was said to be "flat both on top and at the bottom." Sung Chien and Yin Wen apparently felt that this was an appropriate symbol for what they believed in (equality of treatment, nondistinction, etc.).

music (p. 82). The most elevated of the Confucian arts; highly ritualistic and symbolic; usually accompanied by elaborate dance, banners, and panoply.

myriad things (p. 7). A very important expression in early Chinese philosophy, *wanwu* refers to all phenomenal existence. More literally, we might render *wanwu* as "the ten thousand entities." We should note that while *wu* is normally translated as "thing" for consistency's sake, it also includes both the notion of "creature" and of "object."

nature (p. 15). The Chinese word for "nature," in the sense of the natural world, is derived from that for "sky" or "heaven" (*t'ien*). In this translation "nature" is also sometimes used for the Chinese word *hsing*, meaning the character, personality, or disposition of an individual.

nine regions (p. 101). The ancient Chinese divided the whole world into nine regions (like a tick-tack-toe diagram).

"Ninefold Splendors" (p. 171). The regal court music of Shun.

nobleman (p. 309). *Shih* originally meant "retainer" or "knight."

Gradually it came to signify "scholar" or "literatus." It could also mean "soldier," though of a rather exalted sort. Perhaps the best equivalent in English would be "elite." Since, however, "elite" is not available in the singular, we have chosen "nobleman" to convey the sense of class superiority and supposedly elevated character the word carried in early Chinese society. We must note, however, that by Chuang Tzu's time the *shih* were not a hereditary group, in spite of the fact that they began as a warrior caste.

nonaction (p. 6I). On this concept in the *Bhagavad Gītā* and its parallels with *wuwei* in the *Tao Te Ching*, see the Afterword to the latter, pp. I4I–42.

nonfacticity (p. 265). See under **contingent causation** above.

numinous treasury (p. 48). The heart/mind.

Odes, etc. (p. 238). Confucian classics.

ointment for chapped hands (p. 8). Equally effective for sailors in winter and for silkwashers.

parasol tree (p. I7). More specifically, the Chinese parasol tree (*Firmiana simplex*) or *wut'ung*. It had very close associations with lute playing in China, partly because its wood could be used to make that instrument, but also for more metaphysical reasons.

pass (p. I75). A gateway, usually fortified, controlling a vital passageway. See also **Yin** under Names above.

pearl (p. 27I). Placing a pearl or jade in the mouth of a corpse was thought to stave off putrefaction and prolong life in the afterworld.

persuasions (pp. 31, 238). This is a technical term (*shui*), comparable to the *suasoriae* of the classical Greek and Roman orators, that was used during the Warring States period to refer to the counsels of various thinkers who attempted to influence the contending rulers of the day. Confucius was one of the better-known itinerant rhetorician-persuaders of the Eastern Chou period who attempted to influence the policies of various rulers.

petty persuasions (p. 270). The sinographs used to write this expression, which may also be rendered as "small talk," have come to signify "fiction" in Modern Standard Mandarin (probably borrowed back into Chinese from a Japanese calque [semantic borrowing] for the Western literary term). This passage, where the two graphs occur together in combination for the first time, has often been cited as evidence for the existence of fiction during the time of Chuang Chou. This interpretation, however, is both fallacious and anachronistic. It is impossible to demonstrate on the basis of this passage alone or in conjunction with any other contemporary data that the author was even remotely concerned with fiction when he wrote about "petty persuasions." Furthermore, although this tale about the scion of the Duke of Jen catching a huge fish is memorable, parts of it are poorly written, which has caused several commentators to remark that it is a rather late interpolation, even in the context of the derivative Miscellaneous Chapters.

The *Chuang Tzu* itself undoubtedly has the highest degree of fictionality of any literary work before the advent of Buddhism in China (see Mair, "The Narrative Revolution"). Even so, this does not qualify the *Chuang Tzu* to be considered as a conscious or intentional piece of fiction *per se*. See also the previous entry on **persuasions**.

Piebald Thoroughbred (p. 304). The name of a famous horse belonging to the early Chou king Mu that could cover a thousand tricents in a day.

potter's wheel (p. 231). A metaphor for the molding, creative power of nature.

return to the soil (p. 96). The biblical echo is strong: "For dust thou art and unto dust shalt thou return" (Genesis 3:19).

seven sages (p. 241). The Yellow Emperor and his attendants.

seventy-two (p. 142). A mystical number (tied to astronomy and the calendar) that was broadly current throughout Europe and Asia in ancient times.

six pitch-pipes (p. 76). These determined the modes of ancient Chinese music (see also **Yellow Bell**).

six reaches / poles / directions (p. 101). North, south, east, west, up (heaven), down (earth).

six viscera (p. 13). Heart, lungs, liver, kidneys, spleen, and gall bladder (see also **five viscera**).

snipefly (p. 37). An insect in south China that stings horses and cows so fiercely and in such great numbers that the animals sometimes collapse from the pain and loss of blood.

"solitary" (p. 301). The customary humble self-designation of the ruler in traditional China. It literally means "fatherless" or "orphaned" (he ascends the throne upon the death of his father).

son of heaven (p. 31). The ruler.

south-facing (p. 301). The customary orientation of the ruler in traditional China, because south was the direction of warmth and fecundity. The subject, by contrast, faced north. The color of the south is red, that of the north, black.

southwest corner (p. 248). Where the household gods used to be placed.

straw dogs (p. 136). These were placed before the gods during sacrifices to ward off evil spirits. After the ceremony, they would be destroyed.

superior man (p. 78). *Chüntzu*, the ideal person of Confucius; elsewhere also translated as "gentleman."

swallow (p. 195). The information given in the *Chuang Tzu* accords closely with beliefs and customs concerning the swallow in a number of societies. The Taiwanese and the Nepalese, for example, do not consider a newly constructed house to be blessed until a swallow builds its nest under the eaves. It is the sacred quality of the mud-daubed nest that undoubtedly led the author of this passage to refer to it here as an "altar of the soil and grain." Even more remarkable is a personal observation I made during an extended trip to the People's Republic of China in 1983. After three weeks of travel across the length and breadth of the land, one of my companions who happened to be a birdwatcher exclaimed with chagrin, "Oh, heaven! Victor, there are no birds in China!" And, indeed, except for a solitary kite that we had seen flying high in the sky above the remote upper reaches of the Yellow River, we had not seen or heard a single bird for three weeks. When I asked our Chinese guides how this could be, they explained that massive extermination campaigns had reduced the bird population to almost nil ("because birds compete with human beings for grain"). There were also the local "bird-killing kings" who shot or netted as many as a hundred birds a day for sport or food. Four years later, in 1987, the Chinese authorities began to realize what an ecological disaster these misguided policies had spawned—millions of trees were dying from insect infestation, to name only one problem—and so they gradually began to attempt to control the wanton slaughter. But, to return to the conclusion of my 1983 trip, after nearly a month in China, as we reached Canton and were preparing to leave the country, we were overjoyed to behold scattered groups of swallows flying exuberantly in the vicinity of the Canton Historical Museum (formerly a temple that was originally built in 1380 on a commanding height overlooking the city). I was so startled by their existence that I could not help but ask my Chinese host why they, too, had not been killed. "In the first place," he said, "their flight is too fast and jittery for anyone to shoot them easily. Secondly, they help us kill insects that rob us of grain. And finally," he admitted, "they bring good luck." Hence, even in godless communist China, an ancient tradition about the swallow had been preserved—after a fashion.

tattooed; lopped off . . . nose (pp. 62–63). Typical corporal punishments in ancient China.

te (p. xxii). In Confucian or conventional contexts, *te* is translated as "virtue." In Taoist or unconventional contexts, it is translated as "integrity." The most etymologically precise equivalent in English is the archaic word "dough[tiness]."

ten suns (p. 20). This trope is from a myth supposedly dating to the time of the mythical ruler Yao. The simultaneous appearance of ten suns was a disaster because it scorched the crops. Yao had to call upon the mighty archer Yi, a hero of Tai-speaking peoples to the south, to shoot down nine of the suns.

that (p. 175). There are countless speculations about the meaning of this simple word (e.g., the creator, physical form, nature, God [Deus], etc.). I prefer to leave it as ambiguous as its Indic cognate *tat* in the well-known formulation *tat tvam asi* ("that thou art") from the *Chandogya Upaniṣad* (6.8,6) where *tat* ("that") represents the universal principle (*brahman*), *tvam* ("thou") the individual soul (*ātman*), and *asi* is the verbal identification of the two.

theories and techniques (p. 333). "Theory" implies a way of looking at things from a single direction or vantage point (in extreme cases, this may be of a rather secret or esoteric kind); "technique" conveys the notion of device, artifice, strategy, etc. The two words later fused to become a bisyllabic expression signifying various occult arts in medicine, divination, and so forth. Still later, the two syllables taken together as one word came to mean "trick, stratagem."

three armies (p. 122). This is the number of armies permitted to the lords of the large feudal states during the Eastern Chou period. The Chou ruler himself maintained six armies.

three clans (p. 248). Those of one's father, mother, and wife.

Three Dynasties (p. 77). The Hsia, Shang, and Chou.

three luminaries (p. 315). The sun, the moon, and the stars.

timber (p. 38). *Ts'ai* means "timber" and "ability," "talent," or "worth," sometimes "genius."

tread upon fire (p. 175). As in Chapters 2, 6, and elsewhere in the *Chuang Tzu*, the Taoist adept is once again portrayed with the same superhuman abilities cultivated by some Indian yogis and fakirs.

tricent (p. 3). Three hundred paces, exactly equivalent to an ancient Chinese *li* (roughly one-third of a mile ["a thousand paces"]).

true man (p. 239). A Taoist paragon, counterpart of the superior man in the Confucian tradition.

ultimate man (p. 5). The sagely or perfected person of ultimate spiritual refinement and accomplishment; Master Chuang's ideal.

unhewn log (p. 70). For the symbolism of the unhewn log, see Mair, *Tao Te Ching*, p. 139.

viscera. See under **five viscera**.

wandering (p. 5). Probably the single most important and quintessential concept in the *Chuang Tzu*, but often overlooked because it is presented in literary rather than philosophical terms. "Wandering" implies a "laid-back" attitude toward life in which one takes things as they come and flows along with the Tao unconcernedly. The word *yu* is usually translated as "wander(ing)" but is occasionally rendered as "play(ing)," "strolling," or "enjoy(ing) oneself." "Wandering" with someone can also mean to study with or learn from them. In this sense, Chinese thinkers of the Warring States period were very much like their Greek counterparts from the same time who were often peripatetics. When engaged in by Confucians and other "uptight" types, *yu* means simply "traveling" or, at best, "going on an excursion." *Yu* is also cognate with the word for "swim(ming)," so when Master Chuang observes fish swimming (see page 165), he is also watching them playing and wandering freely in their own element. Thus, in the special language of the *Chuang Tzu*, "wandering" amounts to a technical term for that transcendental sort of free movement which is the mark of an enlightened being.

On page 282 it is significant that Sir Sunny Dweller (the hedonist Yang Chu) merely "went" south while Old Longears (the Old Master, Lao Tzu) was doing his transcendental "wandering."

For in-depth studies of *yu* in the *Chuang Tzu*, see Mair's "Chuang-tzu and Erasmus: Kindred Wits" and Michael Mark Crandell's "On Walking without Touching the Ground: 'Play' in the *Inner Chapters* of the *Chuang-tzu*," both in Mair, ed., *Experimental Essays*.

Way (p. 15). Tao. The most etymologically precise equivalent in English is "track." Since the Tao is essentially ineffable, the authors of the *Chuang Tzu* often avoid mentioning it directly.

Wonton (p. 71). The undifferentiated soup of primordial chaos. As it begins to differentiate, dumpling-blobs of matter coalesce. Wonton soup probably came first as a type of simple early fare. With the evolution of human consciousness and reflectiveness, the soup was adopted as a suitable metaphor for chaos. On the connection between wonton soup and cosmic chaos, see Eugene Anderson, *The Food of China*, p. 191 and Norman Girardot's book-length meditation on the theme of chaos in early Taoism (*Myth and Meaning*), especially pp. 29–38, citing Wolfram Eberhard, the great authority on the local cultures of China.

Yellow Bell, Great Tube (p. 76). The names of two of the six pitch-pipes.

BIBLIOGRAPHY

This is by no means an exhaustive listing of works relating to the *Chuang Tzu*. Much airy nonsense has been written about this text in recent years, particularly in Western languages, although there have lately also been some interesting and useful studies. In principle, I would prefer to let Master Chuang speak for himself. The works listed here are thus restricted to those referred to in the Preface, Introduction, and Notes, and others with immediate relevance for those who might wish to pursue questions raised by this book.

AKATSUKA Kiyoshi, tr. and annot. *Sōshi* [*Chuang Tzu*]. Zenshaku Kanbun taikei [Fully Interpreted Chinese Literature Series], vols. 16–17. Tokyo: Shūeisha, 1974–77.

Anderson, E. N. *The Food of China*. New Haven: Yale University Press, 1988.

Brooks, E. Bruce, with the assistance of A. Taeko Brooks. "The Evolution of *Jwāngdž*: A Preliminary Study on Literary Principles." Northampton, Massachusetts: Unpublished manuscript, 1981. 455 pages.

Bryce, Derek, tr. *Wisdom of the Daoist Masters: The Works of Lao Zi (Lao Tzu), Lie Zi (Lieh Tzu), Zhuang Zi (Chuang Tzu)*. Rendered into English from the French of Léon Wieger's *Les Pères du système taoiste*. Llanerch, Felinfach, Lampeter, Dyfed, Wales: Llanerch, 1984.

Chan, Wing-tsit, tr. and comp. *A Source Book in Chinese Philosophy*. Princeton: Princeton University Press, 1963.

CHANG Shih. Chuang Tzu *yü hsientai chuyi* [Chuang Tzu *and Modernism: A Comparison of Ancient and Contemporary Culture*]. Shih-chiachuang: Hopeh People's Publishing House, 1989.

Chang, Tsung-tung. *Metaphysik, Erkenntnis und Praktische Philosophie im Chuang-Tzu: zur Neu-Interpretation und systematischen Darstellung der klassischen chinesischen Philosophie*. Frankfurt am Main: Vittorio Klostermann, 1982.

CH'EN Kuying, tr. and annot. Chuang Tzu *chin chu chin yi* [*A Modern Annotation and Translation of the* Chuang Tzu]. Peking: Chunghua, 1983. A slightly revised reprinting of the edition published in 2 vols. by Taiwan Commercial Press in 1975.

CH'IEN Mu. Chuang Tzu *tsuan chien* [*A Compilation of Notes on* Chuang Tzu]. Taipei: Sanmin, 1974, 4th rev. and enlgd. ed.; first published 1951.

Farrelly, David. *The Book of Bamboo*. San Francisco: Sierra Club, 1984.

FUKUNAGA Mitsuji. *Sōshi* [*Chuang Tzu*]. Chūgoku kotensen

[Selected Chinese Classics], 3 vols. Tokyo: Asahi shinbunsha, 1966–67.

Fung, Yu-lan, tr. *Chuang-tzu: A New Selected Translation with an Exposition of the Philosophy of Kuo Hsiang*. Peking: Foreign Languages Press, 1989; originally published by Commercial Press, 1931.

Giles, Herbert A., tr. *Chuang Tzŭ: Taoist Philosopher and Chinese Mystic*. London: George Allen & Unwin, 1926, second rev. ed.; originally published 1889.

Girardot, N. J. *Myth and Meaning in Early Taoism: The Theme of Chaos (hun-tun)*. Berkeley and Los Angeles: University of California Press, 1983.

Graham, A. C. "Chuang-tzu and the Rambling Mode." In T. C. Lai, ed., *The Art and Profession of Translation*, 61–77. Hong Kong: Hong Kong Translation Society, 1976.

————, tr. *Chuang-tzŭ: The Seven Inner Chapters and other writings from the book Chuang-tzu*. London: George Allen and Unwin, 1981.

————. *Chuang-tzŭ: Textual Notes to a Partial Translation*. London: University of London, School of Oriental and African Studies, 1982.

————. "Chuang-tzu's Essay on Seeing Things as Equal." *History of Religions*, 9.2–3 (November 1969–February 1970): 137–59.

————. "The Date and Composition of Liehtzyy." *Asia Major*, n.s. 8.2 (1961): 139–98.

————. *Disputers of the Tao: Philosophical Argument in Ancient China*. La Salle, Illinois: Open Court, 1989.

————. "How Much of *Chuang Tzŭ* Did Chuang Tzŭ Write?" In *Studies in Chinese Philosophy and Philosophical Literature*, 283–321. Albany: State University of New York Press, 1990.

Hansen, Lars Jul. "An Analysis of 'Autumn Floods' in Chuang-Tzu." In Arne Nalss and Alastair Hannay, eds., *Invitation to Chinese Philosophy*, 113–40. Oslo: Universitetsforlaget, 1972.

Harvard-Yenching Institute Sinological Index Series, Supplement No. 20. *A Concordance to Chuang Tzŭ*. Cambridge: Harvard University Press, 1956.

HUANG Chinhung, annot. and tr. *Hsin yi* Chuang Tzu *tupen* [*Newly Translated Reader on the* Chuang Tzu]. Taipei: Sanmin, 1974.

Knaul, Livia. "Kuo Hsiang and the *Chuang Tzu.*" *Journal of Chinese Philosophy*, 12.4 (December 1985): 429–47.

KUO Ch'ingfan, comp. Chuang Tzu *chi shih* [*Collected Annotations on the* Chuang Tzu]. 4 vols. Peking: Chunghua, 1961.

KURAISHI Takeshirō and SEKI Masao, tr. and annot. *Sōshi* [*Chuang Tzu*]. Chūgoku koten bungaku taikei [Classical Chinese Literature Series], 4. Tokyo: Heibonsha, 1973.

Legge, James, tr. and annot. *The Texts of Taoism*. 2 vols. In *The Sacred Books of the East*, ed. F. Max Müller, vols. XXXIX–XL. Oxford: Oxford University Press, 1891; rpt. New York: Dover, 1962.

Libbrecht, U. "Prāṇa = Pneuma = Ch'i?" In W. L. Idema and E. Zürcher, eds., *Thought and Law in Qin and Han China: Studies Dedicated to Anthony Hulsewé on the occasion of his eightieth birthday*, 42–62. Leiden: E. J. Brill, 1990.

Liou, Kia-hway, tr. *L'Oeuvre complête de Tchouang-tseu*. Paris: Gallimard, 1969.

Lorenzen, David and Russell Maeth. "El *Lièzĭ* y el *Śatakatraya* de Bhartṛhari: Descubrimiento de una relación entre dos textos clásicos de China e India." *Estudios de Asia y África*, 14.4 (1979): 696–707.

Louie, Kam. *Inheriting Tradition: Interpretations of the Classical Philosophers in Communist China, 1949–1966*. Hong Kong, Oxford, New York: Oxford University Press, 1986.

Mair, Victor H., ed. *Chuang-tzu: Composition and Interpretation*. A Symposium Issue of the *Journal of Chinese Religions*, 11 (Fall 1983).

——, ed. *Experimental Essays on Chuang-tzu*. Asian Studies at Hawaii, 29. Honolulu: University of Hawaii Press, 1983 and later reprints.

——. "[*The*] **File** [*on the Cosmic*] **Track** [*and Individual*] **Dough**-[*tiness*]: Introduction and Notes for a Translation of the Ma-wang-tui Manuscripts of the *Lao Tzu* [*Old Master*]." *Sino-Platonic Papers*, 20 (October 1990).

——, tr. and annot. *Mei Cherng's "Seven Stimuli" and Wang Bor's "Pavilion of King Terng."* Studies in Asian Thought and Religion, 11. Lewiston/Queeston: Edwin Mellen, 1988.

——. "The Narrative Revolution in Chinese Literature: Ontological Presuppositions." *Chinese Literature: Essays, Articles, Reviews*, 5.1 (July 1983): 1–27.

——. "Old Sinitic **myag*, Old Persian *maguš*, and English 'Magician.'" *Early China*, 15 (1990): 27–47.

——, tr. and comm. *Tao Te Ching: The Classic Book of Integrity and the Way*. New York: Bantam, 1990.

Malyavin, V. V. *Chzhuan-tsz'i*. Pisateli i Uchen'ie Vostoka [Writers and Thinkers of the East]. Moscow: Glavnaya Redaktsiya Vostochnoi Literatur'i Izdatel'stva "Nauka," 1985.

Mathews, R. H., comp. *Chinese-English Dictionary*. Cambridge: Harvard University Press, 1943, rev. American ed.

OUYANG Chinghsien and OUYANG Ch'ao, tr. and annot. Chuang Tzu *shih yi* [Chuang Tzu *Translated and Explicated*]. 2 vols. N.p.: Hupeh People's Press, 1986.

Porkert, Manfred. *The Theoretical Foundations of Chinese Medicine: Systems of Correspondence.* Cambridge: MIT Press, 1974.

Roth, Harold. "Who Compiled the *Chuang Tzu*?" In Henry Rosemont, Jr., ed., *Chinese Texts and Philosophical Contexts: Essays Dedicated to Angus C. Graham*, 79–128. LaSalle, Illinois: Open Court, 1991.

de Santillana, Giorgio and Hertha von Dechend. *Hamlet's Mill: An Essay on Myth and the Frame of Time*. Boston: David R. Godine, 1983; first published 1969.

SHIH Yunghsiang. *Fochiao wenhsüeh tui Chungkuo hsiaoshuo te yinghsiang* [*The Influence of Buddhist Literature upon Chinese Fiction*]. Chungkuo Fohsüeh yenchiu lunwen tahsi [Chinese Buddhological Research Theses Series], II. Kaohsiung: Fokuang, 1990.

TS'EN Chungmien. *Liang Chou wenshih lun ts'ung* [*Papers on the Literature and History of the Two Chou Dynastic Periods*]. Shanghai: Commercial Press, 1958.

Watson, Burton, tr. *Chuang Tzu: Basic Writings*. New York: Columbia University Press, 1964.

_____, tr. *The Complete Works of Chuang Tzu*. New York: Columbia University Press, 1968.

DELETED PASSAGES

The following passages have been removed from the main body of the text (where their positions are marked by ellipses) either because they are spurious or because they are later commentaries and other types of interpolations that have been mistakenly incorporated into the text. In order to provide a complete translation of the standard edition of the *Chuang Tzu*, however, they are recorded here.

p. 4.   Moreover, if water has not accumulated to a sufficient depth, it will not have the strength to support a large boat. Pour a cup of water into a low spot on the floor and you can make a boat out of a mustard seed. But if you place the cup in the water it will get stuck because the boat will be large in relation to the shallowness of the water. Similarly, if the wind has not accumulated to a sufficient density, it will not have the strength to support large wings. Therefore, only at an altitude of ninety thousand tricents, with so much wind beneath it, can the P'eng ride on the wind. With its back touching the blue sky and no obstacles in its path, the P'eng heads for the south.

p. 16.   In commonality there is use, a kind of use through joining. To join is to attain, and through suitable attainment they are close to the Way.

p. 45.   " 'The center' means the middle place, but it is only destiny that prevents one from being struck."

p. 52.   Therefore the sage, in his conduct of war, might forfeit his state, but would not lose the hearts of his people. His benefits might extend for ten thousand generations, but it would not be for love of man. Therefore, he who delights in linking up with things is not a sage. He who is partial is not humane. He who is negligent of the seasons is not worthy. He who cannot perceive the linkage between benefit and harm is not a gentleman. He who loses himself through pursuit of fame is not a nobleman. He who destroys himself through untruthfulness is not a freeman. Men such as Hu Puhsieh, Wu Kuang, Poyi, Shuch'i, Master Chi, Hsü Yü, Chi T'o, and Shent'u Ti were all servants of freemen. They strove to delight others, but did nothing to delight themselves.

p. 53.   He took punishments as the main body, etiquette as the wings, knowledge as timeliness, and virtue as acceptance. Because he took punishments as the main body, he was lenient in his killing. Because he took etiquette as the wings, he was able to effectuate his policies in the world. Because he took knowledge as timeliness, he handled affairs only when compelled to do so. Because he took virtue as acceptance, it means that he climbed to the tops of hills together with those who had to go by foot, and people truly thought that he had to walk with effort.

p. 87.   Therefore, it is said, "Great cleverness seems clumsy."

p. 101.   That which is lowly, yet must be employed—things. That which is humble yet must be depended upon—the people. That which is minor, yet must be done—affairs. That which is coarse, yet must be set forth—laws. That which is distant, yet must be indwelling—righteousness. That which is intimate, yet must be broad—humaneness. That which is restrained, yet must be amassed—rites. That which is central, yet must be elevated—virtue. That which is unitary, yet must undergo change—the Way. That which is divine, yet must be exercised—heaven.

Therefore the sages contemplated heaven but did not assist it. They found their completion in virtue but were not encumbered by it. They proceeded according to the Way, but made no schemes. They formed their associations in humaneness, but did not rely on it. They clove to righteousness but did not amass it. They responded to the rites and did not conceal them. They engaged in affairs and did not reject them. They applied the laws equally and did not cause disorder. They relied on the people and did not despise them. They depended upon things and did not discard them. Among things, none are adequate for use, yet they must be used.

Those who do not understand heaven are not pure in virtue. Those who do not comprehend the Way will have no point of departure from which they can proceed. How sad are those who do not understand the Way!

What do we mean by the Way? There is the Way of heaven, and there are the ways of men. To remain in nonaction and yet be honored, that is the Way of heaven. To be involved in action and thereby encumbered, such are the ways of men. The ruler is the Way of heaven; his subjects are the ways of men. The Way of heaven and the ways of men are far apart. This is something that must be critically examined.

p. 105.   large, small; long, short; near, far

p. 107.   [The ellipsis on this page does not indicate a deleted passage. Rather, it is meant to show that Yao's question is incomplete because the border warden cuts him short.]

p. 133. "Ultimate music first corresponds to human affairs, conforms to heavenly principles, is carried out through the five virtues, and corresponds to nature. Only then will the four seasons be adjusted and great harmony prevail among the myriad things."

p. 139. If, perchance, one does so, he will receive much recrimination.

p. 146. toiled then exhausted

p. 150. Hidden, but decidedly not hidden of his own volition.

p. 150. Therefore, it is said, "Rectify yourself and that is all."

p. 155. "Therefore the conduct of the great man is not aimed at hurting others, and he does not make much of his humaneness and kindness. When he moves, it is not for profit, but he does not despise the porter* at the gate. He does not wrangle over goods and property, yet he does not make much of his declining and yielding. In his affairs, he does not rely upon others and does not make much of utilizing his own strength, but he does not despise those who are avaricious and corrupt. His conduct may differ from that of the common lot, but he does not make much of his eccentricity. His behavior may follow that of the crowd, but he does not despise the glib flatterer. All the titles and salaries in the world are not enough to encourage him, nor are penalties and shame enough to disgrace him. He knows that right and wrong are indivisible, that minuscule and large are undemarcatable. I have heard it said, 'The Man of the Way is not celebrated; the man of ultimate virtue is not successful; the great man has no self.' This is the pinnacle of restraint."

---

* Who is always looking out for a tip or a bribe.

p. 176. "He who seeks revenge does not break the sword of his enemy and even an irascible person does not bear a grudge against a tile that falls on him. By this means, all under heaven might attain equilibrium. Thus, by following this way, there would be no disorder caused by attacks and battles, no punishments of death and slaughter.

> Do not develop what is natural to man,
> But develop what is natural to heaven.
> By developing what pertains to heaven,
>   virtue is produced;
> By developing what pertains to man,
>   thievery is produced.
> By not wearying of heaven
> And not overlooking man,
> The people will be brought close to the truth."

p. 184. There was a certain Sun Hsiu who paid a call at the gate of Master Pien Sir Ch'ing and complained to him, saying, "When I lived in my village, I was never said to lack cultivation, and when I faced difficulties, I was never said to lack courage. Nevertheless, though I worked in my fields I never met with a good harvest, and though I served my lord I never met with worldly success. I am treated as an outcast in the villages and am driven out of the townships. But what crime have I committed against heaven that I should meet with such a destiny?"

"Haven't you heard how the ultimate man conducts himself?" asked Master Pien. "He forgets his inner organs and is oblivious of his senses. Faraway he is, roaming beyond the dust and dirt of the mundane world, carefree in the enterprise of having no affairs. This is called 'acting without presumption, nurturing without control.' But now you ornament your knowledge to alarm those who are ignorant and you cultivate your person to highlight those who are vile. You are as ostentatious as if you were walking along holding the sun and moon above you. You are fortunate that you have a physical body that is whole and is possessed of all of its nine orifices, that you have not been afflicted midway through life by deafness, blindness, or lameness but can still be compared to the lot of other men. What leisure do you have for complaining against heaven? Begone, sir!"

After Master Sun left, Master Pien went inside. He sat down for a while, then looked up to heaven and sighed. "Why are you sighing, master?" one of his disciples asked him.

"Just now Hsiu came," said Master Pien, "and I told him about the integrity of the ultimate man. I'm afraid that he will be alarmed and bewildered."

"Not so," said the disciple. "If what Master Sun said was right and what you said was wrong, the wrong will surely not be able to bewilder the right. And if what Master Sun said was wrong and what you said was right, then he surely must have come because he was already bewildered. In that case, what mistake did you commit?"

"Not so," said Master Pien. "Of old, there was a bird that alighted in the suburbs of Lu. The Marquis of Lu was pleased with it and offered it beef, mutton, and pork for nourishment. For music, he had 'The Ninefold Splendors' performed, but the bird's eyes began to glaze over with sadness and it was unwilling to eat or drink. This is called nourishing a bird as one would nourish oneself. If, however, we are able to nourish birds as birds should be nourished, we ought to let them perch in the deep forests, float on rivers and lakes, feed on loaches and hemiculters, and dwell in self-contentment, then they will feel safe on level, dry ground, and that is all. Now, Hsiu is a person of slim wit and slight learning. My telling him about the integrity of the ulti-mate man is like using a carriage and horses to transport a mouse or drums and bells to delight a bull-headed shrike. How could he not be alarmed?"

p. 251.   From ants he [learns how] to abandon knowledge; from fish he [learns] the strategy [of mutual forgetfulness]; from sheep he [learns how] to abandon intellection.

p. 303.   "King Wen was imprisoned at Yuli."

p. 335.   The *Odes* describe the will / determination; the *Documents* describe affairs; the *Ritual* describes conduct; the *Music* describes harmony; the *Changes* describe yin and yang; the *Spring and Autumn* [*Annals*] describe obligations.

p. 342.   "Toweringly, he has a surplus."

ACKNOWLEDGMENTS

A substantial proportion of this work was completed during the year (1991–1992) when I was a fellow at the National Humanities Center. The entire staff of the Center was unfailingly helpful to me in facilitating the research that went into the making of this book. I wish particularly to express my gratitude to Karen Carroll and Linda Morgan for typing the whole manuscript from a monumentally messy handwritten first draft. Leave at the National Humanities Center was supported by grants from the National Endowment for the Humanities and by the Mellon Foundation. I am grateful to both of these organizations for their generous assistance.

Linda Loewenthal, who four years ago gave me expert editorial guidance when I was working on the *Tao Te Ching*, has once again provided much needed critical advice for my version of the *Chuang Tzu*. I am deeply appreciative of her patient efforts to wean me away from a natural inclination to scholarly tedium. The format of the book and the present form of the Introduction and other ancillary matter are due to her incisive organizational vision and skills.

Leslie Meredith, Executive Editor at Bantam and in charge

of the Wisdom Editions, deserves thanks for her understanding of what I wanted this book to be, especially on the question of the need for a truly complete translation of the *Chuang Tzu*, and was supportive on various aspects relating to the design of the final product.

I also wish to thank Denis Mair and Jing Wang for reading over the entire translation against the original Chinese text to ensure that nothing was inadvertently omitted. The former, who is a fine poet and premier translator in his own right, made some excellent suggestions for improvement. The latter offered invaluable insights and encouragement in the final stages of the work.

To my son, Thomas Krishna, who has grown into a man while this book was being written, I am grateful for helping me to see things with clarity. To my wife, Liching, who had to endure years of neglect while I was immersed in ancient tomes, I am grateful for all the support and understanding she has shown.

Finally, I wish to acknowledge my indebtedness to the following scholars whose studies on the intellectual history of the Warring States period and on Taoism I have relied upon so heavily in writing the Introduction: E. Bruce and A. Taeko Brooks, Wing-tsit Chan, Yu-lan Fung and Derk Bodde, A. C. Graham, HU Shih, John S. Major, Y. P. Mei, Frederick W. Mote, W. Allyn Rickett, Harold Roth, Anna K. Seidel, Michel Strickmann, and Burton Watson. I have also gained much from the brilliant, iconoclastic deliberations of the Warring States Working Group. The interpretations placed upon their work, however, are strictly my own.